Arno Sonderegger (ed.)

African Thoughts on Colonial and Neo-Colonial Worlds
Facets of an Intellectual History of Africa

Arno Sonderegger (ed.)

African Thoughts on Colonial and Neo-Colonial Worlds

Facets of an Intellectual History of Africa

Neofelis Verlag

German National Library Cataloguing in Publication Data
A catalogue record for this book is available from the German National Library:
http://dnb.d-nb.de

© 2015 Neofelis Verlag GmbH, Berlin
www.neofelis-verlag.de
All rights reserved.

Cover Design: Marija Skara
Printed by PRESSEL Digitaler Produktionsdruck, Remshalden
Printed on FSC-certified paper.
ISBN (Print): 978-3-95808-023-2
ISBN (PDF): 978-3-95808-083-6

Arno Sonderegger (ed.)

African Thoughts on Colonial and Neo-Colonial Worlds

Facets of an Intellectual History of Africa

Neofelis Verlag

German National Library Cataloguing in Publication Data
A catalogue record for this book is available from the German National Library:
http://dnb.d-nb.de

© 2015 Neofelis Verlag GmbH, Berlin
www.neofelis-verlag.de
All rights reserved.

Cover Design: Marija Skara
Printed by PRESSEL Digitaler Produktionsdruck, Remshalden
Printed on FSC-certified paper.
ISBN (Print): 978-3-95808-023-2
ISBN (PDF): 978-3-95808-083-6

Contents

Facets of an Intellectual History of Africa

Reflecting Colonial and Neo-Colonial Worlds

Arno Sonderegger

The plan for this book goes back to a conference devoted to African intellectual history held at the African Studies Department of the University of Vienna last year. It sets out to highlight the history of specific ideas and views on colonialism and post-independence relations as unfolding in the works, thoughts and actions of particular African intellectuals. Papers delivered looked at Africans stemming from various parts of the continent and the African diaspora. Additionally, they emphasized several specific issues relevant to African thought – such as the role of power and privilege in knowledge production, questions of epistemology in an African context, as well as the search for African authenticity and for suitable paths and models of development. The selection of articles included in this volume gives an accurate, though hardly all-embracing, impression of the wide range of topics and personalities that come to mind in any endeavor of writing an intellectual history of Africa in the 20th century.[1]

It is not easy to define intellectual history, because it "is an unusual discipline, eclectic in both method and subject matter and therefore

1 See the conference report by Arno Sonderegger: African Thoughts on (Neo-) Colonial Worlds: Steps towards an Intellectual History of Africa 06.11.2014–07.11.2014 Wien. In: *H-Soz-Kult*, 16.12.2014. http://www.hsozkult.de/conferencereport/id/tagungsberichte-5732 (accessed 13.02.2015). A longer version including names and topics of those selected to the conference but eventually unable to participate, as well as the full program, can be found at: http://afrika.univie.ac.at/veranstaltungen/konferenzen/ (accessed 13.02.2015).

resistant to any single, globalized definition."[2] Its radically transdisciplinary character might be added as further distinctive trait, for neither ideas nor the minds of men and women who operate them, stop according to borders set up by academic disciplines but constantly transgress them. "[C]ontributions to the field of intellectual history", writes Riccardo Bavaj in a recent summary quite to the point, "have been made by a wide array of scholars – these hailing from different national traditions, grounded in varying academic subjects, and employing diverse methodological approaches."[3] The contributions to this volume are no exception. Contributors come from Germany and Austria, from Poland, Italy and France, from Mexico and the US, their disciplinary backgrounds reach from literary studies to sociology, from philosophy to anthropology, from African Studies to history.[4] In his piece on intellectual history, Bavaj rightly deplores that "communication between these various scholars has often proven rather limited."[5] This volume, and the conference from which it sprang, are efforts of boosting such communication. It looks for the common ground on which such inter- and cross-disciplinary dialogue can flourish. To this end it might be useful to think about the basic interests underlying any approach to intellectual history. In connection with reflecting upon the particularities of an Africa-centered intellectual history, it might as well serve as an introduction into this book.

In 1985, Quentin Skinner gave a very short answer to the question: *What is intellectual history*? It simply is "the study of past thoughts." There was, of course, more to his answer. The extended version of his argument ran as follows:

> The study of the great religious and philosophical systems of the past; the study of ordinary people's beliefs about heaven and earth, past and future,

2 Peter E. Gordon: What is Intellectual History? A Frankly Partisan Introduction to a Frequently Misunderstood Field. In: *The Harvard Colloquium for Intellectual History*, Spring 2012. http://projects.iq.harvard.edu/harvardcolloquium/pages/what-intellectual-history (accessed 13.02.2015).

3 Riccardo Bavaj: Intellectual History, Version: 1.0. In: *Docupedia-Zeitgeschichte*, 13.09.2010, pp. 1–19, here p. 3. http://docupedia.de/zg/Intellectual_History (accessed 13.02.2015).

4 Several African scholars selected by the organizers could not attend the conference due to either lacking funds or petty Visa regulations. Unfortunately, those actually attending failed to submit their papers in time.

5 Bavaj: Intellectual History, p. 3.

> metaphysics and science; the examination of our ancestors' attitudes towards youth and age, war and peace, love and hate, cabbages and kings; the uncovering of their prejudices about what one ought to eat, how one ought to dress, whom one ought to admire; the analysis of their assumptions about health and illness, good and evil, morals and politics, birth, copulation and death – all these and a vast range of kindred topics fall within the capacious orbit of intellectual history. For they are all instances of the general subject matter that preoccupies intellectual historians above all: the study of past thoughts.[6]

Studying the past is, of course, something done in the present. It accordingly requires a (self-)critical and reflective stance on behalf of intellectual historians. Skinner distinguished three basically different sorts of doing intellectual history which lend themselves to structuring this introduction: (1) a concentration on what are considerably "unit ideas" or "key terms"; (2) "singling out those texts which have been most influential in shaping our western political tradition and offering as careful as possible an account of how they are put together." This prefigures the making of a classical canon, creating "classic thinkers"; (3) a "focus [...] on the entire social and political vocabularies of given historical periods."[7] In practice, these orientations may well interfere with each other.

Key Terms and Classic Thinkers

Concentrating on key terms has got a somewhat bad reputation in mainstream historical profession. This is due to the idealist bias that marked many works written in the vein of German *Geistesgeschichte* or American *History of Ideas*, often passing over the particular contexts in which the ideas in question were operating, as well as eliding the actual women and men who handled them. There cannot be any doubt, however, that writing the history of certain ideas and terms contextualized has a lot to offer. Reinhart Koselleck's *Begriffsgeschichte* makes this amply clear.[8] More recently, there emerged a new

6 Quentin Skinner: What is Intellectual History? In: *History Today* 35,10 (1985). http://www.historytoday.com/stefan-collini/what-intellectual-history (accessed 11.02.2015).

7 Ibid.

8 Reinhart Koselleck: *Vergangene Zukunft: Zur Semantik geschichtlicher Zeiten*. Frankfurt am Main: Suhrkamp 1989, pp. 114–125; Georg C. Iggers: *Geschichtswissenschaft im 20. Jahrhundert: Ein kritischer Überblick im internationalen Zusammenhang*. Göttingen: Vandenhoeck & Ruprecht 2007, pp. 101–110, 121–144.

interest in the critical reading of human rights and development discourses, which seems important with regard to African intellectual history.[9] Debates about development, human rights or democracy are discussed all over the world, in media and academia, though often abstracted to a 'global' level which is, in fact, more often than not just another way of hiding a Western Eurocentric point of view. A decade ago Frederick Cooper convincingly pointed to the shortcomings of the term "globalization" as an "analytical category", and contrasted it with its success as a "native category".[10] This differentiation between "native" meaning (according to particular contexts and identity politics) and "analytical" meaning (striving for understanding and explanation of a particular phenomenon) is crucial whenever ideology and different world views are on the agenda. The debates about what is called 'global affairs' are carried out within particular ideological frames – discussing certain key ideas in certain ways, setting the limits of what is allowed to be said and thought, and ignoring or marginalizing those who question the status quo.

A lot can be gained by concentrating on both terms and the varying contexts and ways in which they are debated – by African and Western intellectuals alike. The same is true for a whole variety of frequently debated ideas and terms, some of which are explicitly addressed in contributions to this volume (such as, for instance, 'state' or 'art'), but it applies to even more seminal ideas as well. If it is true that colonialism produced not only particular images of Africa stored in what V.Y. Mudimbe called "the colonial library", but a whole distorting way of looking at the continent and its people, then it is essential to challenge the basic ideas of 'Africa' in general and of 'African history' in particular.[11] This is done in several of the pieces that follow. Some

9 Miša Krenčeyová: *Africa and the Rest: Imaginations Beyond a Continent in African Scholarship on Human Rights and Development.* PhD Thesis, University of Vienna 2013, gives a comprehensive account of African voices in the debates; Frederick Cooper: Writing the History of Development. In: *The Journal of Modern European History* 8 (2010), pp. 5–23.

10 Frederick Cooper: *Colonialism in Question: Theory, Knowledge, History.* Berkeley: University of California Press 2005, pp. 92–93.

11 V.Y. Mudimbe: *The Invention of Africa.* Bloomington: Indiana UP 1988; cf. Kwame Anthony Appiah: *In My Father's House: Africa in the Philosophy of Culture.* Oxford: Oxford UP 1992; Ngugi wa Thiong'o: *Something Torn and New: An African Renaissance.* New York: Basic Civitas 2009; Frederick Cooper: *Africa in the World: Capitalism, Empire, Nation-State.* Cambridge, MA: Harvard UP 2014.

address the structures of knowledge production and distribution explicitly, while others treat them implicitly. In some contributions the very relevance of racism comes to the fore. The inherent ambivalence of the matter of 'race' in debates on Africa is due to the formative nature of racial discourse – formative, that is, in the ways we not only represent but perceive the world and its people. Colonialism and Afro-European interactions were crucially important in establishing and shaping the conceptual frames of perception and representation of Africa. Hence, the importance ascribed to "colonial racism" by critical African thinkers from very early on.[12]

By establishing certain individual thinkers as paramount and treating them as classics, one must be careful not to get trapped into writing the history of 'big men' (or 'big women') but to embed the 'classic thinkers' properly in time, space and culture. When Quentin Skinner characterized intellectual history in the sense of treating "those texts which have been most influential in shaping our *western* political tradition",[13] he reveals another point which is crucial from an African perspective: Intellectual history is a field still primarily concerned with Western thought. This invites Eurocentric biases almost inevitably. The work of a great British historian might serve as an appropriate example. When "thinking the twentieth century" or reflecting upon "the forgotten twentieth century" in terms of intellectual history, Tony Judt never bothers to mention any African writers of renown (nor any from Asia).[14] Why? Because being a historian of Europe, no matter how critically minded in intent, still means not being forced to look across the borders of the West. Indeed, Judt looked East but not farther than to Eastern Europe. Such blindness

12 This connection was made in print repeatedly. For early instances see Joseph Ephraim Casely Hayford: *Ethiopia Unbound: Studies in Race Emancipation*. London: Cass 1969 [1911]; George Padmore: *How Britain Rules Africa*. New York: Negro Universities Press 1969 [1936]; Aimée Césaire: *Discourse on Colonialism*. New York: Monthly Review 2000 [1955]; Albert Memmi: *Portrait du colonisé précédé du Portrait du colonisateur*. Paris: Buchet-Chastel 1957. When Frantz Fanon launched his fierce critique on colonialism since the 1950s he was no lonely voice at all; see Frantz Fanon: *Black Skin, White Masks*. New York: Grove 1967 [1952]; id.: *The Wretched of the Earth*. New York: Grove 2004 [1961].

13 Skinner: Intellectual History, my emphasis.

14 Tony Judt: *Reappraisals: Reflections on the Forgotten Twentieth Century*. New York: Penguin 2008; Tony Judt, with Timothy Snyder: *Thinking the Twentieth Century*. New York: Penguin 2012.

has much to do with imperial and colonial pasts forgotten or, at least, not sufficiently reflected.

Bringing Africa into the picture is as essential as decolonizing intellectual history in general, as Nancy Hunt reminded us recently.[15] And it is a good idea to start that project with a fresh look at African intellectual protagonists and key ideas advanced by them,[16] for Tony Judt is right on principle when proclaiming

> The twentieth century was the century of the intellectual: [… of] men and women […] who applied themselves to debating and influencing public opinion and policy. The intellectual was by definition committed – 'engaged': usually to an ideal, a dogma, a project.[17]

African history is by no means short on people who match that definition. Some of them appear in the following pages.

Discourses and Issues

In the wake of the linguistic and cultural turns in the human sciences, academic culture changed markedly. Positivist positions came under heavy critique, and appropriately so, while the new emphasis on culture and representation, performance and expression, gave rise to prominence to a soon influential category: 'discourse'. Effectively introduced by French philosopher-historian Michel Foucault to grasp several distinctive and problematic characteristics of modernity (from madness and science to sexuality, from sanitation to punishment), 'discourse' was to become ubiquitously used.[18] With Palestinian literary scholar Edward Said who combined some of Foucault's ideas with Antonio Gramsci's concept of 'hegemony', discourse analysis reached out onto non-European spaces.[19] Its novelty was twofold.

15 Nancy Rose Hunt: The Affective, the Intellectual, and Gender History. In: *Journal of African History* 55,3 (2014), pp. 331–345, here p. 339.

16 Kwame Anthony Appiah has done exactly this in his recent book on one of the founding fathers of Pan-Africanism, W. E. B. Du Bois (1868–1963), the great African American historian: *Lines of Descent: W. E. B. Du Bois and the Emergence of Identity*. Cambridge: Harvard UP 2014.

17 Tony Judt: *Reappraisals*, p. 13.

18 Cf. Michel Foucault: *L'ordre du discours*. Paris: Gallimard 1972. On Foucault's life and work see Didier Eribon: *Michel Foucault (1926–1984)*. Paris: Flammarion 1989. From a historian's perspective see Peter Burke: *What is Cultural History?* Cambridge: Polity 2008, pp. 53–58.

19 Edward Said: *Orientalism: Western Conceptions of the Orient*. London: Penguin 1995 [1978].

First, *Orientalism* was markedly theoretical in intent – a characteristic that (unfortunately) informs many of the postcolonial studies which take Said's book for their charter –, often at the expense of empirical and historical accuracy. Secondly, in its anti-colonial stance it gave voice to an outspoken partisan approach. In both respects the axis of Gramsci-Foucault-Said informed (and informs) the works of some influential African authors such as V.Y. Mudimbe or, more recently, Achille Mbembe who tend very much, at least in my reading of their works, to fall prey to naïve idealism.[20] It seems, therefore, reasonable to recognize that there are less idealized and less generalizing understandings of 'discourse' available as well, which give due credit to concrete empirical and particular historical contexts.[21] According to J.G.A. Pocock, the focus on

> 'discourse' – meaning 'speech', 'literature' and public utterance in general [...] enables one to write the history of an intellectual activity as a history of actions performed by human beings in a variety of circumstances; actions which have affected other human beings, and have affected the circumstances in which they were performed (if only by making it possible to talk and argue about these circumstances).[22]

It follows that discursive ideas are to be studied in their particular contexts. If we ask, then, which discourse or what 'discursive formations' shaped the long 20th century, it will be easily understood that from an African perspective colonialism looms large.

In the course of several centuries Africa was economically integrated into an emerging capitalist world market on uneven grounds. Over time, she evolved into a sole producer of mineral, agricultural and

20 Mudimbe: *Invention of Africa*; Achille Mbembe: *On the Postcolony*. Berkeley: University of California Press 2001; id.: *Critique de la raison nègre*. Paris: Éditions la Découverte 2013.

21 And there is a critical as well as empirically and historically informed tradition of African historiography that still awaits its rediscovery. It would be a good idea to read again the pioneers of African history – those who accomplished making it into an academic subject, for they said many things that foreshadowed the 'anti-orientalist' critique of later decades, and some things they said much better; see Arno Sonderegger: Nachbetrachtung zur Kolonialgeschichte und Historiographie Afrikas. In: Id. / Ingeborg Grau / Birgit Englert (eds): *Afrika im 20. Jahrhundert: Geschichte und Gesellschaft*. Vienna: Promedia 2011, pp. 228–254, here pp. 231–237; Jean-François Bayart: *Les études postcoloniales: un carnaval académique*. Paris: Karthala 2010.

22 J.G.A. Pocock: What is Intellectual History? In: *History Today* 35,10 (1985). http://www.historytoday.com/stefan-collini/what-intellectual-history (accessed 11.02.2015).

human resources – producing 'products', 'slaves' and 'cash crops', all destined to markets outside the continent, and operating to the benefit of capitalist entrepreneurs. At least in macroeconomic terms, there is no doubt that in the long run Africa and the majority of Africans did not benefit from those various forms of uneven trade but suffered from severe exploitation.[23] According to the Guyanese historian of Africa, Walter Rodney, Europe did actively underdevelop Africa (and other parts of the world) in the course of its capitalist-imperialist expansion that strove for both economic and political hegemony. Starting with the transatlantic slave-trade, "colonialism" changed its outward appearance since the early modern era but persisted over time being "a system which functioned well in the interests of the metropole", by means of "exploitation and oppression", operating as "a one-armed bandit".[24]

Other scholars, African and Western alike, have not professed to this extreme moralistic point of view and offered a more balanced evaluation of the colonial experience, but still, all the serious ones share Adu Boahen's conclusion that "quite clearly the debit side [of colonialism] far outweighs the credit side."[25] The argument of a long-term process of underdeveloping Africa, as proposed by Rodney and, shed off its moralist twist, confirmed by Immanuel Wallerstein's narrative of *the modern world-system*'s development, understands 'colonialism'

23 Important contributions to set the record straight came from African scholars. For macro-level interpretations see Samir Amin: *Unequal Development: An Essay on the Social Formations of Peripheral Capitalism.* New York: Monthly Review 1976 [1973]; id.: *Maldevelopment: Anatomy of a Global Failure.* Cape Town: Pambazuka 2011. The historical research on regional levels since the 1950s is far too numerous to be listed here in detail, as are the contributions of African historians. Kenneth O. Dike and Jacob A. F. Ajayi from Nigeria, Adu Boahen from Ghana, Bethwell A. Ogot from Kenya, Joseph Ki-Zerbo from Burkina Faso, and many other African historians were public figures and would be well worth the attention by intellectual historians of Africa. So far they have been ignored almost completely by *Postcolonial Studies*, most probably because of their dominant focus on left-wing intellectuals. Cf. Robert J. C. Young: *Postcolonialism: An Historical Introduction.* Malden: Blackwell 2001.

24 Walter Rodney: *How Europe Underdeveloped Africa.* Abuja: Panaf 2009 [1973], p. 246–247.

25 A. Adu Boahen: *African Perspectives on Colonialism.* Baltimore: Johns Hopkins UP 1987, p. 108. The last chapter of this small book is entirely devoted to a balanced discussion of the "colonial impact" on Africa, interpreted through the liberal lens of this Ghanaian historian. Cf. Stephen Ellis: *Season of Rains: Africa in the World.* London: Hurst 2011; Frederick Cooper: *Africa in the World*, pp. 90–101.

à la longue durée and gives primacy to economic over political factors, while emphasizing the importance of both.[26] Politics, in this view, develops according to economic changes, and imperialism – i. e. the establishment of colonial empires and of more informal spheres of imperial influence – is both the ideological and praxeological corollary to capitalism.

Against this understanding of colonialism in the long run, one can (and must) distinguish a narrower definition. It has become quite common among colonial historians and historians of Africa to identify colonialism with formalized foreign rule. Understood that way – as colonial rule situated within the formal imperial frame of 'colonial empires' –, colonialism stretched out over almost all of Africa only at the turn of the 19th/20th century, and came to an end in several waves of decolonization already some decades later. Seen in that perspective, African experience of colonial rule was (apart from a few coastal bridgeheads) short-lived. This fact led (and leads) some to consider its impact superficial, marginal and largely irrelevant. Such a view, very widespread in media and policy discourses about Africa (as well as in parts of academic research on Africa that are historically ignorant, *geschichtsvergessen*), is basically wrong – misled, and misleading in consequence.[27] The effects of foreign colonial domination on Africa are strikingly relevant. It is well to remember that decolonization was not complete – not even in political terms, for the sovereignty of African post-colonial states remains precarious, much less in the economic spheres of world capitalism. To underline this fact, the title of this book emphatically speaks of colonial *and neo-colonial* worlds, using a term that fell into disrepute in some corners long ago. Apart from those who ignore the colonial legacies on principle, some serious historians of Africa chose to confine 'neo-colonial' on French policies

26 A short summary of and theoretical reflection on his multi-volume opus *The Modern World-System* can be found in Immanuel Wallerstein: *Historical Capitalism with Capitalist Civilization*. London: Verso 2011.

27 For a convincing critique along those lines targeting at political science approaches in particular, see Patrick Chabal: *Africa: The Politics of Suffering and Smiling*. London: Zed 2009. For critical accounts on the colonial impact on African societies and, in particular, on postcolonial politics by African scholars, see Mahmood Mamdani: *Citizen and Subject: Contemporary Africa and the Legacy of Late Colonialism*. London: Currey 1996; Ngugi wa Thiong'o: The Myth of Tribe in African Politics. In: *Transition* 101 (2009), pp. 16–23.

towards Africa – meaning directly interventionist policies (in diplomatic, financial as well as military senses) by a European state with past formal colonial relationship to some African countries. This is, of course, not the way 'neo-colonial' is understood in the context of this book. And it does not correspond to the way "neo-colonialism" was originally conceived by Kwame Nkrumah:

> The essence of neo-colonialism is that the State which is subject to it is, in theory, independent and has all the outward trappings of international sovereignty. In reality its economic system and thus its political policy is directed from outside.[28]

This visionary of Pan-African unity had a sophisticated understanding of 'outside', already dissolving the simple dichotomies of Black and White, Africa and Europe, and emphasizing their entanglement:

> Under neocolonialism, the economic systems and political policies of independent territories are managed and manipulated from outside, by international monopoly finance capital in league with the indigenous bourgeoisie.[29]

As with the continuing impact of the legacies of formal colonialism, it is well to remember, too, that the establishment of full-fledged colonial empires in Africa was preceded by several centuries of unequal Afro-European relations and interactions.[30] Throughout that history, Africans had a say in the course of events and often spoke out against the currents. For a long time they have been ignored in their originality or treated as only marginally relevant by hegemonic Western discourse. It is time to challenge this state of affairs, for African thinkers of the twentieth century have had a lot to say about the nature and causes of global inequality – and they still do. If we want to come to a more globally informed perspective on colonial and neo-colonial worlds, we should start listening to what Africa and Africans have to say.

28 Kwame Nkrumah: *Neo-Colonialism: The Last Stage of Imperialism*. London: Panaf 1971 [1965], p. ix.

29 Kwame Nkrumah: *Revolutionary Path*. London: Panaf 1973, p. 313.

30 Andreas Eckert / Ingeborg Grau / Arno Sonderegger (eds): *Afrika 1500–1900: Geschichte und Gesellschaft*. Vienna: Promedia 2010.

The Role of the Japanese Model in Ethiopian Political Thought (1900–1936)

Sara Marzagora

In one of the first Amharic-language newspapers ever produced in Ethiopia, renowned intellectual and politician Gäbrä-Ǝgziabher Gila-Maryam (1860s–1914) published a poem praising *zämänawinnät* (the Amharic term used to translate 'modernity') in the following terms:

> He who accepts it, fears no one.
> He will become like Japan, strong in everything.[1]

Ethiopia was, at the time Gäbrä-Ǝgziabher[2] wrote this poem in 1900, the only indigenous polity in Sub-Saharan Africa to have retained its independence throughout the Scramble for Africa, having successfully repelled an Italian invasion attempt at Adwa in 1896. Emperor Mənilək II had been conducting a series of military campaigns to the south-west, south and south-east of the traditional core of the Abyssinian empire, annexing large swathes of territory and negotiating with European powers the demarcation of new state borders.
The issue of *zämänawinnät* was a central one in Ethiopian political thought at the time, and Gäbrä-Ǝgziabher was one of the earliest intellectuals to campaign in favour of a rapid adoption of *zämänawinnät*.

1 Quoted in Richard Pankhurst: The Foundations of Education, Printing, Newspapers, Book Production, Library and Literacy in Ethiopia. In: *Ethiopia Observer* 6,3 (1962), pp. 241–290, here p. 262.

2 There are no surnames or family names in Amharic and Tigrinya. People are referred to by their first name, while their second name is not used for identification purposes, being simply the person's father's first name.

For Ethiopian intellectuals Europe was seen as a major example of how *zämänawinnät* could be achieved, as Gäbrä-Əgziabher argues in other poems.[3] In addition to Europe, though, Gäbrä-Əgziabher is perhaps the first intellectual to explicitly point at Japan as another, and equally important, model to borrow from. The admiration for Japan would remain a central element of Ethiopian intellectual history until the Italian occupation in 1936. This paper discusses the role Japan played in how Ethiopian thinkers defined and discussed *zämänawinnät*. The focus will be not so much on the diplomatic and commercial relations between the two countries, but more specifically on Ethiopian political thought. The topic is still relatively underexplored in Ethiopian historiography, Bahru Zewde and J. Calvitt Clarke being the only two historians to have dedicated comprehensive studies to it.[4]

Historical context

From the medieval period until the late 19th century, education in the Christian highlands was for the majority church-based. A sophisticated and highly codified system of religious education was available for children and young men from surrounding communities, comprising different levels and curricula. Besides churches and monasteries, another prominent centre of knowledge production was the imperial court. This scenario started to undergo significant changes from the latter half of the 19th century, when the first mission schools opened. Protestant and Catholic missionaries started to train recruit and educate Ethiopians, many of whom were given a chance to study in Europe and later came to play a significant role in Ethiopian politics.[5] Missionaries also introduced, in the 1860s, the first printing presses in Ethiopia, publishing mostly religious books and newsletters.

The first Ethiopian government newspaper was launched in 1901 by Emperor Mənilək II. The Emperor gave it the title *Aəmro* ('Intellect' or 'Intelligence') and entrusted the editorship to an Amharic-speaking

3 Pankhurst: Foundations of Education, pp. 260–262.

4 Bahru Zewde: *Society, State and History: Selected Essays*. Addis Ababa: Addis Ababa UP 2008, pp. 198–214; J. Calvitt Clarke: *Alliance of the Colored Peoples: Ethiopia and Japan before World War II*. Rochester, NY: Currey 2011.

5 Bahru Zewde: *Pioneers of Change in Ethiopia: the Reformist Intellectuals of the Early Twentieth Century*. Oxford: Currey 2002, pp. 15–19.

Greek businessman living in Addis Abäba, Andreas E. Kavadia. The Amharic-language newspaper came out weekly, although the publication was irregular until 1924 due to, among other difficulties, the inadequacy of the printing equipment. Initially circulating in a couple of dozen handwritten copies, it later increased its circulation to 200 copies, mostly sold to the nobility and the court. In 1908 Mənilək also founded the first government school in Ethiopia, called Mənilək II School, a primary school for boys. Religious education, though, remained the most vastly available educational facility. The Raguel Church in Ənṭoṭo, on the northern outskirts of Addis Abäba, was to produce a number of graduates who came to exert "much more preponderant influence in the political life of the country than the foreign-educated intellectuals".[6]

After Mənilək's death in 1913, the second phase of expansion of educational facilities and cultural infrastructures was under Empress Zäwditu's rule and *Ras* Täfäri's regency (1916–1930). Täfäri soon founded, in 1923, his own printing press, initially called "The Printing Press of the Heir to the Throne of Ethiopia His Highness *Ras* Täfäri Mäkʷonnən" (*Yä-Ityoppya mängəst alga wäraš yä-ləul Ras Täfäri Mäkʷonnən*) later renamed "*Bərhanənna Sälam* Press" after the flagship newspaper the printing press published from 1925 onwards. *Bərhanənna Sälam* came out weekly and had a circulation of 500 copies, almost all of them sold in Addis Abäba to registered subscribers.[7] Just like Mənilək before him, Täfäri in 1925 also founded a primary school, the Täfäri Mäkʷonnən School, whose first director was Wärḳənäh Əšäte.

Students were sent abroad for studying in a more systematic and organized way: while in 1925 only 25 students were sent overseas, by 1934 the number had risen to 200. The year 1930 saw the establishment of the first government school for girls, the Ətege Mänän School (named after Täfäri's wife). Schools in the provinces also opened, for a total of 21 government schools and 4,200 enrolled pupils in 1936. At the outbreak of the Italian war, Ethiopia had a population of 15 million people, and Addis Abäba was reported to have 90,000 inhabitants in 1938. Cultural infrastructures and institutions were heavily monopolized by the imperial court. With the exclusion of mission stations and foreign legations, private printing presses were non-existent.

6 Ibid., p. 73.

7 Meseret Chekol Reta: *The Quest for Press Freedom: One Hundred Years of History of the Media in Ethiopia*. Lamham / Plymouth: UP of America 2013, pp. 32–33.

All these reforms were implemented under the triple slogans of modernization, unity and state building. These were the three key elements of the political vision of 19th and 20th century emperors, who saw in them effective ideological banners for their own power consolidation. From the point of view of international diplomacy, projecting the image of modernizers and state-builders able to stabilize and develop the region gave the emperors legitimacy and leverage vis-à-vis foreign attempts to extend European influence in Ethiopia, and presented them as credible and like-minded allies and business partners. Domestically, *zämänawinnät* offered the instruments to centralize imperial power on an unprecedented level, thanks to new military technologies, infrastructural development and notions of territorial sovereignty linked to the Western idea of statehood. *Zämänawinnät* in 19th century Ethiopia, then, was eminently a political project of the rulers.[8]

Those early 20th century Ethiopian intellectuals that inherited this ideology, including the role that *zämänawinnät* had acquired within the imperial narrative, rapidly rose to prominence in the government. Of course, they did not count for the totality of early 20th century Ethiopian intellectual landscape: church education and Quranic schools kept training more traditional types of scholars, and numerous public figures remained cold towards the slogans of *zämänawinnät*. But because educational facilities and cultural infrastructures were government-owned and located at the centre of the imperial power in Addis Abäba, the works of the intellectuals close to the government had an impact, circulation and preservation in time that intellectuals from peripheral areas, or intellectuals not in line with government thought, could not achieve. And indeed limited sources are available to document the thought of those intellectuals who were, for reasons of class, ethnicity, religion or gender, distant from the imperial core of the state.

Since *zämänawinnät* was a top-down imperial project in Ethiopia, it was through centralized state institutions that the country's 'modernizers' were shaped and trained. The Emperors presented *zämänawinnät* as one facet of imperial ideology, and so it came to be conceived

8 Andreas Eshete: Modernity: Its Title to Uniqueness and Its Advent in Ethiopia. In: *Northeast African Studies* 13,1 (2012), pp. 1–17.

by many early 20th century intellectuals, who by endorsing the monarchical system gained powerful positions within the government and a high visibility for their works. Of course, there was also a genuinely idealistic aspect to the emperors' and intellectuals' commitment to *zämänawinnät*, but political thought and cultural production were never independent from political opportunism and calculations. The relationship between intellectuals and government remained problematic and uneasy throughout the period under consideration, and all the major intellectuals until the 1960s came to prominence through state institutions and through demonstrating at least a certain degree of loyalty to those institutions.

Ethiopia's new intellectual class was the first to be exposed to Western education, to have a distinctively urban lifestyle, and to operate in the international political environment defined by statehood. The first generation of 20th century Ethiopian thinkers comprised of men born in the 1860s, 1870s or 1880s, whose formative period was under Mənilək II and whose main period of intellectual and political activity were the 1910s, 1920s and 1930s. Their biographies have been extensively studied by Bahru Zewde, who refers to them as Ethiopia's "pioneers of change".[9] The most prominent members of this generation were Gäbrä-Həywät Baykädaň (1886–1919), Wärḳənäh Əšäte (1864–1952), Täklä-Hawaryat Täklä-Maryam (1884–1977), and Həruy Wäldä-Səlasse (1878–1938). Although their relationship with the imperial rulers was not always an easy one, they all came to occupy high positions in the Ethiopian government. Their role as Ethiopia's 'Japanizers' will be explored in the next paragraph. Another important 'Japanizer' was Käbbädä Mikael (c. 1914–1999),[10] who belonged to a younger set of intellectuals that came to prominence only after the end of the Italian occupation in 1941.

All of these intellectuals sought to theorize a uniquely Ethiopian way to *zämänawinnät* and an alternative development model to the one European colonial powers imposed throughout the rest of Sub-Saharan Africa. In order to achieve this, they "called for an *appropriate appropriation* of Western modernity on Ethiopian grounds, rejecting anything

9 Bahru: *Pioneers of Change.*

10 For biographical information on Käbbädä Mikael, see Reidulf K. Molvaer: *Black Lions: The Creative Lives of Modern Ethiopia's Literary Giants and Pioneers.* Lawrenceville, NJ: Red Sea 1997, pp.73–82.

that goes counter to Ethiopia's culture and honour".[11] *Zämänawinnät* would be achieved by the amalgam of what were considered the best elements of Western culture and what were considered the best elements of Ethiopian culture. The West was considered as a cultural area from which Ethiopia could borrow on equal terms, and although pride in Ethiopian cultural roots never waned, pre-1936 Ethiopian political thought is characterized by a rather open Europhilia. Of course, though, Ethiopian thinkers knew that their country's independence was still under threat, and indeed they embraced *zämänawinnät* also for strategic reasons. Only by developing rapidly could Ethiopia defend its independence against foreign colonial aggressions. Belief in evolutionary progress and modernization, as divulged in the West, was readily adopted by Ethiopian intellectuals, its teleology being consonant with Ethiopia's already-existing historical and political narratives strongly influenced by Christianity.

Ethiopia's 'Japanizers'

Embracing uni-linear social evolutionism meant, for Ethiopian thinkers, to conceive of their country as trailing behind Western nations in the single, universally valid, development path regulating the lives of all human societies. The need for Ethiopia to 'catch up' with the West led to the search for an appropriate model – a country that, starting off as a "little nation" (in Käbbädä Mikael's terminology)[12] like Ethiopia, managed to gain a place among the world's "big nations". This model was identified as Japan, and enthusiasm for the Japanese example was so widespread before the Italian occupation that historians frequently refer to pre-war intellectuals as Ethiopia's "Japanizers".[13] The term needs to be qualified, as pre-war intellectuals were admirers of Japan in so far as it offered a blueprint to reach the levels of economic growth and technological-scientific progress of Europe and

11 Teshale Tibebu: Modernity, Eurocentrism, and Radical Politics in Ethiopia 1961–1991. In: *African Identities* 6,4 (2008), pp. 345–371, here p. 357.

12 Käbbädä Mikael: *Ityopyanna mərabawi sələṭṭane / Ethiopia and Western Civilization / L'Éthiopie et la civilisation occidentale* [trilingual publication]. Addis Abäba: Bərhanənna Sälam 1949.

13 The first historian to use the terms "Japanizers" and "Japanization" seems to have been Addis Hiwet: *Ethiopia: From Autocracy to Revolution.* London: Review of African Political Economy 1975, p. 68.

the United States. In this sense, pre-war thinkers were 'Westernizers' as much as they were 'Japanizers', and their admiration for Japan was an extension of their admiration for what they saw as Western modernity. Japan and Europe were abstract models or patterns, and of course in neither case did Ethiopian intellectuals want their country to become a copy of Japan or Europe. While the ultimate objective pursued by pre-war Ethiopian intelligentsia was for Ethiopia to be recognized among the world's power-brokers, this ascent would have to be based on the safeguard of the country's own traditions. Japan was conceived, in this sense, as a temporary transitional guidance towards building a uniquely Ethiopian form of modernity.

The general Europhilia of early 20th century Ethiopian authors was attenuated by a series of pragmatic and ideological considerations that made Japan a valuable counter-model. First of all, the most significant threats to Ethiopian political and economic sovereignty were coming from European powers, so that "modernity's best teachers were also those who most threatened Ethiopia's independence".[14] It is more difficult to exactly assess the extent to which Western racism influenced pre-war Ethiopian political thought. Racially prejudiced descriptions of Ethiopian primitiveness coexisted with a Western fascination for Ethiopia as the legendary land of "black Caucasians"; Western depictions of Ethiopia oscillated between these two poles from Adwa to the 1930s. There appeared to have been a widespread outrage in Ethiopia at the discriminatory attitudes of white foreigners,[15] but European racism is seldom discussed or comprehensively analyzed in the intellectual production of the era, and it does not seem to be a dominant concern in the Ethiopian intellectual agenda.

While European Social Darwinists perceived the world in terms of the struggle between 'races of high social efficiency' and 'races of lower social efficiency', Ethiopian thinkers did not elaborate much on the racial and biological aspect of this concept, and adopted Social Darwinism in its sociological version as the struggle between 'nations' not 'races'. By a law of nature, Ethiopian intellectuals argued, stronger and more advanced nations will take over weaker ones, in

14 Clarke: *Alliance of the Colored Peoples*, p. XV.

15 Ibid., p. 17.

a perpetual struggle where only the fittest nations survive. In 1925, Wärḳənäh Əšäte (1864–1952) warned that "no individual nation can survive for long without basic knowledge. It will either lag behind or advance forward. If that nation lags behind, it will be overtaken by a stronger nation".[16] Käbbädä Mikael later echoed Wärḳənäh by explaining that "a nation assures the safeguard of its liberty by fighting courageously, but as another more civilised nation rises up against it, fearlessness and courage can do nothing against ability and it will succumb".[17]

Although racial issues were not central in Ethiopian political thought, the brief and ill-fated alliance between Ethiopia and Japan in the pre-1935 years was certainly framed, partly at least, from the racial point of view as a solidarity agreement between non-white peoples. Clarke suggests that it was the Japanese that particularly emphasized the racial connotation of the alliance and "began seductively speaking of leading an alliance of the world's colored peoples against white imperialism".[18]

Japan had an added bonus too, as it did not only offer an example of a "little nation" successfully becoming "big", but also of a transition to modernity able to retain local customs and culture. Teshale remarks how in the view of Ethiopian pre-war intellectuals "Japan appropriated Western modernity without losing its Japanese soul".[19] The most appealing aspect of the Japanese model was its successful hybridizing of external and internal inputs. This held particularly true at the level of the political macrostructure, Japan having successfully reinvented the monarchy as one of its main modernizing drives – exactly what Ethiopian intellectuals hoped to achieve in their own country. Early 20th century Ethiopian thinkers, in line with pre-existing traditions of Ethiopian political thought, identified the nation with the monarchy, and conceived the monarchy as the primary force of modernization. These thinkers were all organically linked to the imperial tradition, and proposed a reform scheme solidly implanted in Ethiopian

16 Quoted in Peter Garretson: *A Victorian Gentleman and Ethiopian Nationalist: The Life and Times of Hakim Wärqenäh, Dr. Charles Martin*. Rochester, NY: Currey 2012, p. 127.

17 Käbäddä: *Ethiopia and Western Civilization*, pp. 4–5.

18 Clarke: *Alliance of the Colored Peoples*, p. 13.

19 Teshale: Modernity, Eurocentrism, p. 357.

time-honoured political structure with the Emperor at the top. Both the intellectuals directly employed in the government and those "only peripherally attached to the state apparatus" advocated for Ethiopia a "modernization from above".[20]

All of the major first-generation 20th century intellectuals praised Japan at one moment or another. Gäbrä-Həywät Baykädaň (1886–1919) concluded his *Aṭe Mənilək-nna Ityopya* ('Emperor Mənilək and Ethiopia') with the advice to *Ləjj* Iyasu (r. 1913–1916) to follow the example of the Japanese government. In another point, Gäbrä-Həywät comments that

> when the Japanese Government finds someone willing to go to Europe to learn it supports them by giving them money. […] As a result the people [of Japan] opened their eyes. They became rich, strong and respectable. […] China and Asia have been following the path of Japan with great enthusiasm.[21]

Regent *Ras* Täfäri, who became Emperor in 1930 with the regal name Haylä Səlasse, reportedly had a personal fascination with Japan.[22] His newspaper *Bərhanənna Sälam* regularly published articles advocating the adoption of the Japanese model. In the teleology of progress, Ethiopia's lag over Japan was quantified at 60 years: "sixty years ago", remarked *Fitawrari* Deressa Amänte on a 1927 issue of *Bərhanənna Sälam*, "Japan was in the same state as Ethiopia".[23] The urge to mathematically measure Ethiopia's delay shows the extent to which the problem of Ethiopia's backwardness was tackled through a positivistic mindset.

Wärḳənäh Əšäte reasserts all the main elements of 'Japanization' in his speech at the opening of the Täfäri Mäkʷonnən School in 1925:

> Realizing that to be successful in life they ought to imbibe European knowledge and imbibe it fast, [the Japanese] began to work diligently and were able to reach in sixty years the level of development that it has taken others centuries. Let us follow this amazing and praiseworthy example of far-sightedness and resoluteness of an entire people.[24]

20 Bahru Zewde: *A History of Modern Ethiopia, 1855–1974*. London: Currey 1991, p. 110.

21 Quoted in Richard Pankhurst: Misoneism and Innovation in Ethiopian History. In: *Ethiopia Observer* 7,4 (1964), pp. 287–320, here p. 309.

22 Clarke: *Alliance of the Colored Peoples*, p. 12.

23 Quoted in Bahru: *Society, State and History*, p. 205.

24 Quoted in ibid., p. 204.

And he continues: "The reason behind the success of the Japanese to successfully defend their independence is their mastery of knowledge and education in due time."[25]

The peak of Ethiopia's Nippophilia was the period between Haylä Səlasse's coronation and the Italian invasion (1930–1935). In those years, the two intellectuals that moved the most concrete steps towards actualizing this desired "Japanization" were Həruy Wäldä-Səlasse (1878–1938) and Täklä-Hawaryat Täklä-Maryam (1884–1977). Həruy, as Haylä Səlasse's Minister of Foreign Affairs, was the leader of an Ethiopian diplomatic mission that visited Japan in 1931, following a treaty of friendship and commerce signed by the two countries in 1927 and the presence of a Japanese delegation at Haylä Səlasse's coronation in 1930. Həruy's trip, lasting from 5th November to 28th December 1931, undoubtedly marks the highest point of Ethio-Japanese relations. The main objective of the visit was to develop closer commercial ties and stimulate Japanese investments in Ethiopia. Həruy was particularly hopeful to arrange for Ethiopia to import cheap everyday goods from Japan.[26] The Ethiopian delegation received a very warm welcome. In the forty days they spent in Japan, Həruy and his party attended a number of high-profile receptions and visited factories, offices, industrial farms, zoos, theatres, railways, shrines, museums, and military training schools. As part of his visit, Həruy met Emperor Hirohito, to whom he announced:

> Our Ethiopian Emperor is deeply impressed with Japanese Empire's remarkable and great progress of the last sixty years, and is moved with surprise that the Japanese Empire accomplished such a great deed in such a short time. […] He is determined to advocate to his whole nation to take the Great Japanese Empire as the best model.[27]

His Japanese sojourn impressed Həruy so much that, back in Ethiopia, he quickly put together a booklet titled *Mahdärä Bərhan Hägär Japan* ('The Place of Light: the Country of Japan'), published in 1932, praising the Japanese example. Həruy writes that it is surprising that two nations with such similar histories had remained for such a long time oblivious of each other. He proceeds to list the similarities between

25 Quoted in Garretson: *Victorian Gentleman*, p. 127.

26 Clarke: *Alliance of the Colored Peoples*, p. 45.

27 Quoted in Bahru: *Society, State and History*, p. 205.

the two countries. Both Ethiopia and Japan had been ruled by long and uninterrupted imperial dynasties. Hirohito is the 124th monarch of the Jimmu dynasty, while Haylä Səlasse is the 126th of the Solomonic line. Both empires had itinerant capitals for centuries. The Tokugawa Shogunate (1600–1868), as a period of decentralized political authority, is comparable to the Ethiopian *Zämänä Mäsafənt* (1769–1855). In his reassertion of centralized imperial power, Meiji was similar to Mənilək II. *Mahdärä Bərhan Hägär Japan* was promptly translated into Japanese by Oreste and Enko Vaccari, and the Japanese translation was published in Tokyo in 1934, with a preface penned by the Japanese Minister of Foreign Affairs Kijūrō Shidehara.[28]

Täklä-Hawaryat's contribution to Ethiopia's pro-Japanese momentum is mostly linked to the 1931 constitution, which Täklä-Hawaryat was asked by Haylä Səlasse to draft. Täklä-Hawaryat declares in his autobiography to have consulted copies of the German, Italian, Japanese and English [*sic*] constitutions,[29] but in the resulting text the Japanese influence proved by far the greatest. Täklä-Hawaryat's draft was subsequently reviewed by Həruy, *Ras* Kassa and Haylä Səlasse himself.[30] Educated for many years in Russia and reputed to be a Russophile, it is dubious to what extent Täklä-Hawaryat really shared Həruy's profound admiration for Japan. Täklä-Hawaryat believed that Ethiopia had more poignant political models in the countries of Eastern Europe and the Mediterranean area, with which it always maintained close links due to, among other things, the common Orthodox Christian faith.[31] On top of this, Täklä-Hawaryat seemed to have been worried that increased commercial ties with Japan would have antagonized European countries – and, as we shall see, his fears would prove long-sighted.[32] The circumstances surrounding the drafting of the 1931 constitution are not well documented, but, although Täklä-Hawaryat certainly produced a first comprehensive draft, it has been suggested that it was Həruy who played a decisive role in revising it along the lines of the Meiji model.

28 Clarke: *Alliance of the Colored Peoples*, p. 45.

29 Bahru: *Society, State and History*, p. 208.

30 Ibid., p. 208.

31 Clarke: *Alliance of the Colored Peoples*, p. 57.

32 Ibid., p. 56.

In whatever way the drafting process went, the result was that many of the articles of the 1931 constitution are closely modelled on the articles of the Meiji constitution, and a clause-by-clause analysis of the two texts reveals striking similarities. Two examples are given here.[33] In the Meiji constitution, the third article of the first chapter reads that "the Emperor is sacred and inviolable", while in the Ethiopian 1931 constitution the fifth article of the first chapter states that "by virtue of His imperial blood as well as by the anointing which He has received, the person of the Emperor is sacred, His dignity is inviolable and His power indisputable". In the Meiji constitution, the seventh article of the first chapter reads that "The Emperor convokes the Imperial Diet, opens, closes and prorogues it, and dissolves the House of Representatives" and is echoed in the eight article of the second chapter of the Ethiopian constitution, which proclaims:

> It is the Emperor's right to convene the deliberative Chambers and to declare the opening and the close [sic] of their sessions. He may also order their convocation before or after the usual time. He may dissolve the Chamber of Deputies.[34]

Bahru notices that both constitutions were granted from above, "not won by popular struggle from below", and were intended "more as vehicles of strong monarchical government than as platforms for genuine popular representation".[35]

The Ethiopian constitution was, if anything, more authoritarian, and

> the chapters on the rights and duties of citizens are masterpieces in qualification: […] the guaranteeing of civil liberties is coupled with such nullifiers as 'within the limits provided for by the law' or 'except in cases provided for in the law'.[36]

Clarke so comments in this regard:

> Ethiopia's Constitution concentrated and made more emphatic the Emperor's traditional, absolute and Imperial power than did Japan's. Ethiopia's Emperor held executive power over the central and provincial governments, and the

33 For a full list, see James C.N. Paul / Christopher Clapham: *Ethiopian Constitutional Development*. Addis Ababa: Haile Selassie I UP 1967, pp. 326–338, or Bahru: *Society State and History*, pp. 210–213, or Clarke: *Alliance of the Colored Peoples*, pp. 172–173.

34 Ibid.

35 Bahru: *Society, State and History*, pp. 206–207.

36 Ibid., p. 206.

newly created parliament, which had only powers of discussion, provided no check on him.[37]

The commercial ties and political alliance between Japan and Ethiopia would not survive pre-World War Two international tensions. Italy invaded Ethiopia in 1935, and although in Japan popular support for Ethiopia was strong, the Japanese government could not risk alienating a powerful potential ally like Italy. After the liberation of Ethiopia in 1941, the old generation of Japanizers had either died (Həruy) or lost influence in the government (Wärḳənäh and Täklä-Hawaryat), and the new generation of younger intellectuals looked rather towards the UK and USA than towards Japan.

Conclusions

The way Ethiopian intellectuals related to Japan in the first half of the 20th century highlights two general characteristics of Ethiopian political thought. The first is the centrality of the monarchy. The case of the 1931 constitution shows that the most appealing trait of the Japanese paradigm was the possibilities it offered to reinvent the political significance of the monarchy by presenting it as the main driving agent of modernization. In other words, Japan offered the example of a successful top-down, monarchy-driven progress, and it was precisely this model that Ethiopian intellectuals envisioned to replicate in their own country. In Ethiopian intellectual circles, *ʒämänawinnät* was exclusively conceived to be an effect of kingship. The possibility of achieving it outside of kingship was never considered – and this holds true for Ethiopian political thought well into the 1960s. As a result of this, however, the intellectuals ended up being politically, economically, and ideologically co-opted by Haylä Səlasse's regime – a collusion that historians like Bahru Zewde and Richard Reid see as an element of failure.[38]

The second characteristic is that Ethiopian intellectuals approached world history and cultural alterity in a teleological and reductionist

37 Clarke: *Alliance of the Colored Peoples*, p. 38.

38 Bahru: *History of Modern Ethiopia*, pp. 110–111; Richard Reid: Review of Peter Garretson's 'A Victorian Gentleman & Ethiopian Nationalist: the Life and Times of Hakim Warqenah, Dr Charles Martin'. In: *Reviews in History* 1388 (2013). http://www.history.ac.uk/reviews/review/1388 (accessed 23.01.2014).

manner. The Ethiopian Japanizers only had "the faintest acquaintance with Japanese history".[39] The comparisons with Japan and attempts to emulate Japan's historical trajectory "suffered all too often from inadequate understanding of pre-Meiji Japanese history".[40] The argument that Ethiopia and Japan were comparable societies was based on an assimilationist reading of Japanese history, which selectively picked elements of apparent similarity and overlooked the vast differences that existed between pre-Meiji Japan and the Ethiopia of the 1920s and 1930s. The Japanizers' claim that Ethiopia and Japan were, until the 1868 Meiji restoration, at the same stage of social development was, Bahru remarks, essentially mistaken.[41] Bahru concludes that "the impassioned pleas of the 'Japanizers' remained a subjective urge unsupported by objective reality".[42]

Käbbädä Mikael was one of the few in the post-occupation period to still demonstrate faith in the viability of the Japanese model; his *Japan əndämən sälät̤t̤änäčč* ('How Japan modernized' but also translatable as 'How Japan became civilized', considering that *sələt̤t̤ane* is often translated as 'modern civilization'), published in 1953/54, was the last major contribution to the Japanizing cause. From one point of view, Käbbädä reiterates and even expands the elements of similarity between Ethiopia and Japan. To Həruy's list, he adds that both Ethiopia and Japan were visited by the Portuguese roughly at the same time, and reacted to the Portuguese evangelization attempts by forcing them out of the country in order to safeguard local religion traditions. After the Portuguese incursion, Käbbädä reasons, both countries remained isolated from the external world for two and a half centuries. However, Käbbädä also accounts for the differences between Ethiopia and Japan, noticing that Japan was more developed than Ethiopia at the time of renewed contact with Westerners in the mid-19th century. Käbbädä writes at the time when one of the main objectives of pro-*zämänawinnät* Ethiopians, to develop their country's military and economic sector enough to effectively repel foreign attacks, had already failed. The five traumatic years of Italian occupation (1936–1941) have already invalidated the main rationale

39 Bahru: *Society, State and History*, p. 209.

40 Bahru: *Pioneers of Change*, p. 4.

41 Bahru: *Society, State and History*, pp. 208–209.

42 Ibid., p. 210.

behind the adoption of the Japanese model, i. e. to preserve Ethiopia's independence.

After Käbbädä, the Japanese model did not disappear, but started being discussed in different terms. In the pre-war period the Ethiopian intellectuals spurred their ruling class to 'do just like Japan'. From the 1950s onwards, the discourse on Japan shifted towards an *ex post* assessment of 'why Japan managed to modernize and we did not'. Despite this bitterness, the fascination with Japan as a possible developmental model, or as a useful comparison pole for Ethiopia, lasts to the present day, both in daily conversations between educated urban Ethiopians (as I experienced during my stays in Addis Abäba) and in scholarly publications.[43]

43 Messay Kebede: Japan and Ethiopia: An Appraisal of Similarities and Divergent Courses. In: Katsuyoshi Fukui / Eisei Kurimoto / Masayoshi Shigeta (eds): *Ethiopia in Broader Perspective: Papers of the 13th International Conference of Ethiopian Studies*. Kyoto: Shokado 1997, pp. 639–51; Donald Levine: Ethiopia and Japan in Comparative Civilizational Perspective. In: Ibid., pp. 41–51; Merid W. Aregay: Japanese and Ethiopian Reactions to Jesuit Missionary Activities in the Sixteenth and Seventeenth Centuries. In: Ibid., pp. 676–698; Getachew Felleke: Education and Modernization: An Examination of the Experiences of Japan and Ethiopia. In: Seifudein Adem (ed.): *Japan, a Model and a Partner: Views and Issues in African Development*. Leiden / Boston: Brill 2006, pp. 67–104; Seifudein Adem: Is Japan's Cultural Experience Relevant for Africa's Development? In: Ibid., pp.187–222; Donald Levine: Ethiopia, Japan, and Jamaica: A Century of Globally Linked Modernizations. In: *International Journal of Ethiopian Studies* 3,1 (2007), pp. 41–51.

Africa and Neoliberal Circuits of Intellectual Value Production

Thinking through the Work of Issa Shivji[1]

Paulina Aroch-Fugellie

After a couple of pages dedicated to reduce Africa to the fetishistic mind, to the incapacity of its inhabitants to attain the level of abstraction proper to monotheist religions or to Western art, Georg Wilhelm Friedrich Hegel, in his *Philosophy of History* solemnly declares: "At this point we leave Africa, not to mention it again. For it is no historical part of the world; it has no movement or development to exhibit".[2] Although this view of Africa is supposed to be long-ago superseded, it remains present in both academic and popular discourse. Mass media equate the continent to abjection and lack, to a violent space of lawlessness, to famine and pernicious disease. Africa is reduced to the sphere of mere biological –indeed animal – survival, below and beneath civilization and history.

At an apparently opposite end of the spectrum, speculative capital has managed to popularize a coexisting idea of Africa as the land of capital's future, a land of potential, of virtuality, and above all, of mobility. Going over the last two years of the coverage that the popular British weekly newspaper *The Economist* has given to the continent, we find a bombardment of story after story of IBM, Google

1 I thank Brían Hanrahan (Deep Springs College, CA), whose ideas in conversation were crucial for the development of the present text.

2 Georg Wilhelm Friedrich Hegel: Introduction to the Philosophy of History, trans. from German by John Sibree. In: *Great Books of the Western World*, ed. by Robert M. Hutchins. London: Encyclopedia Britannica 1952, pp. 151–201, here p. 199.

or Microsoft penetrating Africa, of Chinese capital venturing in and gliding through, of potential markets ready to be untapped only by those entrepreneurs savvy enough to have the necessary foresight.[3] It calls to attention that of all the new information and communication technologies, mobile phones, with their connotations of flexibility, mediation and mobility itself have become so widely popularized in Africa, and this so heavily advertised.

In sum, today Africa is shoveled out of history in two ways. First, by way of absolute abjection, by being produced and reproduced as the realm of the infra-human: infra-human meaning here both a precariousness that reduces people at the very best to mere survival and modes of life not yet codified according to the liberal humanist ideals that are the very same ones to co-structure these conditions in the first place. Second, we are confronted with mobile, hyper-fluid African outposts of futurity, forts and bridgeheads of a kind of clean de-historicized next-wave capitalist future, in an otherwise swamp of disease and war. So long as we understand history not as a particular moment in time but as the dialectic invocation of one moment in and through another, then we may say that history continues to be systematically denied to the continent.

In the context of this book's quest towards an intellectual history of Africa, I want to examine Africa's place (or its displacement) in the global imaginary today, as concerns both the question of history and the question of intellectual practice. I address the period spanning from the emergence of the New International Division of Labor in the late 1960s to the present day. I will explore some macro-logical narratives on the place and function of Africa in terms of the wider global imaginary; and, thereafter, I will focus on the work of Tanzanian activist and scholar Issa Shivji: on how he acts, on how he reflects, and on how he does both together in terms of that wider constellation.

3 See, for example, one recent article in *The Economist*, where both text and photograph convey the idea of Africa's direct passage from a land of absolute wilderness to one of technologized futurity (Innovation in Africa: Upwardly Mobile. In: *The Economist*, 14.02.2013. http://www.economist.com/node/21560912 (accessed 30.10.2014). Another example, among many, of both picture and text playing into such an image of the continent has appeared in the same journal: Information Technology in Africa: The Next Frontier. In: *The Economist*, 23.08.2012. http://www.economist.com/news/business/21571889-technology-companies-have-their-eye-africa-ibm-leading-way-next-frontier (accessed 30.10.2014).

I.

In the 1960s there was a shift that reorganized the spatial logistics of the global political-economy. New transport, information and communication technologies made it cheaper to subdivide "manufacturing processes into a number of partial operations at different industrial sites throughout the world".[4] Countries of the North Atlantic now focused on the service sector and geared towards consumption, while Asia and Latin America became increasingly interpolated as providers of cheap industrial labor power rather than suppliers of raw materials.[5] With the emergence of this New International Division of Labor, the differentiated roles of each were clearly demarcated: the Global South was to be the ground for the valorization of capital – producing surplus value in industry, while the North Atlantic would be consolidated as the place of value's appropriation and accumulation.

Yet it is only catachrestically that Africa as a homogenous whole can be included in that Global South. As James Ferguson has argued, today most industries in Africa are set up in the form of extractive enclaves that are alienated from their immediate surroundings. These are capital intensive mining and oil sites, walled-off from neighboring society, insulated from the local economy and often guarded by paramilitary forces.[6] As Ferguson elaborates, the French colonial distinction between "useful" and "unusable" Africa is pertinent now more than ever.[7]

4 Folker Fröbel / Jürgen Heinrichs / Otto Kreye: *The New International Division of Labour*. Cambridge: Cambridge UP 1980, p. 45.

5 Ibid., p. 403. They list Africa alongside Asia and Latin America, since their objective is not to focus on the distinctions within the Third World, but rather on that between the Third and the First. Likewise, and as will become more pertinent further on in this paper, while they do deal with the question of unemployment in the Third World, their emphasis is mainly on how these changes have brought structural unemployment to the countries of the North Atlantic region.

6 James Ferguson: Globalizing Africa? Observations from an Inconvenient Continent. In: Id.: *Global Shadows: Africa in the Neoliberal World Order*. Durham: Duke UP 2006, pp. 25–49, here pp. 34–38.

7 Ferguson's distinction is via the work of William Reno. He refers to "the two different Africas that French colonialism once distinguished as '*Afrique utile*' and '*Afrique inutile*' – or 'usable/useful Africa' and 'unusable/useless Africa' as Reno (1999) has reminded us" (ibid., p. 39).

> Usable Africa gets secure enclaves – noncontiguous "useful" bits that are secured, policed, and […] governed through private or semiprivate means. These enclaves are increasingly linked up, not in a national grid, but in transnational networks that connect economically valued spaces dispersed around the world in a point to point fashion. / The rest – the vast terrain of "unusable" Africa – gets increasingly nongovernmental states […] open to banditry and warlordism.[8]

This "unusable" and, even, 'useless' part of Africa constitutes the vast majority of the continent, in terms of territory, but mostly in terms of population. Whereas earlier work-intensive industrial capitalist mining – as in the case of the Zambian copper belt – brought with it a social investment in housing, schools and hospitals required for its own fulfillment, contemporary capital-intensive enclaves are socially thin, bringing little employment to Africans and hiring only a reduced amount of foreign high-skilled workers.[9]

The inhabitants of "unusable Africa" are thus paradigmatic of what Michael Denning has – in a different context – referred to as the precariousness and disposability of human life for contemporary capitalism.[10] 'Useless' Africa is not a zone beyond the grasp of the global economy, but constitutive of the latter. Just as Walter Rodney's historiography has established that the dependent, export-oriented economies were produced in tandem with, in, by and for colonialism itself,[11] today, the steep relief of contemporary African economies is not an aberration of the norm, but the required inequality that allows for the norm: the norm of competition amongst zones of differentiated taxing regulations, differentiated prices of labour, differentiated life expectancies.

It is with these insights in mind that we can conceive neoliberalism as operating on a triadic geo-economic structure which concentrates accumulation of surplus value in the North Atlantic and industrial production in Asia and Latin America. Africa appears then as the abject other of an economy which nonetheless is fundamentally dependent on it. The vast terrain of Africa's 'useless' territories, its "disposable lives", its "precarious lives" provide an excess labor force

8 Ferguson: Globalizing Africa?, p. 39.

9 Ibid., pp. 36–37.

10 Michael Denning: Wageless Life. In: *New Left Review* 66 (2010), pp. 79–97, here p. 79.

11 Walter Rodney: *How Europe Underdeveloped Africa.* Abuja: Panaf 2009 [1973].

in permanent indebtedness that underscores the speculative logic of the global economy, embodying a state of abjection such that it indexes exploitation itself as a privilege.[12]

II.

So, on this basis, let me now argue that a parallel triadic structure underpins global circuits of intellectual value production. The North Atlantic concentrates Theory in the universal sense, while Latin America and Asia's role is to yield an intellectual production of the particular (for example, fiction, or theory considered of exclusive local interest). In this reading, Africa is then shown to be the land of the *infra-theoretical*, on whose exclusion the value-as-differential of Theory, Theory's scarcity value ultimately rests. Thus, if, at the time of Hegel, Africa was the place of absolute *absence* – the foundational foreclosure that allowed for the emergence of History elsewhere –, in today's hegemonic imaginary, Africa is deployed as a place of such absolute *presence* that it remains unable to enter the second order discourse appropriate for self-reflexivity.

As Edward Said and Gayatri Spivak have elaborated, second order discourse is a paradigmatic place for the constitution of the subject status.[13] Africa operates as the negative space allowing Western Theory as a Universal to achieve its closure. Deployed as the land of the infra-theoretical, Africa fulfills the need for what in mathematical Set Theory would be called the "Theory Complement" (T'), that is, an exterior to the set "Theory" (T), within a given "Universe" (U = T + T'). Serving merely a structural function to delineate the contours of theoretical production elsewhere, the deployment of Africa as pure absence is not only a violence to African intellectual history, but also a violence to history as such: it is the largest scale testament to how the idealist tradition in Western thought has been erected at the cost of and on the basis of a radical separation between history and theory.

12 The terms "disposable lives" and "precarious lives" are taken from Denning: Wageless Life, p. 79.

13 Edward W. Said: *Orientalism: Western Conceptions of the Orient.* London: Penguin 1995 [1978]; Gayatri Chakravorty Spivak: More on Power/Knowledge. In: *Outside in the Teaching Machine.* New York: Routledge 1993, pp. 25–51.

The disassociation between Western Theory and its historical specificity is what has always allowed Theory to operate as a universal, yet that disassociation is more heightened today than ever before. In his book *Considerations on Western Marxism*, Perry Anderson writes that the bond between theory and practice even in Marxist intellectuals began to quiver after the First World War and "[b]y the [...] Second World War [...] the distance between them was so great that it seemed virtually consubstantial with the tradition itself".[14] Anderson is particularly critical of the professionalization and academic affiliation of most contemporary intellectuals.[15] He also criticizes attempts such as that of Theodor Adorno in *Negative Dialectics*[16] to find a perfectly closed autonomous systematicity, which wasn't there in Marx's own work to begin with – Anderson therefore refers to that trend of Marxism as an "esoteric" one. In sum, for Anderson postwar Western Marxism "had no anchorage within the social class for whose benefit theoretical work in Marxism alone has ultimate meaning".[17] I appreciate Anderson's emphasis here on the importance of approaching theoretical production not only in its own self-legitimating terms. Anderson deploys the pragmatic dimension of theoretical discourse as vital for the completion of its meaning. I believe that both the semantic and the pragmatic dimensions of theory are important to consider as we take steps towards an intellectual history of Africa. Since theory is one of the most consecrated modes of circulation of contemporary intellectual production, its historical purpose, reason and function in context cannot be ignored.

Historiography is capable of actually producing theory. A historiography of intellectual practice in Africa produces theory *post facto* because economic and semiotic values in capitalism pivot around the

14 Perry Anderson: *Considerations on Western Marxism*. London: Verso 1979, p. 29.

15 Anderson goes on to elaborate on the changing historical conditions that cut the ties between social struggles and intellectual practice in the countries of the North Atlantic region. One of the most striking features that Anderson detects "about the whole tradition from Lukacs to Althusser [...] is the overwhelming predominance of professional philosophers within it", an academic emplacement of theory that, as he observes, was emphatically scorned by earlier Marxists of the Second International, such as Rosa Luxemburg (ibid., p. 52).

16 Theodor W. Adorno: *Negative Dialectics* (1966), trans. from German by E. B. Ashton. New York: Continuum 1983.

17 Anderson: *Considerations*, p. 44.

sphere of production, but are only *realized* as values in circulation. By engaging in a historiography of African intellectual practices, we legitimize and set into circulation a *pre-existing* intellectual history, the value of which has not yet been actualized as such in North-Atlantic circuits of scholarly value. Crucial here is the fact that, although African cultural production has been increasingly present in academic spheres outside the continent for the past few decades, it has been limited to the role of object enunciated, exotic fetish, or commodity for the mere appropriation and accumulation of cultural capital for scholars in the North Atlantic. An intellectual history of Africa can serve to legitimate the continent as a site for self-reflexive and critical enunciation, for the production of theory in the aforementioned sense.[18]

III.

I have decided to focus the last pages of this text on the work of contemporary Tanzanian political economist Issa Shivji. His work is solid ground from which to argue that African intellectual production, while on the one hand wanting admittance to the enabling global circuits of production and consumption of cultural capital is, on the other hand, in a privileged position when it comes to the production of meaning – the socially relevant and historically transformative function of theory that Anderson finds so poignantly absent in postwar Western Marxism, not to mention in contemporary theory in general.[19]

18 Hence, the mere formal gesture on our part, the very fact and nature of our undertaking, produces theory as an object of study, so long as we understand theory as a congealed moment of abstraction in the dialectics between a subject's experience of and reflection on the world; a discourse that proceeds according to established methods, builds on shared referents and traditions of thought, and, crucially, is received and accepted as such by a particular society.

19 I have stressed contemporary Marxism's lack of a social anchorage to adequately produce meaning because the maxim of this philosophical tradition is the transformation (rather than mere interpretation) of the world. Yet this lack of anchorage is a widespread characteristic in contemporary thought and by no means limited to Marxism. While Jonathan Culler elaborates on post-structuralism's derailment into hyper-formalist and self-referent acrobatics of thought in a number of First World academic niches, Frederic Jameson speaks of a basic break between signifier and referent in postmodern society; see Jonathan Culler: Structure of Ideology and Ideology of Structure. In: *New Literary History* 4,3 (1973), pp. 471–482; Frederic Jameson: *Postmodernism or the Cultural Logic of Late Capitalism*. London: Verso 1991.

In 2007, having been involved in NGO activism for over 15 years, Issa Shivji published *Silences in NGO Discourse: The Role and Future of NGOs in Africa*, a book that examines nongovernmental organizations in Africa as a key element of the neo-colonialist project. After a historical account of the advance of NGOs in the continent – an advance traceable in figures such as the 400 percent British government increase for funding NGOs overseas between 1984 and 1994 – Shivji puts forward the thesis that "the proponents of neoliberalism saw in charitable development the possibility of enforcing the unjust social order they desired by consensual rather than coercive means".[20] Therefore, he argues, NGOs are to the neoliberal project what Christian missionaries were to the colonialist one: the human face at the forefront of the imperialist enterprise. Let us not forget also, that NGOs are the form of governmentality that prevails in all of "unusable Africa", in the zones of widespread banditry and warlordism to which Ferguson referred.

The first of the "five silences" of NGOs that Shivji addresses is their unrevised emergence as a reaction of the international donor community to the nation-state centered period in African history.[21] Secondly, the author addresses the NGO activists in Africa, mostly urban elites, and only a small sub-portion of them acting out of desire for genuine political transformation. Another subset, argues Shivji, is constituted by altruistic or morally motivated individuals that nonetheless tend to be ignorant of the complicities implicit in the actions in which they engage. Yet, by far the largest subgroup of NGO activists is formed by career-driven individuals. In a continent in which work opportunities in the private sector are lacking and governments thinning out, NGOs increasingly function simply as a source of income.[22]

The third silence Shivji mentions is the fact that, being donor funded, NGOs must follow donor agendas. These donors, legitimated as 'civil society' are at worst foreign government agencies and at best a non-African civil society. Given that in countries such as Zambia, 70% of the government's revenue consists of foreign aid, national sovereignty is seriously put into question. But it is in regard to the last

20 Issa G. Shivji: *Silences in NGO Discourse: The Role and Future of NGOs in Africa.* Nairobi: Fahamu 2007, p. ix.

21 Ibid., p. 30.

22 Ibid., p. 31.

two "silences of NGO discourse" that Shivji directly addresses the function of the intellectual and the historical purpose of knowledge production as critique. What the author terms the "fourth silence" is that NGOs are issue-based. In true identity-politics style, the organizations target the surface symptom of a problem such as gender violence or child malnutrition and, in disavowing the larger structural ties of such issues in society and history, allow for the problem to continue reproducing itself. This myopic approach can be maintained so long as there persists a rift between academic research and activist agendas. That divorce between critical thought and political action is by all means deliberate, as Shivji bluntly puts it "our erstwhile benefactors tell us: 'just act, don't think; and we shall fund both'".[23]

The fifth silence also relates to the disablement of praxis and the de-historization of discourse. Shivji refers in this last point to the vagueness of the missions written out by NGOs. In their vagueness, NGO mission statements celebrate moral principles in the abstract; their floating signification is what allows for the naturalization of neoliberal values.[24] This hegemonic appropriation of terms such as 'freedom', 'self-governance' or 'civil-society' as understood by neoliberalism, can only be counteracted by being historicized. Issa Shivji describes how NGO discourse seems to have internalized Fukuyama's idea of the end of history, the idea that we live in a "permanent present", in which "the hegemony of the imperialist North is declared permanent" and where "[a]ny historical understanding of our present state is ridiculed and dismissed", "reduced to a blaming exercise" or "tolerated as a token to [...] create the illusion of diversity".[25] Shivji interrogates the NGO slogan that summons us to 'Make Poverty History' by asking "but how can you make poverty history without understanding the history of poverty?"[26] As Shivji states,

23 Ibid., p. 35.

24 See Ernesto Laclau: The Death and Resurrection of the Theory of Ideology. In: *MLN* 112,3 (1997), pp. 297–321. Despite later variations, in 1997 Ernesto Laclau holds that floating and empty signifiers are, for all practical purposes, the same: "In the case of a floating signifier we would apparently have an overflowing of meaning while an empty signifier, on the contrary, would ultimately be a signifier without a signified. But if we analyze the matter more carefully, we realize that the floating character of a signifier is the only phenomenal form of its emptiness" (ibid., p. 306).

25 Shivji: *Silences in NGO Discourse*, pp. 37–38.

26 Ibid., p. 37.

only in understanding the present as history can we have any hope of changing it.[27] Hence, what contemporary hegemonic discourse as articulated in NGO rhetoric forecloses is the political force of history as a *function* of the present.

By historicizing the notion of civil society Shivji questions the widespread presupposition of 'civil society' as a 'harmonious whole'.[28] Such an assumption comes from both activist and scholarly locations in the West, particularly in Anglo-America today – I am thinking, for example, of the work of Canadian political philosopher at Queen's University, Richard Day. In his book *Gramsci is Dead*, which had a direct impact on the Occupy Wall Street movement, Day attributes the failures of the contemporary left to their retrograde forms of organization in political parties and trade unions, and proposes instead to follow the informal modes of organization proper to civil society, which he views as "non-universalizing, non-hierarchical, non-coercive relationships based on mutual aid and shared ethical commitments".[29] Shivji questions the possibility of such uninterested and unmarked forms of organization, since he understands civil society historically – as the realm of economic relations emerging with the birth of the bourgeoisie – and examines the re-emergence of the concept – also historically – in terms of its growing popularity in public discourse in the era of structural adjustment programs. Therefore, he is able to conceive of civil society as a "terrain of contradictory relations".[30]

By questioning the artificial division of state and civil society, Shivji reassesses the nationalist period in Africa and, in direct opposition to the World Bank's diagnosis of the African state as the villain of the continent's declining economic performance, actually proposes to understand the nationalist moment in African history as the constitutive contradiction, the exception, the relative outside, or what he terms "the fundamental antithesis" to the imperialist project.[31] Thinking of Theodor Adorno's proposition that ideology is based

27 Shivji: *Silences in NGO Discourse*, p. 38.

28 Ibid., p. 28.

29 Richard J. F. Day: *Gramsci is Dead: Anarchist Currents in the Newest Social Movements*. London: Pluto 2005, p. 9.

30 Shivji: *Silences in NGO Discourse*, p. 28.

31 Ibid., p. 1; cf. ibid., p. 20.

on constitutive exclusions and that to contest an ideology is to negate its negation, to push it towards the realization of its own promise, Shivji's persisting praxis in NGO activism in and through his severe critique of it, as well as his invocation of the nationalist project as a history to be owned, in the full sense of the term, are carried out in true negative dialectical fashion, as a way of invoking a particular history to actualize its promise in the present. While conscious of the "politically authoritarian, economically rapacious, internationally compradorial and nationally dictatorial" degenerations of African nationalisms in course of time, Shivji is still able to build upon the intellectual and political legacy of his countryman Julius Nyerere to call forth an exception to that project that was nonetheless possible, however provisionally.[32]

In working to destroy the system by pushing it to fulfill its own promise, Shivji is following the path of negative dialectics. Yet, unlike Adorno's negative dialectics, this is not a finished project, not an "esoteric" one, to use Perry Anderson's term. Shivji's is an unfinished project because it is open to history, an intellectual history of praxis. Shivji reintroduces the value of history into a largely self-referential or merely descriptive corpus of academic thought and in so doing produces knowledge as critique.

Conclusion

African theory has a history. Its intellectual praxis is not an absent but a disavowed tradition. As readers and scholars engaging in and with this tradition we leap into its retroactive constitution. To focus on the value of reception in the retroactive constitution of a philosophical cannon is to accept the responsibility that in interpreting African intellectual history we are participating in it: we are granting that past a historical, even an ontological reality, just as the selected pasts enable our political positioning and projects in the present.

Shivji's *Silences in NGO Discourse* entails a theoretical praxis that contributes to undoing the meaning of Africa as pure absence and, in so doing, may help undermine – even if in the most circumscribed of manners – the whole triadic structure to which I referred at the beginning of this article. The intersections of intellectual reflection

32 Ibid., pp. 11–13.

and political action in Shivji's trajectory also relativize the alleged escape from instrumental reason of much contemporary Theory in the North Atlantic tradition.

Reassessing his work and that of other African theorists is a way to push for the entrance of African knowledge production into valued global circuits, but also to question the nature and function of the circuits themselves, to ask what the uses of intellectual history are to the present status quo, and to recall the contingency of that history as we participate in its production.

In Search of 'African Aesthetics'

Academic Perspectives on Art, Culture and the African Way of Appreciating

Lena Dallywater[1]

In modern African historiography, three intellectual currents have significantly changed writing about Africa: firstly, the global black intellectual movement, expressed in the politics of Pan-Africanism and in cultural developments, such as the Harlem Renaissance, secondly, the tradition of indigenous writing within Africa itself, and thirdly a current that began in the 1940's in the era of decolonization and combined the two strong forces of overseas history in Europe and of nationalism in Africa.[2] This new historiography affirmed the possibility of African history and began to reclaim the history of the pre-colonial and colonial period. Measured against the size of today's historiographical output in general, we are still confronted with a disproportionately small number of extensive research projects and comprehensive publications on both periods, as well as on post-colonial developments, from a multi-centered perspective. Few authors have systematically analyzed the impacts of cultural and racial essentialism on representations of Africa, which is present both in the derogative discourses of Eurocentrism as well as in the affirmative gestures of Afrocentricity, in the rather uncared-for realm

1 My thanks go to the members of the working group *Global History* at Leipzig University for their valuable contributions to the outline of this paper.

2 Toyin Falola: African Historical Writing. In: Alex Schneider / Daniel Woolf (eds): *The Oxford History of Historical Writing*, vol. 5: Historical Writing since 1945. Oxford: Oxford UP 2011, pp. 399–421.

of (philosophical) aesthetics. Previous writings were limited in either scope or multi-perspectivity; mostly the necessary step from "othering to listening"[3] had not been taken. This turn is, however, not only necessary to gain insights into structures of knowledge production and the social embeddedness of academic disciplines, but also to include African perspectives into a discourse still dominated by former colonial powers and its neo-colonial offshoots, that is, Western discourse.

In this paper I describe the manifold elements that constitute the debates about 'African Aesthetics' (along with related concepts) by identifying exemplary groups of actors who, with individual social, political and economic backgrounds, have engaged with the topic and have established their own theoretical approaches since the 1960s. By doing so, the following questions shall be tentatively answered: First, from which social and intellectual background do the scholars come that have been promoting conceptualizations of African, Black, and Pan-African aesthetics? Secondly, can recurring motifs and ideas be identified in the texts of the authors under consideration? And finally, which challenges are directly and indirectly expressed with regard to the (similarly biased) terms 'African' and 'aesthetics'? Both the social and intellectual dimension of 'African Aesthetics' hence build the core of this analysis, as the particular life way of the academics translated itself into a specific body of thought. The paper focuses on actors rather than on ideas. This biographical approach promises to reveal the complexity of intellectual networks and the mutuality of influences that is so often overlooked in the systematic disciplines. With taking two case studies in different settings as examples and illustrations of the overall argumentation, I will link up the multiple debates and give an insight in commonalities, differences and transatlantic entanglements. The four perspectives chosen for this paper of course cannot give an exhaustive overview of all possible positions in the debate on 'African Aesthetics'. The selected scholarly pieces, two from a francophone background (Cameroon), two from an anglophone country (Nigeria), represent larger strands of literature and allow for a glimpse of the complex academic debate.

3 Miša Krenčeyová: Who Is Allowed to Speak About Africa? A Reflection on Knowledge, Positionality, and Authority in Africanist Scholarship. In: *Africa Insight* 44,1 (2014): Special Issue Development Through Knowledge, pp. 7–21.

Most academic treaties start with a definition of the subject under consideration, but trying to give a definition of 'aesthetics' already leads to the core challenge of this paper. Aesthetics seem to have no clearly defined place, location, responsibility, or scope – neither in society nor in academia. Whereas in everyday experiences aesthetics form part of representations in national and private cultural institutions, are prominent in practices of maintaining the beauty of the body, can be found in descriptions of traditional and contemporary arts and crafts, and even appear in foreign cultural policies, a comparable kaleidoscope of approaches can be found in academia. Sometimes aesthetics constitute an acknowledged discipline, in other contexts form part of various other research fields. The term itself has lost its sharp definition within the past centuries, as Schneider argues,[4] and this under-definition invites for multiple contributions which create a complex and dispersive debate. Especially when it comes to aesthetic conceptualizations about, or from non-European regions, a knot of interwoven meanings and conflicting explanations can be noticed. Areas of tension in the debates about 'African Aesthetics', for instance, span from Eurocentric and Afrocentric worldviews, over debates about 'authenticity', discourses about epistemologies and 'African Philosophy', to questions of diaspora and minority identities and to forms of racial and cultural nationalism.

Efforts to define the scope and characteristics of 'African Aesthetics' have been made for example by scholars with African descent in the US, who are more or less explicitly connected to an 'Afrocentric' approach.[5] Points of reference are to a great extent the Black Arts movement and related forms of ethnic or racial nationalism of the 1960s and 1970s in the US, which put "an emphasis on the need to develop [...] a distinctly African American or African culture that stood in opposition to white culture or cultures".[6] Proponents of such schools of thought hold that every cultural group has its own

4 Norbert Schneider: *Geschichte der Ästhetik: Von der Aufklärung bis zur Postmoderne.* Ditzingen: Reclam 2005, pp. 18–19.

5 Molefi Kete Asante: Location Theory and African Aesthetics. In: Kariamu Welsh-Asante (ed.): *The African Aesthetic: Keeper of the Traditions.* Westport: Greenwood 1993, pp. 53–62.

6 James Edward Smethurst: *The Black Arts Movement: Literary Nationalism in the 1960s and 1970s.* Chapel Hill / London: UNC 2005, pp. 14–15.

way of reacting to beauty and art and of perceiving, creating, appreciating, defining and understanding them, since different cultural groups develop different ways of life. Other strands of thought claim universal patterns in the perception of beauty and aesthetic preferences and state a deep human layer, a universal 'base zone' which carries our cultural impressions.[7] As Hauke Dorsch remarks rather deridingly, the European academic discourse is "celebrating anti-essentialist identities",[8] and in recent years the number of endeavours to establish an "intercultural philosophy" and the promotion of concepts of 'universal' or 'global aesthetics' is increasing.[9] Such anthropological ultimate groundings are again frowned upon within postmodern and post-colonial thought, where aesthetic claims of validity are rather expressed in strategies of positioning, localization and asserting one's claims within aesthetic institutions.[10]

While postcolonial approaches put an emphasis on the need to deconstruct ethnocentric narratives, ask for more awareness of the "intellectually debilitating effects"[11] of (especially) Eurocentrism and point to the ideological content of representations, the realm of aesthetics seems to be an area where culturalism often prevails. Since the end of the 20th century postmodern artists and academics have been proposing notions such as "post-black art" to describe contemporary artistic practices of a new generation of black art-makers.[12] Authors concerned with theoretical approaches to aesthetics not uncommonly

7 Wolfgang Welsch: *Blickwechsel: Neue Wege der Ästhetik*. Stuttgart: Reclam 2012. Cf. Ellen Dissanayake: *Home Aestheticus: Where Art Comes from and Why*. Washington: University of Washington Press 1995; Frederick Turner: *Beauty: The Value of Values*. Charlottesville: University of Virginia Press 1991.

8 Hauke Dorsch: *Globale Griots: Performanz in der afrikanischen Diaspora*. Berlin: Lit 2006.

9 Urs Stäheli: Spezialeffekte als Ästhetik des Globalen. In: Gregor Schwering / Carsten Zelle (eds): *Ästhetische Positionen nach Adorno*. Paderborn: Fink 2002, pp. 191–213; Welsch: *Blickwechsel*.

10 Norbert Schneider: Ästhetische Geltungsansprüche. In: Friedrich Jaeger / Burkhard Liebsch / Jörn Rüsen / Jürgen Straub (eds): *Handbuch der Kulturwissenschaften*, vol. 1. Grundlagen und Schlüsselbegriffe. Stuttgart: Metzler 2004, pp. 266–276.

11 Ella Shohat / Robert Stam: *Unthinking Eurocentrism: Multiculturalism and the Media*. London / New York: Routledge 1994, p. 1.

12 Nana Adusei-Poku: The Multiplicity of Multiplicities – Post-Black Art and Its Intricacies. In: *Darkmatter Journal* 9,2 (2012): Post-Racial Imaginaries. http://www.darkmatter101.org/site/2012/11/29/the-multiplicity-of-multiplicities-%E2%80%93-post-black-art-and-its-intricacies/print/ (accessed 06.02.2013).

repel those attempts. Hence, it is not only the case that the discussion of aesthetic matters has no central location in society or academia, the academic debates that can be observed are moreover complex and rather disordered and reveal multiple tensions related to identity. They deal with culturalism, universalism, essentialism, blackness, whiteness, tradition, modernity and last but not least with 'Africanity'.

'Esthétique(s) Africaine(s)'

In Yaoundé, Cameroon, there is a kaleidoscope of approaches to 'aesthetics'. To grasp and explain the multifaceted discussion here, two conceptualizations of 'Esthétique(s) Africaine(s)' by Engelbert Mveng and Mbog Mbombog Bassong will be portrayed. Their individual paths will serve as examples for the various entanglements that shaped their understandings of the function, form and epistemology of African Art.

The Jesuit priest, artist and scholar Engelbert Mveng has published several books and essays on (Black) African Art and Craft. Mveng, a Cameroonian intellectual who was assassinated on April 22, 1995,[13] was born in 1930 in a small village in South Cameroon as son of a protestant farmer. He was registered at a catholic school and aroused interest among the missionaries because of his outstanding intellect.[14] The young scholar continued his education in Yaoundé, studied philosophy in Belgium, and commenced studies in theology in France. In this period Mveng succeeded to publish his *History of Cameroon* (1963) at the Editions Présence Africaine. Since then he has published numerous books on religion, African art, Pan-Africanism, as well as Negro-African and Cameroonian history. Since 1965 Mveng has been a professor at the University of Yaoundé and subsequently director of the Department of History in 1984. During this period, public lectures and meetings with students occasionally turned into heated debates, as Mveng harshly pointed his finger on "the anthropological

13 Jean Paul Messina: Engelbert Mveng. La plume et le pinceau: Un message pour l'Afrique du 3em millénaire (1930–1995). In: *Presses de l'UCAC* (*Université Catholique d'Afrique Centrale*, Yaoundé) 2003. http://fr.missionerh.com/index.php?option=com_content&task=view&id=4519&Itemid=136 (accessed 14.03.2014).

14 Ibid., pp. 19–22.

poverty of African man".[15] He was engaged in the cultural movement of *négritude* and godson of Alioune Diop, a Senegalese writer and editor who was a central figure in this movement.[16] Mveng was also among the pioneers of African theology and a strong believer in the necessity and possibility of inculturation, not only with regard to Christianity but also related to art and culture. In his role as active artist he initiated the *Atelier d'arts nègres* in Yaoundé.[17]

After Mveng's unexplained death in 1995 a "disconcerting silence" was installed around the Jesuit Priest.[18] As a result, Mveng became a myth for Cameroonian intellectuals and stimulated the thoughts and dreams of young African scholars. He remains an iconic protagonist of the first generation of African theologians and "continues to haunt the conscience of intellectuals".[19] Apparently, Mveng created an "Mvengism"[20] in his circle of influence, and his publications hint to a wide scope of international influences and a large network of scholarly cooperation. The examination of his life and work in the international academic community is fractional. A distinctively important treaty is Mveng's essay *Problématique d'une esthétique négro-africaine* (1975) that starts with a quite 'classical' definition of aesthetics.[21] Mveng points out that the question (*'problème'*) of aesthetics is

15 Antonietta Cipollini: Engelbert Mveng: Libérer l'Afrique de sa pauvreté anthropologique. 15.01.2012. http://fr.missionerh.com/index.php?option=com_content&task=view&id=4519&Itemid=136 (accessed 08.07.2014).

16 Méroë-Africa, Membres & Intervenants, Comité des Sages: Engelbert Mveng. http://www.universitepopulairemeroeafrica.org/Engelbert-Mveng (accessed 08.07.2014). Alioune Diop also played an important role in the founding of the magazine, later publishing house, *Présence Africaine.*

17 Cipollini: Mveng.

18 Messina: Mveng, p. 13.

19 Cipollini: Mveng, my translation. A similar assessment is made by Messina: Mveng, p. 14: "Du fond de sa tombe, Engelbert Mveng trouble le sommeil des vivants."

20 Messina: Mveng, p. 17.

21 "L'esthétique est à la fois science et art. Elle a pour objet les norms du Beau telles qu'elles s'expriment à travers les oeuvres d'art. Son domaine embrasse donc la totalité des expressions artistiques et littéraires" (Engelbert Mveng: Problématique d'une esthétique negro-africaine, 2ième partie: Culture et civilisations. In: *Ethiopiques. Revue négro-africaine de litterature et de philosophie* 3 (1975). http://ethiopiques.refer.sn/spip.php?article490 (accessed 25.01.2015)). Cf. Université d'Abidjan, Institut de littérature et d'esthétique négro-africaines [ILENA]: *Colloque sur littérature et esthétique négro-africaines, Abidjan, Côte d'Ivoire 1974.* Abidjan: Les Nouvelles Editions Africaines 1979. The text reproduces Mveng's lecture at the *Colloque sur l'esthétique négro-africaine*, organized by ILENA, the *Institut de Littérature et d'Esthétique Negro-Africaines*

basically a question of artistic and literary creativity. He emphasizes though that it is not only a problem of definition, judgment, identification and appreciation of an oeuvre, but that it is a problem of cultural identity, of civilization. Therefore, the problem of aesthetics is the problem of "our time" par excellence. Mveng argues that at this moment, where humanity finds itself shaken in its once indisputable bases, people develop the need to more and more question themselves, their destiny, their creative genius and heritage of civilization. He summarizes: "It is true, in the abundance of research in the social sciences, aesthetic questioning today seems the most subtle, the most radical one which puts a challenge on the same ideologies of protest."[22] Aesthetics is also the key to the great cultural revolutions and central for the struggle for authenticity and *négritude*.[23]

His book on African art and craft, *L'art et l'artisanat africains* (1980), provides further insights into his visions and ambitions. It aims at promoting "*L'art négre*" as instrument for dialogue, within Africa and beyond. Mveng emphasizes the African's ability to express, in all sovereignty, the creative continuity of his cultural identity, and accentuates that the development of civilization of all peoples cannot do without the invaluable contribution of the Black African creative genius.[24] According to Mveng, African art, as it is discovered in modern times, appears as a total art. "It represents man. It

at Abidjan University, Côte d'Ivoire, in December 1974. Another contributor to the *Colloque* is Alassane Ndaw, former professor of philosophy and dean of the *Faculté des Lettres* of Cheikh Anta Diop University, Dakar. Cf. http://www.africultures.com/php/?nav=personne&no=8300 (accessed 22.06.2014). This shows the close connections between scholars in Yaoundé and Senegal.

22 Mveng: Problématique d'une esthétique.

23 "C'est qu'á la verité, dans le foisonnement des recherches en Sciences Humaines, l'interrogation esthétique semble aujourd'hui la plus subtile, la plus radicale, celle qui met en contestation jusqu'aux idéologies mêmes de la contestation. Elle est aussi la clé des grandes révolutions culturelles. Elle est au centre de notre lutte pour la Négritude et l'Authenticité" (Mveng: Problématique d'une esthétique).

24 Engelbert Mveng: *L'art et l'artisanat africains*. Yaoundé: Clé 1980, pp. 43, 151–152. References to the idea of 'artistic genius', as introduced and popularised by the philosopher Immanuel Kant, can be assumed when Mveng alludes to the "Negro-African genius" throughout his book. He mentions the term 'aesthetics' however only twice in the book, in combination with 'africaine' only once: "[…] révèlent un sens esthétique exceptionnel" (ibid., p. 18); "nous avons appelée la universelle de creation esthétique négro-africaine" (ibid., p. 26).

represents the entirety of man."[25] And because African art represents an irreplaceable dimension of the universal genius of humanity, it must be saved. Interestingly, Mveng refers to 'Africanity' as much as to 'universality': "Now the Negro art became the heritage of a universal culture".[26] Evidently, and complementary, Mveng's Christian education and occupation also have an impact on his thinking. He emphasizes the essentially religious dimension of black African art and the role of the artist as "almost priestly" in the proceeding of his book.[27] To summarize, we can hence name some decisive influences on Mveng's theoretical work: his Christian upbringing and education, his career in the French higher education system, the *négritude* movement and Senghor's conceptualizations of "universal culture", and ideas of universality and the "artistic genius" in general. Also his studies of ancient Egypt and the role of art and culture for cultural revolutions have certainly shaped his visions.

Another author who engages with ideas of "Esthétique Africaine" at the present time is Mbog Mbombog Bassong, a trained Geologist and Planetologist. Bassong is the descendant of a strongly Christianized family in Cameroon. Today however, he is a representative of the spiritual order of the Mbog, a syncretic neo-traditionalist confraternity. The second decisive turning point in his life was meeting Cheikh Anta Diop, the notorious Senegalese scholar who criticized the Eurocentric bias of previous scholarship on Africa and placed the ancient Egyptians in the genetic and cultural context of Africa,[28]

25 Original: "L'art africain que l'on découvre dans les Temps Modernes apparaît comme un art total. Il représente l'homme. Il représente tout l'homme" (Mveng: *L'art*, p. 15). Remark: The statements can be both interpreted as a) African Art representing every human being or b) African Art representing every aspect of every African.

26 Original: "Désormais, l'art nègre est devenu patrimoine de la culture universelle" (Mveng: *L'art*, p. 20). Hereinafter Mveng refers to the work of the German 20th century anthropologist Leo Frobenius who occupied himself with African art and was an inspiration for the Senegalese philosopher Léopold Sédar Senghor.

27 "On a souvent souligné la dimension essentiellement religieuse de l'art négro-africain. L'artiste qui est le créateur de ses oeuvres, est donc un personage quasi sacerdotal." (Mveng: *L'art*, p. 90.)

28 Cheikh Anta Diop: *Nations nègres et culture: de l'Antiquité nègre égyptienne aux problèmes culturels de l'Afrique noire d'aujourd'hui*. Paris: Présence Africaine 1954; cf. François-Xavier Fauvelle: *L'Afrique de Cheikh Anta Diop: Histoire et idéologie*. Paris: Karthala 1996; François-Xavier Fauvelle-Aymar / Jean-Pierre Chrétien / Claude-Hélène Perrot (eds): *Afrocentrismes: L'histoire des Africains entre Égypte et Amérique*. Paris: Karthala 2000.

in Paris in 1986, shortly before his death. In this meeting he became aware of the importance of history for the awakening of Africa. According to Bassong's biography, he then decided to break with the Christian model and to discover African knowledge.[29] Thus it is not surprising that a strong Afrocentric orientation can be found in both Bassong's books and on his website, although Diop's theses, and the related 'Black Athena debate',[30] are contested in the scientific community.[31]

Currently Bassong works for the Cameroonian ministry of culture. Despite being a regionally active delegate, without an actual office in the capital Yaoundé, all my contact persons in academia (even those living in diaspora), other ministries, and in the ministry of culture immediately knew his name and rated him as "strong".[32] In contrast to other Yaoundé-based scholars he has a multifaceted website with his biography, videos, interviews, academic articles and other reflections, a regularly updated blog, a site for free books, and a function for commentaries, which has been used actively. He is listed on *facebook*,

29 Mbog Mbombog Bassong: Biographie, dated 01.01.2012. http://mbombog.wordpress.com/about/ (accessed 16.06.2014).

30 The debate started soon after the publication of Martin Bernal: *Black Athena: The Afroasiatic Roots of Classical Civilization.* New Brunswick: Rutgers UP 1987.

31 For an assessment of Bernal's theses see Mary R. Lefkowitz / Guy MacLean Rogers (eds): *Black Athena Revisited.* Chapel Hill / London: University of North Carolina Press 1996. Far more positive towards Bernal: Jaques Berlinerblau: *Heresy in the University: The Black Athena Controversy and the Responsibilities of American Intellectuals.* New Brunswick: Rutgers UP 1999; Wim M.J. van Binsbergen: Black Athena and Africa's Contribution to Global Cultural History. In: *Quest, Philosophical Discussions: An International African Journal of Philosophy* 9/10,2/1 (1996), pp. 100–137. Diop's approach, which is often related to Bernal's view, though quite different in its main hypotheses, is discussed in Leonhard Harding / Brigitte Reinwald (eds): *Afrika – Mutter und Modell der europäischen Zivilisation? Die Rehabilitierung des schwarzen Kontinents durch Cheikh Anta Diop.* Berlin: Reimer 1990; Andreas Eckert: Wem gehört das Alte Ägypten? Die Geschichtsschreibung zu Afrika und das Werk Cheikh Anta Diops. In: Wolfgang Reinhard (ed.): *Die fundamentalistische Revolution. Partikularistische Bewegungen der Gegenwart und ihr Umgang mit der Geschichte.* Freiburg i. Brsg.: Rombach 1995, pp. 189–214; Arno Sonderegger: *Die Dämonisierung Afrikas: Zum Despotiebegriff und zur Geschichte der Afrikanischen Despotie.* Saarbrücken: VDM 2008, pp. 564–567.

32 This observation is based on conversations before, during and after a research stay in Yaoundé in October 2013. The word "strong" was used in a dialogue with a scholar who introduced himself as "Prof. Kook", professor of philosophy and linguistics with Cameroonian descent whom I met at Sorbonne University, Paris, on June 2, 2014 in Paris (further contact with the professor could however not be established).

youtube, *amazon*, *vimeo*, and various other platforms, which makes it easy to gain some information about him; however, the well-versed reader may wonder about the trustworthiness of the given information, as it clearly serves a self-promotional purpose.

In his book *L'Esthétique de l'art africain* (2007) Bassong analyses the aesthetics of what he calls "*l'art africain*". His analysis is based on studies of the symbolic forms of African art and their functional complexity, starting in antiquity and moving into the present. In his approach he follows Théophile Obenga's thoughts on *La philosophie africaine de la période pharaonique* (1980) that follows the tradition of Diop's emphasis on ancient Egypt.[33] It is furthermore inspired by the two Cameroonian philosophers Marcien Towa and Fabien Eboussi Boulaga, and the Beninese philosopher Paulin Hountondji.[34] To elaborate on how and why 'African Art' operates in the field of the regulation of traditional political societies, Bassong consults history, anthropology, communication sciences and even neurobiology and quantum physics.[35] His ambition is to draw conclusions for an epistemology of African art and to give a foundation, a better theory for the practice of art which gives the modern artist access to the African discourse on the real, without cutting the intuitive and affective dimension of artistic creation.[36] In Bassong's opinion African thought needs an epistemological overhaul for which it is appropriate to assert one's pretensions to the ethical, aesthetic, and hermeneutic truth.[37]

33 Théophile Obenga is a Cameroonian scholar who currently lives and works in Paris. In the early 1990s, Obenga has also collaborated with the already portrayed, very influential, priest and scholar Mveng, who is mentioned in Bassong's text, together with the Senegalese thinker Senghor, who seems to have a constant presence in all books of Cameroon origin concerned with questions of art and aesthetics. See Mbog Mbombog Bassong: *Esthétique de l'Art Africain*. Paris: L'Harmattan 2007, p. 15; see also ibid., p. 19, 22.

34 Bassong: *Esthétique de l'Art Africain*, p. 119.

35 Ibid., p. 14. He has published books on African epistemology and nomocracy in pre-colonial Africa (both 2007), African thinking (2012), African economy and African knowledge (both 2013), African religion (2014), as well as online essays on African sociology and African philosophy; a book on meteoroids in Cameroon is forthcoming.

36 "Il nous semble souhaitable que dans la pratique, l'artiste moderne s'aménage un espace théorique ouvert à la portée du discours africain sur le Réel, sans toutefois se couper de cette dimension intuitive et affective de la creation artistique." (Bassong: *Esthétique de l'Art Africain*, p. 9.)

37 "Tel est aussi cet autre enjeu de la présente contribution, à savoir, donner à

Compared to Mveng, who refers to African art, but hardly mentions the term 'aesthetics', he uses "aesthetics" often throughout the book. In the last paragraph of the book Bassong offers a definition of the aesthetics of (black) African art, which in his opinion

> demonstrates a mastery of the laws of complexity, that is to say the integration of different categories of being [...] in a same unit of composition of the art work, the transformation of the social chaos in order and the apprehension of the general dynamic of the elements of the universe in movement within a multidimensional space. That's all, the aesthetics of African art.[38]

Both authors thus refer to certain figures and schools of thought that can be summarized: (1) influences of the French Africanist discourse; (2) Léopold Sédar Senghor's conceptualization of *négritude* and *culture universelle*; (3) francophone Afrocentrism that points to the importance of pharaonic Egypt for African philosophy (Cheikh Anta Diop, Théophile Obenga); (4) Paulin Hountondji's reflections on 'Africanity' and criticism of 'ethnophilosophy'; (5) German idealist philosophers and anthropologists (Immanuel Kant, Leo Frobenius); (6) religiously informed ideas of the 'universe' as understood in Christian and Mbog belief systems; (7) ideas on cultural production and revolution that are inspired by socialist thought. If and how these influences vary from the entanglements of scholars in other contexts will be depicted in the following.

'African Aesthetics'

Both anglophone authors portrayed in this study, Godfrey Okechukwu Ozumba and John Isola Ayotunde Bewaji, grew up in Nigeria. They are of similar age, and received their PhDs in philosophy at the University of Ibadan, Nigeria. Both have made attempts to outline the characteristics of 'African aesthetics' in recent years. Ozumba

la pratique de l'art un point de depart, une assise, mieux une théorie, aux fins d'y renouveler des constructions dignes d'intérêt scientifique La pensée africaine appelle une refondation épistémologique pour laquelle il apparaît opportune de faire valoir ses *pretentions à la vérité éthiques, esthétiques et herméneutiques*." (Ibid., p. 10.)

38 Original: "L'Esthétique de l'art d'Afrique noire apporte la preuve d'une maîtrise des lois de la complexité, c'est-à-dire l'intégration des différentes categories de l'être (animal, vegetal, mineral, invisible) dans une meme unite de composition de l'oeuvre d'art, la transformation du chaos social en ordre et l'appréhension de la dynamique générale des elements de l'Univers en movement dans un espace pluridimensionnel. C'est bien tout cela, l'esthétique de l'art africain." (Ibid., p. 212.)

is the incumbent head of the Department of Religious Studies and Philosophy at the University of Calabar, which was set up in 1976 as one of the new seven Universities that were to be established in consequence of the National Development Plan of the Federal Military Government of Nigeria.[39] Until 1979 the Department of Religious Studies and Philosophy ran a combined honors degree in Religious Studies and Philosophy which was afterwards split up into two separate programs. Ozumba graduated with a BA in philosophy from the University of Calabar, where he also received Master's degrees in first political economy and then philosophy. In 1995 he attained his PhD in philosophy at the University of Ibadan with a thesis on *Quine's Theory of Ontological Relativity*. Since then he has been working in the philosophy unit of the Department of Religious Studies and Philosophy in Calabar where he achieved professorship in 2005 and the current position as head of department in 2009. He was born in 1960 in Aba, Abia State, a major urban settlement in Southeast Nigeria. Presumably he grew up in a Christian environment, as his books and theories are either dedicated to God/Jesus or explicitly reflect Christian sets of beliefs.[40]

Ozumba has published several books on ethics, epistemology, logical positivism, and philosophy of language and various articles on education, gender, orality and African philosophy/epistemology, spiritualism, and the human soul, to name but a few topics. Ozumba spent one sabbatical lectureship in 1999 at Nnamdi Azikiwe University, 300 kilometers from Calabar, and later another sabbatical at the University of Cape Coast in Ghana. This stay resulted in a joint *Journal of Integrative Humanism* where Ozumba and colleagues discuss the respective method developed by him.[41] Other hints to transnational work or

39 It grew out of the University of Nigeria at Nsukka that was founded only three years earlier, in 1973. Academic work at the University of Calabar started with the faculties of Arts, Science and Social Science in October in 1976 with an initial enrolment of 896 students. See University of Calabar: About UNICAL. History. http://www.unical.edu.ng/pages/about/?nav=history (accessed 21.06.2013).

40 Godfrey O. Ozumba / S. Yekini Alabi: *Landmarks in Aesthetic Studies: A Book of Reading*. Makurdi: Microteacher 2007, p. vi, where both the Almighty God as well as Jesus are acknowledged. Ozumba also indicates reading and writing of Christian literature as hobby in his CV.

41 Godfrey O. Ozumba: *Philosophy and Method of Integrative Humanism*. Calabar: Jochrisam 2010.

research experiences cannot be found in his CV.[42] Ozumba's visibility for other scholars is based on the academic internet platform *academia.edu* where he uploads his numerous papers and a CV with a list of publications. Two new books from 2014 can be purchased online, his numerous other publications however cannot be found or ordered (even though they have an ISBN), and getting to know his thoughts on *Landmarks in Aesthetic Studies* was only possible due to the kindness of the author himself, who has personally sent me the book at no charge from Nigeria. Hence, whereas Ozumba is frequently cited in local journals and scores high click-through-rates on *academia.edu*, his academic activities and perception are rather restricted (yet) in their boundary-spanning outreach.

The bibliography to his article *Outlines of African Aesthetics* (2007) conveys a similar picture.[43] Works cited are mainly printed in Nigeria or are Ozumba's own previous works.[44] Ozumba holds the opinion that philosophy is a universal discipline, though has cultural and ideological partitioning. He emphasizes the varieties of perception arising from historical experience. But rather than neutrally reflecting upon these varieties he deplores the waning African sense of appreciation due to the dominating Western lifestyle which leaves only a "latent stump of the African aesthetic mindset".[45] Throughout the article culturalizing and universalizing statements alternate, for example when Ozumba defines "African aesthetics" as "the African's way of appreciating nature, creating aesthetic objects, evaluating and improving on nature's aesthetic raw materials for the overall improvement of their well being", which is hinged on "*man's* multilayered relationship that is in tune with God, nature, spirit and ancestors".[46] Ozumba holds

42 The list of contributors to the edited volume *Landmarks in Aesthetic Studies* suggests the same. All contributions to the book of readings came from scholars situated either at Calabar University or at Abakaliki University nearby.

43 Godfrey O. Ozumba: Outlines of African Aesthetics. In: *Sophia: An African Journal of Philosophy and Public Affairs* 9,2 (April 2007), pp. 153–158. http://unical-ng.academia.edu/GodfreyOzumba (accessed 19.10.2012). Remark: I am referring to the online version. I only got to know through contacting Prof. Ozumba that the paper had been published in *Sophia: An African Journal of Philosophy and Public Affairs*. The journal is based at the University of Calabar, Nigeria.

44 Only one edited volume from London and a book that has been published by a Singaporean company can be found.

45 Ozumba: Outlines of African Aesthetics.

46 Ibid., p. 154.

that because philosophy is a universal mode of thinking and aesthetics a universal experience, the African philosopher can examine Western aesthetics that provide the needed tradition of written documentation, and, in an "inside out approach", know what contents correspond with what in the African concepts of aesthetics.[47]

His overall ambition to "delineate the possible contours through which African aesthetics can be handled as a documented academic discipline",[48] is certainly influenced by his reading and teaching of the philosophy of Immanuel Kant and several 19th century philosophers, who intended to establish aesthetics as an independent philosophical discipline. His aim is intertwined with a Pan-African aspiration for Africa's independence from Western hegemony. According to Ozumba, African aesthetics shall be based on "the African's" worldview, which is his metaphysics and socio-political reality.[49] Correspondingly, his aim is to articulate and export on a conscious political level, maybe through the African Union, the African values and aesthetic traits that will make the world a better place. This shall be Africa's contribution to qualitative globalization. Hence 'African Aesthetics' are explicitly promoted to strengthen the 'African' position in global structures of knowledge production.[50]

A second example for academic conceptualizations of 'African Aesthetics' is the works of John Ayotunde Isola Bewaji, currently head of the philosophy section in the Department of Language, Linguistics, and Philosophy at the University of the West Indies, Mona, Jamaica. Founded in 1948 as a College of the University of London, the University of the West Indies achieved full university status in 1962. It offers a wide range of programs with a special emphasis on Caribbean issues. Bewaji came to the university as a Rhodes Visiting Lecturer in Philosophy in 1991, and has since taught courses ranging from the

47 Ozumba: Outlines of African Aesthetics, p. 154.

48 Ibid., p. 153.

49 Ozumba himself uses the singular form. Indeed neither the precise definition of the scope of this 'Africanity' nor the empirical foundation of his reflections, seem to be crucial for his project. In other publications the equation of "African" and "Nigerian", through formulations like "African, nay Nigerian" appears frequently.

50 He emphasizes, for example, that "[i]t shows that Nigerians, nay, African scholars can hold their own anywhere, anytime and in any discipline" (Ozumba / Alabi: *Landmarks in Aesthetic Studies*, p. iv).

Theory of Knowledge, *Philosophy of Art* to *Advanced African Philosophy*.[51] Additionally he is founding President of the International Society for African Philosophy and Studies, was John Simon Guggenheim Fellow from 2010 to 2011, Jay Newman Visiting Professor of Philosophy of Culture at Brooklyn College, USA, and founding editor of the *Caribbean Journal of Philosophy*. Bewaji underwent his undergraduate training in Nigeria – he received his BA and MA in philosophy at the University of Ife, and, like Ozumba, attained his PhD in philosophy at the University of Ibadan.[52] Afterwards he taught philosophy at the University of Ife and at Ogun State University. Bewaji was born in a small town in Ijesa land, which is now the Osun State of Nigeria, and he too grew up in a Christian environment as the son of an elder and co-founder of the Apostolic church, which is a pentecoastal, revivalist and evangelical denomination: "'[S]trict' Christian mytho-epistemic, social-spiritualistic, moral and religious values and metaphysical belief" shaped his childhood and youth.[53]

In the preface to his book *Beauty and Culture: Perspectives in Black Aesthetics* (2003), Bewaji states that writing about African and African Diaspora philosophy of art was challenging because he has not studied African art as specialization nor has he taken part in artistic activities. In fact, his involvement in the academic field of aesthetics rather happened by chance.[54] According to Bewaji the task of working on

51 The University of the West Indies at Mona, Jamaica: Department of Language, Linguistics and Philosophy. http://www.mona.uwi.edu/dllp/ (accessed 25.06.2013); Id.: History. http://www.mona.uwi.edu/about/history.php (accessed 25.06.2013).

52 If Bewaji who received his PhD in Ibadan in 1991, and Ozumba who received his degree in 1995, have personally met and influenced each other directly needs further investigation.

53 John Ayotunde Isola Bewaji: *Black Aesthetics: Beauty and Culture: An Introduction to African and African Diaspora Philosophy of Arts*. Trenton, NJ: Africa Research and Publications 2013, p. 5. On career, position and work of Bewaji see also *African Studies Quarterly*: John A.I. Bewaji. http://www.africa.ufl.edu/asq/v2/jbewaji.htm; *Africa World Press, Inc. & The Red Sea Press, Inc. Black Aesthetics*. http://www.gf.org/fellows/16912-john-ayotunde-tunde-isola-bewaji; *Mona Online Research Database*: Dr. John Ayotunde Isola Bewaji. http://mord.mona.uwi.edu/staff/view.asp?pid=9849 (all accessed 25.06.2013).

54 He had been asked to fill the gap created by the absence on leave of the lecturer of an African Art History course at the Edna Manley School of Visual and Performing Arts in Jamaica. Later he was invited to deliver a public lecture by the Philip Sherlock Centre for Creative Arts as part of the African History Month programme in 1996.

African and African Diaspora arts is not easy, as most texts have been mainly descriptive and have ignored the critical, analytic, and philosophical implications of the artistic objects and thus there is not much precedent to guide the discussion.[55] He therefore aims to "fill the yawning gap" and to shed light on the nature and meaning of both African philosophy and artistic expression in Africa and the diaspora and to examine the mutual interdependence of both.[56]
Bewaji broaches the issue of African Aesthetics in a new edition of his book published as *Black Aesthetics: Beauty and Culture* (2013), in an additional chapter on "Arts, Memory and Identity". Three elements contribute to African Aesthetics: (1) the skill and the mental faculty that produces artistic forms; (2) the final outcome of the effort, the extent of finesse, and truth of representation; (3) the moral or ethical element of art.[57] The motivations for the new edition, and his dedication to the topic in general, are the "grown recognition of the importance of taking African aesthetics into consideration on its own terms" and the "need for Africana peoples to begin to take a closer look at aesthetics from the Africana perspective or whatever is left of it".[58] Moreover Bewaji wants to stimulate further work in the area of African philosophy of art and get to a better understanding of philosophy of art in general.[59]
Just like Ozumba, he uses profoundly negative wording with regard to Western philosophy, which in his opinion "has become unduly abstract, professionalistic, irreverent, idiosyncratic, eccentric,

55 John Ayotunde Isola Bewaji: *Beauty and Culture: Perspectives in Black Aesthetics: An Introduction to African and African Diaspora Philosophy of Art.* Ibadan: Spectrum 2003, p. 29.

56 The presumption of his book hence is "that there is African philosophy, that there is artistic expression in Africa, that there is a fundamental way in which artistic expression is determined, influenced by, and/or is a function of African philosophy, and that artistic expression influences […] African philosophy" (ibid., p. 1).

57 Bewaji: *Black Aesthetics*, p. 314.

58 Ibid., synopsis backcover. The term 'Africana' commonly refers to a concept of an 'African experience' that encompasses Africa and the African-American and African-Latin diaspora and which has a Pan-African perspective. Bewaji's integration of the Afro-Caribbean perspective also happens against the background that in his work he has been inspired and supported by the legendary "guru of West Indian art" Prof. Rex Nettleford, then Vice-Chancellor at the University of the West Indies; cf. ibid., p. xiii.

59 Ibid., p. xiii.

irrelevant, pedantic, inaccessible, muddled and parasitic".[60] African philosophies on the other hand have in Bewaji's opinion been remarkably different "in the positive sense of being sensitive to the environment in which it was developed and in which it is applied".[61] But in contrast to Ozumba's publications, the works cited in his book reflect a global scope of ideas taken into consideration for his conclusion. More specifically, Bewaji's career path can be described as transnational – having moved from Nigeria to Jamaica, having been visiting scholar in New York and Gaborone, as well as being a member of the advisory council on culture at the Russian Academy of Arts in St. Petersburg. He and his work are widely present on the internet, and his books are available in Western libraries as well as in online book shops. His academic environment is globally connected, and the bibliographical references reflect his various relations to scholars and currents of thought in the US, on the African continent and in Europe, mainly the United Kingdom. Accordingly the focus of his Pan-African perspective is put on past and present entanglements of the African continent and its diaspora, and in his books Bewaji uses both the terms "African Aesthetics" and "Africana aesthetics" interchangeably.

Transatlantic Entanglements and Tentative Conclusions

When looking at the academic conceptualizations of aesthetics and the corresponding biographies of their authors, significant differences and similarities in their scholarly traditions, theoretical influences, and transnational entanglements can be noted. Moreover the impact of social backgrounds and academic networks becomes more obvious. We can summarize that (1) all authors grew up in a Christian environment and most maintained tight bonds to religious practices and/or institutions during their life. (2) The degree of international visibility and accessibility (e.g. through internet presentations, publications) varies significantly. Whereas Bewaji and Bassong are present in online platforms and bookshops to a large degree, Ozumba is rather invisible for foreign scholars, and his publications are hardly accessible outside his country. Strong local academic communities

60 Ibid., pp. 3–4.

61 Ibid., p. 4.

could be detected in all case studies but the comparison of the two scholars from Nigeria, Ozumba and Bewaji, points to the crucial role of international networks and transnationally oriented universities for the embedded transsocietal and transcultural contexts. (3) Connections and networks are closely linked to the language used in the academic context, which can be observed in the Cameroonian-French-relations as well as Nigerian-Jamaican-relations. Both discursive formations have overlapping contents, but are to a large degree organized separately from each other. (4) Embedded transnational academic networks, stays abroad and scholarly entanglements beyond borders allow a striking influence on the scope of works cited and on the amount of own citations.

Concerning recurring motifs and ideas in the texts of the authors under consideration, it can be concluded that (1) essentialist and culturist views are still put forward in different contexts. In all examples the idea of a shared African essence can be found. (2) At the same time, references are made to conceptions of universality. (3) Ideas on cultural production and revolution that can be named socialist, serve as inspiration. (4) In all cases a recurring pattern is the reference to some sort of 'humanism': for example, to traditions of a new humanism as promoted in the texts of Léopold Sédar Senghor, or own conceptualizations of an integrative humanism in the work of Godfrey Ozumba. (5) The reference to Ancient Greek and Egyptian philosophy and culture, seen as foundation of African philosophy and promoted by scholars like Cheikh Anta Diop and reverberating in the 'Black Athena debate', is present in both discursive formations, but more prominently among the Cameroonian authors. The renowned Beninese philosopher Paulin Hountondji was part of the philosophy colloquium[62] in Yaoundé in the 1980s. His critical ideas on African philosophy most definitely had an impact on the last two generations of Yaoundé-based thinkers in that realm.

What makes the realm of 'aesthetics' interesting research is the antagonisms that appear in the texts and biographies of the authors

62 See Bassong's "Bibliographie Sommaire" in Id.: *La Méthode de la Philosophie Africaine.* Paris: L'Harmattan 2007: "Actes du colloque de philosophie de l'École Normale Supérieure, Yaoundé, 4–8 avril 1983, avec la participation de […] Hountondji, Paulin." His famous *Sur la 'philosophie africaine': Critique de l'ethnophilosophie* (Paris 1976) has been re-published in Yaoundé in 1980.

outlined above. Aesthetics is an open arena to reflect about 'Africanity' inviting multiple actors and contributions to the debate. It is also a domain that is highly loaded with biased terms and double-sided presumptions. In the mixture of different traditions of thought, tensions occur between overcoming Eurocentrism on the one hand, and employing epistemologies of the former colonizers on the other hand. Moreover religiously informed ideas of the 'universe' collide with culturist assertions of 'Africa' and 'Africanity'. Differences between anglophone traditions in the realm of 'African aesthetics', and francophone discourses on '*esthétique(s) africaine(s)*' are striking. Due to the persistent influence of Senghor's thoughts and the positive connotation of *négritude* in francophone countries, the term '*nègre*' for example can still be frequently found in the writings of Yaoundé-based authors. In English publications the term 'negro', which has been objected by the American Civil Rights Movement, has by the majority been replaced with 'black' or 'African'.[63] Also, positive references to the 'West', in the form of positive imaginations of Germany and references to German thought (Enlightenment philosophers, *Sturm und Drang* literates, or anthropologists), are more prominent in the works of the Cameroonian authors.

Clearly, global connections raise new questions about understandings of beauty, taste and works of art. Journeys across continents, global interrelation of media and a world-market for art and beauty make aesthetic experiences of the 'Other' as well as experiences of 'other Aesthetics' part of a process of mutual awareness. Those confrontations of 'Otherness' channel the focus on cultural transfers and intercultural interactions as main source for social transformation and change. But they also lead to the search of culturally defined groups for anchors of identity in a dispersive and changing world. It is thus not surprising that aesthetic claims are indeed asserted to a greater extent in recent decades, as the multifaceted examples above indicate. The under-determination of the term aesthetics[64] allows it to become an arena for rivalries of interpretation, a strategy of

63 Tom W. Smith: Changing Racial Labels: from 'Colored' to 'Negro' to 'Black' to 'African American'. In: *Public Opinion Quarterly* 56,4 (1992), pp. 496–514.

64 Schneider: *Geschichte der Ästhetik*, pp.18–19 argues that the term has lost its sharp definition within the past centuries.

self-staging, intertwined with structures of power and hegemony.[65] But, whereas some of the aforementioned approaches to analyze culture and philosophy are based on strong binary oppositions, and hence limit themselves in considering contradictory or multifaceted perspectives, the last decades have, in the same degree, been a fertile soil for new paths in the investigation of cultural practices, politics, and representations.

In the context of postcolonial thinking the foundation to examine transcultural phenomena from a multi-sided perspective has been built. Already in 1993 Paul Gilroy asserted that the polarization between essentialist and anti-essentialist theories of black identity has become unhelpful.[66] His conceptualization of a "Black Atlantic" and his remarks on the mutability of identities and the "inescapable hybridity and intermixture of ideas" are as poignant and relevant today.[67] Indeed, a culture is not closed neatly within a space but exceeds it, as intellectual products enter foreign territories and representatives of cultural space establish themselves well beyond the borders of their homeland.[68] Cultural and societal phenomena have distinguishable and isolatable aspects, although historical and current processes of exchange, influence and reciprocal reception shape them.[69] New paths for the analysis of transcultural phenomena doubtlessly need to be found in both 'Western' as well as 'non-Western' academia. V.Y. Mudimbe's striking work on *The Invention of Africa* (1988) laid the groundwork for questioning of what comes after the 'post-' of poststructuralism, postmodernism, and postcolonialism. With the

65 Schneider: Ästhetische Geltungsansprüche, pp. 266–276.

66 Paul Gilroy: *The Black Atlantic: Modernity and Double Consciousness*. Cambridge, MA: Harvard UP 1993, p. ix. See also the works of Hountondji, who suggests to dismantle myths of Africanity and to reduce the concept of Africa to its primal simplicity in order to reveal the extreme complexity of the intellectual, cultural, political and social life of the continent (Paulin J. Houtondji: *African Philosophy: Myth and Reality*. Bloomington / Indianapolis: Indiana UP 2002).

67 Gilroy: *Black Atlantic*, p. ix.

68 Michel Espagne: Comparison and Transfer: A Question of Method. In: Matthias Middell / Lluis Roura i Aulinas (eds): *Transnational Challenges to National History Writing*. Basingstoke: Palgrave Macmillan 2013, pp. 36–53, here p. 23.

69 Hannes Siegrist: Perspektiven der vergleichenden Geschichtswissenschaft: Gesellschaft, Kultur und Raum. In: Hartmut Kaelble / Jürgen Schriewer (eds): *Vergleich und Transfer: Komparatistik in den Sozial- Geschichts- und Kulturwissenschaften*. Frankfurt am Main: Campus 2003, pp. 305–340.

increasing awareness of cultural difference and cultural interrelatedness, literary, media, and philosophical investigations now have the potential to challenge paradigms of stereotyping.[70] If such research on interrelations and exchanges in the field of aesthetics can – or should – circumvent the utilization of various universalisms on the one hand and radical culturalism on the other hand for hegemonic or counter-hegemonic, yet always ideological strategies of self-staging and positioning, is an open question.[71] Certainly it can promote the rather fragmented academic debate and open it up for new diversified perspectives to study 'African aesthetics' in a new global order.

70 V. Y. Mudimbe: *The Invention of Africa: Gnosis, Philosophy, and the Order of Knowledge*. Bloomington: Indiana UP 1988. Cf. Michael Janis: *Africa after Modernism: Transitions in Literature, Media, and Philosophy*. New York: Routledge 2008.

71 Henning Melber: What Is African in Africa(n) Studies? Confronting the (Mystifying) Power of Ideology and Identity. In: *Africa Bibliography 2013* (2014), pp. vii–xvii.

Virtues for All, State for No One?

Jomo Kenyatta's Postcolonial Political Imagination

Anaïs Angelo

In August 1961, the colonial Governor of Kenya, Sir Philip Mitchell advised Jomo Kenyatta (1893–1978) to take some time reacclimatising himself before stepping back into politics again; "so many things had changed in his long absence."[1] In 1952, Kenyatta had been arrested suspected of being a leader of the Mau Mau movement. After a year-long trial many thought unfair and unlawful, he was found guilty and sentenced to seven year's imprisonment.[2] To the colonial authorities, Kenyatta was "the African leader to darkness and death" as the then Governor Sir Patrick Muir Renison described him; to his fellow nationalists and Kikuyu people, however, he would eventually become a political martyr.[3] Kenyatta was imprisoned in the remote area of Lodwar for seven years, and then restricted in Lokitaung for two more years. Before this forced absence, he had lived in self-imposed exile for sixteen years in Great Britain, where he pursued a literary and political career. In the 1920s he started out as a representative of the Kikuyu Central Association in London, and as a journalist for the Kikuyu newspapers he founded *Muigwithania* (The Reconciler). In London, where he arrived in 1928, Kenyatta was quick to understand that he lacked the authority and political legitimacy to

1 Montagu Slater: *The Trial of Jomo Kenyatta.* London: Secker & Warburg 1955, p. 10.

2 On Kenyatta's trial, see Slater: *Trial of Jomo Kenyatta*; John M. Lonsdale: Les Procès de Jomo Kenyatta: destruction et construction d'un nationaliste africain. In: *Politix* 17,66 (2004), pp. 163–197.

3 Jeremy Murray-Brown: *Kenyatta.* London: Allen & Unwin 1972, p. 301.

be heard: the British ignored him.[4] Instead, he dedicated himself to voice the Kikuyu cause through writing: his PhD thesis *Facing Mount Kenya* (1938) became the touchstone of his literary production as well as his political career, and two other pamphlets: *My People of Kikuyu and the Life of Chief Wangombe* (1942) and *Kenya: The Land of Conflicts* (1945). After 1945, that is to say just a year before his return to Kenya, Kenyatta did no longer publish anything, except, much later, a collection of speeches.[5]

Upon his release in 1961, Kenyatta's political imagination could only be grasped through a work that stemmed from a different historical and political context, and even from a different geographical perspective. Kenyatta was no postcolonial thinker; he doubted at some point he would live long enough to see the fruits of the struggle for independence, and never made use of the term either.[6] The vision of politics he defended was bound to a Kikuyu past few of his younger fellow-politicians would comprehend. At Kenya's independence in 1964, he was believed to be 73 years old, and had been away from the cradle of nationalist politics for twenty-five years. To many of his political contemporaries, he was an aging man whose ideas seemed to come from another era.[7] Yet, he remained in power for the next fourteen years. To historians, there seems to be a missing link between his becoming 'Doctor Jomo Kenyatta' and his late, but quick ascension to power, as if nothing could have altered the ideas he laid down some nineteen years before. Ironically, few historians deemed the study of his political imagination worthy.[8] Although Kenyatta's "tons

4 Bruce J. Berman / John M. Lonsdale: The Labors of Muigwuithania: Jomo Kenyatta as Author, 1928–45. In: *Research in African Literatures* 29,1 (1998), pp. 16–42.

5 Jomo Kenyatta: *Facing Mount Kenya*. New York: Vintage 1965 [1938]; id.: *My People of Gikuyu and the Life of Chief Wangombe*. London: Luttersworth 1942; id.: *The Land of Conflict*. London: Panaf Service 1945; id.: *Suffering Without Bitterness: The Founding of the Kenya Nation*. Nairobi: East African Publishing House 1968.

6 Malcolm MacDonald: Transcript of interview with Dame Margery Perham given to the Oxford University Colonial Records Project at Queen Elisabeth House in Oxford, on 25th June 1970; Margery Perham Papers, BRIT. EMP., S. 533, Oxford University Archives.

7 John Lonsdale: Henry Muoria, Public Moralist. In: Wangari Muoria-Sal / Bodil F. Frederiksen / John Lonsdale / Derek R. Peterson (eds): *Writing for Kenya: The Life and Works of Henry Muoria*. Leiden: Brill 2009, pp. 3–58.

8 John Lonsdale: Jomo Kenyatta, God & the Modern World. In: Peter Probst / Heike Schmidt / Jan-Georg Deutsch (eds): *African Modernities: Entangled Meanings in Current*

of private papers and books" might have been "confiscated by the state, either to be lost thereafter or destroyed", a striking consistency appears throughout the ideas he expressed in his early publications and later political speeches. This deserves attention; as the historian John Lonsdale reminded, one ought to reconcile his biography with his political theology; one ought to understand which ideas guided his actions.[9]

Confronting Kenyatta's writings and speeches, this article attempts to unveil the rich and complex interaction of his imagination of what we now call the postcolonial society and his understanding of the constraints of realpolitik. Building on Lonsdale's seminal article *Jomo Kenyatta, God & the Modern World* dedicated to Kenyatta's political imagination, I want to argue that Kenyatta's conception of authority, imbued with conservative moral values, and of leadership that he considered could not dent moral autonomy, lead him to erect the *family* as the ultimate base and limit of his politics of state building. Firstly, I attempt to situate the 'family' in Kenyatta's early writings.

Debate. London: Currey 2002, pp. 31–66, here p. 34. Paradoxically, his early writings have caught the scholars' attention. Kenyatta's strong stance in favor of clitoridectomy in the 1930s was a direct answer to such threats. On this issue see Murray-Brown: *Kenyatta*, chapter 11; John Lonsdale: The Moral Economy of Mau Mau: Wealth, Poverty and Civic Virtue in Kikuyu Political Thought. In: Bruce J. Berman / John M. Lonsdale: *Unhappy Valley: Conflict in Kenya & Africa*. Athens: Ohio UP 1992, pp. 386–395; Bruce Berman: Ethnography as Politics, Politics as Ethnography: Kenyatta, Malinowski, and the Making of Facing Mount Kenya. In: *Canadian Journal of African Studies* 30,3 (1996), pp. 313–344; Bruce Berman / John Lonsdale: Custom, Modernity, and the Search for Kihooto: Kenyatta, Malinowski, and the Making of Facing Mount Kenya. In: Robert J. Gordon / H. Tilley (eds): *Anthropology, European Imperialism and the Ordering of Africa*. Manchester: Manchester UP 2007, pp. 173–198; Bodil F. Frederiksen: Jomo Kenyatta, Marie Bonaparte and Bronislaw Malinowski on Clitoridectomy and Female Sexuality. In: *History Workshop Journal* 65,1 (2008), pp. 23–48. This must be read in the context of Kikuyu precolonial thought, well studied as well. See in particular Lonsdale: Moral Economy of Mau Mau; John Lonsdale: Contest of Time: Kikuyu Historiography, Old and New. In: Axel Harneit-Sievers (ed.): *A Place in the World: New Local Historiographies from Africa and South Asia*. Leiden: Brill 2002, pp. 201–254; Greet Kershaw: *Mau Mau From Below*. Oxford: Currey 1997; Yvan Droz: *Migrations Kikuyus: des Pratiques Sociales à l'Imaginaire*. Paris: Editions MSH 1999; Derek R. Peterson: *Creative Writing: Translation, Bookkeeping, and the Work of Imagination in Colonial Kenya*. Portsmouth: Heinemann 2004; Bodil F. Frederiksen: The Present Battle is the Brain Battle. Writing and Publishing a Kikuyu Newspaper in the Pre-Mau Mau Period in Kenya. In: Karin Barber (ed.): *Africa's Hidden Histories: Everyday Literacy and Making the Self*. Bloomington: Indiana UP 2006, pp. 278–313.

9 Lonsdale: Jomo Kenyatta, God & the Modern World, p. 34.

Next, I explore the intellectual legacy of his writings *after* independence, and confront, in the third section, the discourse of moral virtues with regard to the logics of state-building. In the fourth and final part, I attempt to locate the transfer of the 'family' onto the politics of state building.

Kenyatta's Pre-independence Writings: The Family between Sociability and Authority

In 1929, recalling his amazement at the opening of the British Parliament in London, Jomo Kenyatta urged his readers to "learn well to trust or rely upon one another among your own selves, so that you may be trusted and respected ('feared') by other nations."[10] Calling for trust, Kenyatta was not simply pushing for moral and political unity. He was establishing trust as the pre-condition for a community to exist. Yet, trust could not be institutionalized: it could only be achieved through self-reliance, it could neither be given nor negotiated. During his London years, Kenyatta was as impressed by the British art of parliamentary debates, as appalled by their readiness to break commitment. He saw in the colonisation of Kikuyu land a crisis of trusteeship.[11] For a stateless society like the Kikuyus, trust was the key to survive and maintain dignity.[12] It was not just a functional ornament of social relationships: it drew the boundaries of inclusion and exclusion in a community. As such, Kenyatta had to define sociability and authority in ways that mutual trust would not be impaired. This was a tricky task, for the Kikuyu moral economy rested, primarily, on the supremacy of individual achievement. Kenyatta was confronted with a problem that haunted Kikuyu politics: how to define an authority that would not weaken mutual trust?[13]

10 Quoted in *Muigwithania*, July–August 1929, vol. 2, no. 2, p. 8, DC/MKS/10B/13/1, Kenya National Archives (KNA). I relied on the English translation by A. R. Barlow, Church of Scotland lay missionary, and kept Barlow's own hesitations regarding the translation, which explains the words in parenthesis (as for the subsequent references).

11 John Lonsdale: Ornamental Constitutionalism in Africa: Kenyatta and the Two Queens. In: *The Journal of Imperial and Commonwealth History* 34,1 (2006), pp. 87–103, here pp. 95–97.

12 Ibid., p. 93.

13 Lonsdale: Moral Economy of Mau Mau, p. 400.

Kenyatta took great pains to situate individualism in a larger reflection on sociability. To him, individualism erected as a social and behavioural maxim, was no doubt a product of colonial decadence. With the publication of *Facing Mount Kenya*, his academic supervisor, the social anthropologist Bronislaw Malinowski, reflected he "might have been tempted to advise the writer to be more careful in using such antitheses as 'collective' vs. 'individual,' in opposing the native outlook as 'essentially social' to the European as 'essentially personal.'"[14] In Kikuyu society, Kenyatta explained, individuality was subsumed under "three governing principles": the family group (*mbari*, or *nyomba*), the clan (*moherega*), and the age-grading system (*riika*).[15] At the same time, individuals were the ultimate owners of land. That did not entail, however, any right to claim authoritative status.[16] Kenyatta was endorsing a specific trait of Kikuyu thought that Lonsdale described as "possessive individualism in the service of the community".[17] This was carefully underlined throughout Kenyatta's thesis: individual land ownership should not be confused with individual *right* over land. No individuality could express itself outside of tribal authorities, namely the authority of the council of elders (*kiama*), which was paramount to ensure that well-being of the family – once the individual owner has built a family – is not jeopardized.[18] In the colonial politics of the time, this meant that individual ownership was necessary to protect the rights of a minority, the Kikuyu, against the white settlers. But the elders' supreme right and discretionary control over land ownership – that traditional authority Kenyatta was competing for – ought to be safeguarded.[19]

14 Bronislaw Malinowski: Introduction. In: Kenyatta: *Facing Mount Kenya*, pp. vii–xiv, here p. xi. Bronislaw Malinowki taught anthropology in the United Kingdom (London School of Economics) and in the United States. He was the founder and defender of anthropological functionalism, which considers society as a living organism, where social relationships are regulated by institutions; each institution playing a particular function that maintains society as a coherent body. Functionalism aims at uncovering regular patters of behaviors, while myths and beliefs are seen as malleable and changing ornaments.

15 Kenyatta: *Facing Mount Kenya*, p. 1–2.

16 Ibid, pp. 21–22, 98. On Kikuyu culture and individualism, see Droz: *Migrations Kikuyus*, p. 154; Yvan Droz: L'Ethos du Mûramati Kikuyu: Schème Migratoire, Différenciation Sociale et Individualisation au Kenya. In: *Anthropos* 95,1 (2000), pp. 87–98.

17 Lonsdale: Moral Economy of Mau Mau, p. 374.

18 Kenyatta: *Facing Mount Kenya*, p. 31.

19 Lonsdale: Moral Economy of Mau Mau, p. 376.

The distinction between individual and tribal authority compelled further precisions. Kenyatta not only denied individual rights, but condemned individualist behaviour. As he explained: "Let each person take his own road, that is the way by which we shall lose (throw away) our country."[20] A year earlier, in 1928, Kenyatta implored his *Muigwithania*'s readers to "remember that 'Members of the same family do not lose their identity'."[21] Society could only survive through the household, and individual property through the family. A prosperous society was a prosperous family, itself the guardian of a prosperous land. Society, family and land were thus depending on each other.[22] Only the nature and source of authority was left to be defined. To do so, Kenyatta distinguished ownership from use of land: he drew the line between private ownership and collective boundaries. More significantly, he distinguished the family both from the collectivity and the tribe.

He highlighted that the family, vested with land rights, would ultimately prevail over the collectivity that only demarcated territorial boundaries.[23] A collectivity embodying general good yet made of atomized voices was a European invention; it had no relevance to decide over land issues. Kenyatta set the family apart from the tribe: "the Gikuyu system of land tenure was never tribal tenure, nor was there any customary law which gave any particular chief or group of chiefs any power over lands other than the lands of their own family groups."[24] There could be no collectivity further than the supreme authority of the family: "Realise that there is nothing equal to a man's home, for it is it that leads him and is also his base"[25], he wrote in

20 Jomo Kenyatta: Our Land. In: *Muigwithania*, May 1929, vol. 1, no. 12, DC/MKS/10B/13/1, Kenya National Archives (KNA).

21 Jomo Kenyatta: Let Us Agree among Ourselves and Exalt the Kikuyu. In: *Muigwithania*, November 1928, vol. 1, no. 7, DC/MKS/10B/13/1, KNA.

22 For detailed anthropological studies of the relationship between land and generational organization, see Anne-Marie Peatrik: Un Système Composite: l'Organisation d'Age et de Génération des Kikuyu Précoloniaux. In: *Journal des Africanistes* 64,1 (1994), pp. 3–36; Droz: *Migrations Kikuyus*, p. 116; Kershaw: *Mau Mau From Below*, pp. 66–68.

23 Lonsdale: Moral Economy of Mau Mau, p. 335, highlights these contradictions.

24 Kenyatta: *Facing Mount Kenya*, pp. 32, 26–27. Yet again, Kenyatta invoked or condemned the term 'tribe' at his own convenience throughout the rest of his book.

25 Jomo Kenyatta: Muigwithania' Journey. In: *Muigwithania*, May 1929, vol. 1, no. 12, DC/MKS/10B/13/1, KNA.

Muigwhitania. Only the family could be the fertile soil of political and economic sociability. Furthermore, it only could ensure trust among individuals, by providing reliability within society, in contradiction to European commerce which "serve[s the] interest of their party which rob all the other."[26] Kenyatta contrasted the cohesion of Gikuyu customs to the Europeans' "good jobs and good money".[27] He warned that the "time of being helped is coming to end", for when a man would have to leave this good job, he would be left with unreliable friends quick to forget the glory of the past. His ancestry too would fade away, and "HE WILL BE REDUCED TO EATING THE VERY SKIN OF HIS BODY".[28] Individual autonomy and dignity relied on home and land. In *My People Kikuyu*, Kenyatta would insist: "[a] good name, rather than material reward, was what every warrior looked for."[29] Trust was an internal, almost intimate process which no alien or superseding social or authoritative structure other than the family could ensure.

From Pre-colonial Kikuyu Moral Debate to the Kenya Nation

His distrust for individuals proved to be an enduring political dynamic: two decades later, former British High Commissioner and friend Malcolm MacDonald would confirm Kenyatta's belief in a personal letter to him: "I know that you think (quite rightly) that individuals are unimportant" and "agree with you about the unimportance of individuals – except for the rare few, and Mzee Jomo Kenyatta is one of those few."[30] We touch here on an important aspect of Kenyatta's political imagination: politics are a matter of families, not individuals. Individuals *on their own*, i. e. isolated from tribal institutions, have neither power nor any political relevance. Trust too remained a relevant feature of his speeches. Speaking at a KANU seminar on 29 June 1962, not even a year after his release from restriction, he

26 Kenyatta: Let Us Agree among Ourselves.

27 Jomo Kenyatta: Money Making (or, Quest of Possessions). In: *Muigwithania*, December 1928 – January 1929, vol. 1, no. 8, DC/MKS/10B/13/1, KNA.

28 Ibid.

29 Kenyatta: *My People Kikuyu*, p. 17.

30 Malcolm MacDonald to Jomo Kenyatta, November 19th 1964: MAC/44/1/2 MacDonald Papers, reproduced by kind permission of the Trustees of the Malcolm MacDonald Papers, and of the University of Durham.

bluntly denounced corrupted political behaviour: "If a person can buy another, he too can be bought. If a person can offer himself to be bought by a leader, he is no better than a prostitute and cannot be trusted."[31] Trust had to remain rooted in a moral community.

The moral community Kenyatta exalted in his post-independence speeches was not dissimilar to that of *Facing Mount Kenya.* To guide Kenya on the postcolonial road, Kenyatta spoke of "Africanism", an idea directly inspired from his earlier writings:

> I submit that the Africanism to which we aspire in this country is the Africanism which combines the best from the past, present and future: the Africanism which seeks to fulfil what our people want to be, to do and to have. Indeed, this is the Africanism to which I dedicated my book […] in my early days in the political field, when I said that: 'The dead, the living and the unborn will unite to rebuild the destroyed shrines'.[32]

The parallel is all the more obvious when it comes to land and tribal issues. During the 1964 independence celebrations, Kenyatta reasserted that land was not only the "greatest asset" for economic development in Kenya; it also ensured "our survival and salvation."[33] Although he reaffirmed that "all tribal land is entrenched in the tribal authority", he quickly added that the tribe should not replace the state, for "[a]t no time did the African tribes, or groups of tribes, see the State in the same way as the Greek City States. At no time did African tribes see themselves as tinpot 'nations'."[34] Kenyatta's use of the past was just as malleable as it was in *Facing Mount Kenya*, except that he could now use it to serve his political interests.[35]

The glow of the pre-colonial past could mask, justify or decry, depending on convenience, the contradictions of postcolonial Kenya. One visible contradiction that ought to be concealed after independence was the breach between the freedom fighters (ex-Mau Mau) and the

31 Kenyatta: *Suffering without Bitterness*, p. 185.

32 Jomo Kenyatta: Statement in the Capacity of the President of KANU, August 13th, 1964. In: Ibid., pp. 226–231, here p. 227.

33 Jomo Kenyatta: Television Broadcast on September 11th, 1964. In: Ibid., pp. 232–234, here p. 232.

34 Kenyatta: August 13th, 1964. In: Ibid., p. 229.

35 On the malleable use of the past, see John Lonsdale: The Prayers of Waiyaki; Political Uses of the Kikuyu Past. In: David M. Anderson / Douglas Hamilton Johnson (eds): *Revealing Prophets: Prophecy in Eastern African History.* London: Currey 1995, pp. 240–291; Lonsdale: Contest of Time.

loyalists. Kenyatta's calls to "forget and forgive" the past have been widely noticed by historians, who pointed out that this was a convenient strategy to burry his ambiguous relationship to the Mau Mau movement, while drowning the freedom fighter's cause in the larger struggle for independence.[36] Forgetting the past was justified by the need for national unity: "all (a long history of setbacks and sufferings, of failure and humiliation) can be forgotten, when its outcome is the foundation on which a future can be built."[37] But his notion of unity was as instrumental as confused.

On the one hand, unity depended on the constant dedication to nation-building: "Whether this age of African opportunity becomes in fact the age of African achievement, depends on how we move, as one united team, towards a common goal."[38] Consequently, tribalism was vilified: "unity cannot be taken for granted. […] There are some people who remain tribalists at heart, and who regard unity as their enemy."[39] On the other hand, unity did not dethrone tribalism; Kenyatta juggled with concepts. He was quick to admit that the colonial past could not be wiped away – just as he had done in *Facing Mount Kenya*, certainly because he knew the colonizers were part of his audience. He acknowledged tribal politics mattered under the cover of a culturalist argument: "Every man has the right to take a pride and interest in his tribe – its history, its culture and its customs."[40] He appealed to tribal feeling clothed in terms of a more democratic representation.[41] Yet again, when tribal animosities risked damaging his

36 See in particular Murray-Brown: *Kenyatta*; Elisha Stephen Atieno-Odhiambo: The Production of History in Kenya: the Mau Mau Debate. In: *Canadian Journal of African Studies* 25,2 (1991), pp. 300–307; Elisha Stephen Atieno-Odhiambo / John Lonsdale (eds): *Mau Mau & Nationhood: Arms, Authority & Narration.* Athens: Ohio State UP 2003.

37 Jomo Kenyatta: Speech on Kenyatta Day, October 20th, 1964. In: Id.: *Suffering without Bitterness*, pp. 240–245, here p. 241.

38 Jomo Kenyatta: Opening Address at the Kenya Institute of Administration, August 19th, 1965. In: Ibid., pp. 281–284, here p. 282.

39 Jomo Kenyatta: Speech on Madaraka Day, June 1st, 1965. In: Ibid., pp. 274–277, here p. 276.

40 Jomo Kenyatta: Speech on Madaraka Day, June 1st, 1966. In: Ibid., pp. 308–315, here p. 313.

41 Kenyatta was already at pain to establish a parallel between Kikuyu culture and Western democracy in *Facing Mount Kenya* (see p. 33). As for his post-independence speeches, the references to "democracy" are multiple. See Kenyatta: *Suffering without Bitterness*, pp. 229, 231, 260–261, 306, 347.

politics, he argued for unity. An *aide mémoire* preparing his forthcoming tour of Western province in April 1964 advised him:

> Western Region people consider themselves neglected by government. They urge redistribution of portfolios to give them an additional Minister. Your underlying theme, therefore, might be on UNITY, and that the strength of the State and Government depends on the loyalty of the people to their laws and respect for Human Rights and property.[42]

Kenyatta was taking advantage of the unsettled status of African traditions in a republican context. As tribal logics drove political behaviours, African traditions served to legitimate the independent state. He compared Kenya's state institutions to tribal authorities. The parliament "must give full modern expression to the traditional African custom, by serving as the place where the Elders and the spokesmen of the people are expected and enabled to confer."[43] When it came to the justification of the one-party state in 1964, he argued that just as tribes had, from time immemorial, united against crises, the tribal council "was at once a Government and an expression of the very personality of each and every citizen."[44] The connection between tribal council and the state was "justified on the grounds that only therein could people find peace and security."[45] Nevertheless, the frontier between the nation and the tribe were fuzzy, barely clarified on the grounds that "we have our own concept of Ujamaa, springing from our own culture here."[46] Confronted with the accusation that his "African socialism" meant nothing at all, Kenyatta replied that

> The essential of our African socialism can be defined as inspiration. We are seeking to inspire dedication, not in pursuit of an ideology or in search for power, but for the welfare of humanity.[47]

42 Tours of Western Province (Friday, 23rd April – Sunday 25th April [1965]), Aide Memoire, KA/4/9, KNA.

43 Jomo Kenyatta: Speech for the State Opening of Parliament, December 1964. In: Id.: *Suffering without Bitterness*, pp. 259–264, here p. 260.

44 Kenyatta: August 13th, 1964. In: Ibid., p. 229.

45 Ibid.

46 Jomo Kenyatta: Speech for the State Opening of the Parliament, November 2nd, 1965. In: Id.: *Suffering without Bitterness*, pp. 285–293, here p. 286.

47 Speech by His Excellency the President at Diplomatic Corps, Luncheon July 29th, 1965, KA/4/9, KNA.

These were not merely empty words. Kenyatta had never been a man of ideology. He was part of a movement of moral re-foundation, which was not limited to Kikuyu politics. At the time of his encounter with Bronislaw Malinowski indeed, colonial doctrinal thoughts were undergoing change, becoming increasingly self-reflexive as well as more critical. With the help of anthropologists who saw there an opportunity to promote their own research agenda, colonial administrators started to rethink colonization, its progress, its techniques and its legitimacy. This "second colonization" aimed at rationalizing and modernizing colonization by fostering scientific knowledge, and promoting, as a result, of "a colonial science".[48] Colonial science was not about ideology – it was about moral virtues, which Kenyatta exalted almost as a personal signature to his speeches – quite visible when one compares the notes prepared for his speeches, generally by an assistant minister or the general attorney and the delivered version. Just as he had done in *Facing Mount Kenya*, he continued to warn against the pervasiveness of "colonial mentality" and advised "to be vigilant, and to re-dedicate yourselves today to building a nation deeply rooted in our own thoughts and ideas [so as to preserve] in many arts the African traditional forms and culture."[49] He condemned the detribalizing attraction to towns – he himself disliked staying in Nairobi – people leaving "their land unattended", an "attitude […] not only negative, but [which] promotes biggest waste in Kenya today", and a "disgrace to […] manhood and to our society."[50] To carry on African traditions, he called for respect to elders' authority, for a disciplined code of

48 Terence O. Ranger: From Humanism to the Science of Man: Colonialism in Africa and the Understanding of Alien Societies. In: *Transactions of the Royal Historical Society (Fifth Series)* 26 (1976), pp. 115–141; Paul Cocks: The Rhetoric of Science and the Critique of Imperialism in British Social Anthropology, c. 1870–1940. In: *History and Anthropology* 9,1 (1995), pp. 93–119; Jack Goody: *The Expansive Moment: The Rise of Social Anthropology in Britain and Africa 1918–1970*. Cambridge: Cambridge UP 1995; Véronique Dimier: Enjeux institutionnels autour d'une science politique des colonies en France et en Grande-Bretagne, 1930–1950. In: *Genèses* 37,1 (1999), pp. 70–92; Frederick Cooper: Development, Modernization, and the Social Sciences in the Era of Decolonization: the Examples of British and French Africa. In: *Revue d'Histoire des Sciences Humaines* 10,1 (2014), pp. 9–38.

49 Jomo Kenyatta: Speech for the O. A. U. Day, May 25th, 1964. In: Id.: *Suffering without Bitterness*, pp. 218–219, here p. 218.

50 Jomo Kenyatta: Television Broadcast, September 11th, 1964. In: Ibid., pp. 232–234, here pp. 233–234.

behaviour, all that could elevate African's dignity abroad, and "contribute to the world [with] a new philosophy."[51]

His conception of politics was not only imbued with this moral discourse – his whole vision of state and society where confined to the cradle of moral virtues: the family. Political loyalty and obedience to state authority were clothed with moral virtue. Addressing administrative officers in March 1965, Kenyatta did not mince his words: "Those of you who fail to give your best are not only betraying yourselves and a shame to your families, but you are also failing in the trust which I as Head of the Republic of Kenya have placed in you."[52] Loyalty was invoked whenever law and order mattered, or when it was about joining opposition – and thus abandoning "past loyalty to Kenya nationalism."[53] At stake was more than setting apart good from evil, pros and cons. Distinctions drawn from and through moral virtues define in fact social frontiers, frontiers between individuals, between exclusion and inclusion within the new 'postcolony'. Making politics an affair of civic virtue, law and order became a matter of individual behaviour – not of collective action. Kenyatta expressed it clearly during the 1964 republican celebration: "All of us must safeguard the integrity of our State. And we must look on law and order not just as an institution of society, or a code of behaviour, but as the outward image of our self-respect."[54] The society Kenyatta defended was certainly not a nation, yet not a tribe either. It was inherently atomized; his conception of authority too.

Postcolonial Kenya: Virtues for All, State for No One?

Fragmented authority does not mean that there is no authority at all. Following on Lonsdale's observation that Kenyatta imagined himself as a Kikuyu elder, that his authority was not at all an authority for all and ended when others' "moral equivalence" began, I want to argue that Kenyatta never considered authority – and, by extension, the

51 Kenyatta: December 1964. In: Ibid., p. 257.

52 H.E. the President's Talk to Administrative Officers, March 12th, 1965, KA/4/9 KNA.

53 Jomo Kenyatta: Broadcast Address to the Nation, April 26th, 1966. In: Id.: *Suffering without Bitterness*, pp. 302–307, here p. 302.

54 Kenyatta: December 1964. In: Ibid., p. 257.

state – as an instrument of social change.[55] His authority as President did not expand beyond the realm of security, law and order. He repeated several times that "you must know that Kenyatta alone cannot give you everything. All things we must do together." Concurrently, the state was not accountable to its citizens:

> We reject a blueprint of the Western model of a two-Party system of Government because we do not subscribe to the notion of the Government and the governed being in opposition to one another, the one clamouring for duties and the other crying out for rights.[56]

Individuals ought to seek their own means to accomplish themselves: "It is [...] the responsibility of each individual to ensure that he grows up into a person who can fit into his national society, thereby living contentedly with his fellow human beings."[57] Authority, state and society where bound, not so much by a traditionalist than a functionalist conception of community making, directly inspired by his anthropological studies with Malinowski, where social cohesion comes first, myth and history second; at the same time, it was also bound to a conservative and static understanding of the rule of law.[58]

Kenyatta placed the Kikuyu principle of personal accomplishment at the basis of state-building in Kenya, hence exalted it in virtually all his post-independence speeches. In line with his contempt for communist values, and his ideal of a self-regulated society, he considered "self-help" (or self-mastery) as the cement of social order. Heading to London for the last independence conference in 1963, he reasserted the supremacy of land property right – a principle that quickly became the crux of the politics of independence – in front of Kenyan businessmen crowded in Nairobi City Hall. He explained that if the state was to protect property, at no point did it mean nationalization: "You must not interpret my remarks as implying nationalisation. We consider that nationalisation will not serve to advance the cause of

55 Lonsdale: Jomo Kenyatta, God & the Modern World, pp. 49, 63.

56 Jomo Kenyatta: Broadcast on September 21st, 1963 and Statement in the Capacity of the President of KANU, August 13th, 1964. In: Id.: *Suffering without Bitterness*, pp. 209–211, here p.211 and pp.226–231, here p. 227.

57 Speech by His Excellency the President at Diplomatic Corps, Luncheon July 29th, 1965, KA/4/9, KNA.

58 Henry Tudor: *Political Myth*. Portsmouth: Praeger 1972, pp. 46–52.

African socialism."[59] He maintained the line he had always taken since the early days of his political commitment: the supremacy of land property and the necessity to work for it. In the same speech on economic policy, he stated that

> [t]he land is the place where the ordinary man and woman can do most to build the nation. When one farmer increases his cultivations and improves his farm by harder work, it is a personal achievement. When ten thousand farmers follow his example, it becomes a national achievement.[60]

Successful business only, itself closely depending on working the land, could lead to successful nation-building. All the state could and ought to do, was to enable "individual men and women" – Kenyatta rarely referred to these individuals as citizens – to "[exercise] their personal initiative and for the fulfillment of their individual ambitions."[61] Kenyatta transferred, or rather enlarged, the principle of possessive individualism, the same he praised in *Facing Mount Kenya*, to the new Kenya republic. Individual undertaking ('self-help') only could lead to individual achievement (the ethos of the *mûramati*). Speaking to the Kenyan youth in 1966, he summarized this position: "Not everybody can reach the top of his profession and not everybody can enter the profession of his choice. […] There is work in Kenya for all, but you must go out and seek it."[62] The solution to unemployment depended "equally on the efforts of the many thousands of our countrymen whose livelihood comes from the land."[63] Already in December 1964, he had stated: "Do your work honestly and well. For the State's obligation to you is no greater than your obligation to your fellow-men."[64] So the creation of opportunities was not the business of the state, which aimed only at protecting the integrity of property. This also implied that any attack against property was an attack against the state. In a speech celebrating the birth of the Republic of Kenya,

59 Jomo Kenyatta: Speech in the Nairobi City Hall on Economic Policy, September 29th, 1964. In: Id.: *Suffering without Bitterness*, pp. 235–239, here p. 238.

60 Jomo Kenyatta: Speech for the State Opening of the Parliament, February 15th, 1967. In: Ibid., pp. 332–339, here p. 336.

61 Ibid.

62 Address by His Excellency the President at the Youth Festival on October 16th, 1966 at 2.30 p.m., KA/4/11, KNA.

63 Kenyatta: February 15th, 1967. In: Id.: *Suffering without Bitterness*, pp. 332–339, here p. 335–336.

64 Kenyatta: December 1964. In: Ibid., p. 255.

the notions of property and crime were barely masked by the ornamental, internationally acceptable expressions of 'human rights' and 'unlawfulness':

> We must gear ourselves to a fundamental belief in individual human rights, as the basis of respect. And this respect must be extended, beyond what a man is or what he does, to what he *owns* and cherishes. Without respect for property, security of property, chaos can swiftly come to any State. [...] We are all moving now towards a common goal. We need, therefore, respect for a new social conscience, in which the *criminal* is not just a candidate for punishment or pity, but a traitor to our purpose and an object of scorn.[65]

With the state considered as an instrument of control, self-accomplishment could only be achieved outside of the realm of authority and power: at the margins of the state. At no point was self-accomplishment an ideology of state.

Kenyatta considered community-making by the state as impractical and illusionary: since communal sense did not exist outside the individual, no authority could foster and protect it. The state was at best "in the hearts and spirit of the people".[66] The leitmotiv of 'virtues for all, yet state for no one' was adapted to all government's politics. As for concrete development issues, such as land possession and agriculture: it was "not the intention of government to go on pumping money indefinitely into large scale farmers in this area if these farmers do not follow the rules of good husbandry and the advice of the extension staff."[67] Banks could not "make something out of nothing and the government cannot by order, or 'fiat' grant to a printed piece of paper a value independent of the backing which it possesses".[68] Individuals should obey state legislation – "there is no hope in our country if individuals take upon themselves to grab land" – and yet "it should be made clear to everyone that we will not be able to give everyone land."[69]

65 Ibid., p. 254 (my emphasis).

66 Speech by His Excellency the President at the Opening of the Secondary School and Technical Block at Starehe Boy's Central, July 15th, 1966, KA/4/11, KNA.

67 Speech to be delivered by the Minister for Finance On Behalf of His Excellency the President on the Occasion of the Opening of the Eldoret Show on 4th March, 1966, KA/4/11, KNA.

68 Speech by His Excellency the President Mzee Jomo Kenyatta at the Opening of the Central Bank on the 14th September, 1966, KA/4/11, KNA.

69 Notes for the President on the Occasion of the Presentation of Certificates to the Former Squatters on November 25, 1966, KA/4/11, KNA.

Back to the Family

Subsequently, Kenyatta's vision of leadership was ingrained in the domestic realm of the family. His often quoted apostrophe to political opponent and former Mau Mau Bildad Kaggia "What have you done for yourself?" illustrates well that, to him, family and home are primordial objectives for a self-respecting man.[70] I wish to push the argument further, and emphasize that the politics of the state start in the family household. More particularly, they start in the field, as Kenyatta claimed:

> I work during the day, and then after work I go home to my *shamba* and have a look at my bananas, potatoes, poultry and other things. If you elect somebody who spends all his time in Nairobi doing nothing: what good is that? What does such a person – whether an M.P. or a City Councillor or a KANU official – show us he is doing back at his home and in his *shamba*, where his parents are? Of what use is it roaming about in Nairobi in bars and hotels? This only brings poverty and prostitution in this country. Many of you write letters blaming the women, saying that these women prostitutes are spoiling Nairobi, but you do not tell the truth. It is the men who are prostitutes.[71]

By comparing state building to farming, Kenyatta set up the family not only as the ultimate social basis of the state itself, but as the ultimate frontier his leadership could not cross: "I am prepared to serve you with the life which is still left in me. I have not come to rule you so as to tell anyone do this and do that", would he tell his welcoming crowd in 1946.[72] After independence, and advocating politics of *Harambee* (literally 'let's pull together' in Swahili), he repeatedly insisted that "you must know that Kenyatta alone cannot give you everything."[73] The rhetoric of governing oneself, deep-rooted in the household, was elevated to the realm of state-building:

70 Kenyatta and Kaggia were arrested and jailed together. See Kaggia's own records of the event in Bildad M. Kaggia / W. de Leeuw / M. Kaggia: *The Struggle for Freedom and Justice*. Nairobi: Transafrica 2012, p. 271. Lonsdale highlighted the tension between leadership and self-mastery when he wrote that Kenyatta "made room for the self-mastery of others, by no means for all Kenyans but for all the more important ethnic vassals who, having had done with trifling, aspired to realize their ambition under an elder's shade." (Lonsdale: Jomo Kenyatta, God & the Modern World, p. 63.) Cf. Hervé Maupeu: Kikuyu capitalistes. Réflexions sur un cliché Kenyan. In: *Outre-Terre* 2,11 (2005), pp. 493–506.

71 Kenyatta: *Suffering without Bitterness*, p. 347; cf. p. 305.

72 Lonsdale: Henri Muoria, Public Moralist, p. 279.

73 Kenyatta: *Suffering without Bitterness*, p. 217.

> I tell you this: nation building is not a matter of having money to employ, or of having authority to wield. It is a matter of patriotism and pride. In your work, whatever this is, and in your homes and in your districts, the smallest efforts to build and to improve are most important.[74]

Kenyatta's praise of the virtues of the family dated from *Facing Mount Kenya*. His definitions of the family were nonetheless fuzzy and imprecise, perhaps because the family was, at that time already, a new concept in a new environment. Resulting from the colonization of the fertile White highlands, shortage of land hindered the formation of new and large *mbari* (clans) that structured pre-colonial Kikuyu society, thus reduced to the patrimonial families who could afford acquiring and cultivating land. The Kikuyu society did not disappear, but disintegrated. It basic unit shrank, and its ideal democratized: the *mûramati*, the Kikuyu accomplished man, owner of land and family man aspiring to leadership, was no longer subjected to the authority of the *mbari*, the clan. With the disintegration of clanship, the family took over the control and regulation of social relations.[75] This transformation was described by Kenyatta in *Facing Mount Kenya* – yet without being able to solve the internal contradictions it posed to his understanding of Kikuyu history.[76] At that time, his aim was to revive the ethos of personal accomplishment, while he himself aspired to be recognized as a *mûramati*, as the legitimate leader of his "clan".[77] In *Facing Mount Kenya*, he associated the family group to the *mbari*, literally the lineage or extended family, and gave a rather minimalist definition: the family "brings together all those who are related by blood; namely a man, his wife or wives and children and also their grand- and great-grandchildren."[78] This was a surprising definition, for Kikuyu society was regulated by rituals, not by blood ties.[79]

'Family' was a Janus-faced concept. On the one hand, it demarcated acceptable sociability, by safeguarding the sanctity of ownership of land and its owners. It encompassed two opposite forces, individualism

74 Ibid., p. 258; cf. pp. 273, 287, 347.

75 Droz: *Migrations Kikuyus*, p. 117. I thank Yvan Droz for his helpful insights on this question.

76 See Berman / Lonsdale: Custom, Modernity, and the Search for Kihooto.

77 Lonsdale: Jomo Kenyatta, God & the Modern World.

78 Kenyatta: *Facing Mount Kenya*, p. 1.

79 Peatrik: Système Composite.

and tribalism. It restricted individuals from thinking that individual achievements would give them the right to have "authority to wield". And it was erected as the antithesis of tribalism, which, for the reasons previously explained, Kenyatta never considered a self-sufficient right to authority. At no point, however, was the family in contradiction with individualism and tribalism – or ethnicity. Ethnicity would remain the guiding strength from which Kenyans had to "[learn] how to master themselves in modern times", the only force to prove "that Kenya was a moral community precisely because its people were not detribalized."[80] But family boundaries set the frontiers of the state and of authority, as a state could never replace the people's duty to rule their own lives.[81]

The important, though ambiguous role *the family* plays in Kenyatta's political imagination may shed new light on his strategy of state building. From his return to Kenya to his accession of power, Kenyatta gradually built his power not only on the most prominent Kikuyu families, but on what some called a "Kiambu mafia", as most powerful actors of the Kenyatta state would come from Kiambu, his home-district.[82] With the achievement of independence in 1963, he pushed the alliances further, nominating Charles Njonjo (son of the former colonial chief Josiah Njonjo) as his Attorney General, and appointing the sons of former chiefs to various ministries.[83] His personal physician, Njoroge Mungai, was a close cousin and led different prominent ministries throughout the Kenyatta regime. He was married to a sister of James Gichuru, founder of the Kenya African Union, Kenyatta's dear and reliable friend, a prominent politician and minister. His "inner cabinet" was constituted by Kikuyus from his

80 Lonsdale: Jomo Kenyatta, God & the Modern World, p. 51.

81 On the tension between state and ethnicity see John M. Lonsdale: KAU's Cultures: Imaginations of Community and Constructions of Leadership in Kenya after the Second World War. In: *Journal of African Cultural Studies* 13,1 (2000), pp. 107–124, here p. 121.

82 On Kenyatta's first marriages, see Murray-Brown: *Kenyatta*. On the notion of "mafia" state, see Michaela Wrong: *It's Our Turn to Eat: The Story of a Kenyan Whistle Blower*. London: Fourth Estate 2009. On the politics of the chiefs, see Marshall S. Clough: *Fighting Two Sides: Kenyan Chiefs and Politicians, 1918–1940*. Niwott: UP of Colorado 1990.

83 On the moral legitimacy provided by the association with former chiefs, see David W. Throup: The Construction and Destruction of the Kenyatta State. In: Michael G. Schatzberg (ed.): *The Political Economy of Kenya*. Portsmouth: Praeger 1987, pp. 33–74.

hometown Kiambu.[84] The quote attributed to James Gichuru, himself from Kiambu, is meaningful: "It is not by accident that Kiambu was made the seat of power, it is not that they like it, it is because the god of the Kikuyu decided that Kiambu would be the head, Murang'a the stomach and Nyeri the legs."[85]

Kenyatta's definition of the family might be fuzzy, it emphasizes nonetheless that family is not so much a matter of blood ties than a community of interests, rooted in land and bound by shared moral virtues.[86] This fuzziness corresponds, as matter of fact, to his intellectual background in functionalist anthropology: family matters as a *functional* organ of society; not as an essential social body. One may read the patrimonial family not as a result but as the precondition of economic policies. In the context of a scramble for land, it was bound to preserve the colonial pattern of "small-peasant farming on an individual basis".[87] But, as Robert Buijtenhuis underlined, Kenyatta had always been a moderate, and a political rather than an economic nationalist.[88] One may assume that he judged the preservation of the colonial economic legacy the only road to the preservation of Kikuyu self-mastery.

84 Njonjo, Mbiu Koinange and Mungai were referred in 1969 as the "inner cabinet", i.e. Kenyatta's "closest advisers […] often making decisions without consulting ministers or even Kenyatta." By 1969, 30% of Kenyatta's cabinet was Kikuyu; in 1964, the President, the Attorney General, the Foreign minister, the Defence minister, the Finance minister, the Commissioner of Police, as well as the elite presidential guard, Mr Bernard Njinu and his bodyguard Wanyoike Thungu were all from Kiambu, to mention only these few. Furthermore "nine of the twenty-two permanent secretaryships [of the Civil Service, on which Kenyatta heavily relied to rule the country], four of the then seven [Provincial Commissioners] also [were] of the same tribe." Both quotes are from Moderchai Tamarkin: The Roots of Political Stability in Kenya. In: *African Affairs* 77,308 (1978), pp. 297–320, here p. 302.

85 Emman Omari: When They Were Kings: How Kiambu's Power Men Ruled. In: *Daily Nation*, 15.06.2011. http://www.nation.co.ke/counties/When-they-were-kings-How-Kiambu-power-men-ruled-/-/1107872/1181458/-/jobdxmz/-/index.html (accessed 06.02.2015). Murang'a and Nyeri, along with Kiambu, Meru and Embu, constitute the Central Province, heart of the Kikuyuland.

86 It is meaningful that Duncan Ndegwa, first secretary to the Cabinet and Head of the civil service devoted a large part of the first hundred pages of his autobiography to Kikuyu culture (Duncan Ndegwa: *Walking in Kenyatta Struggles: My Story*. Nairobi: Kenya Leadership Institute 2011).

87 Robert Buijtenhuijs: *Mau Mau Twenty Years After: the Myth and the Survivors*. The Hague: Mouton 1973, p. 31. Cf. Colin Leys: *Underdevelopment in Kenya*. London: Heinemann 1975, chapter 3.

88 Buijtenhuijs: *Mau Mau*, p. 54.

Conclusion

My final argument can be summarized as follows. Kenyatta's post-independence speeches were clearly inspired from his earlier writings. Although all remained enmeshed with political purposes, they revealed a model of society and authority Kenyatta defended and erected as a political chart. Kenyatta did not believe in community building, because he saw individual interests as paramount. At the same time, he did not believe individuals could wield authority alone. He liked repeating that there are no things for free, and people must work for themselves and should not expect any help from the state. His conception of authority as state leader was thus confined to law and security – at no point was it an instrument of social transformation. By the same token, his moral authority remained rooted in the moral economy of the family. Therefore, I argue that Kenyatta was no nationalist thinker, but he was no tribalist either. We must take his denunciation of tribalism seriously. He was a *mûramati*, a family man; and, to accomplish himself, a man of power. Being Kikuyu, Kenyatta acted within a particular cultural frame, that of Kikuyu society which shaped him profoundly, although his political imagination was augmented by the Western influences he experienced both in Kenya and abroad. Important as Kikuyu culture was to his personal development and his political imagination, one should not forget that Kikuyu moral economy was constantly negotiated and that it underwent profound changes in Kenyatta's lifetime.

The Making of Biko

Martyrdom and the Creation of an African Intellectual

Myra Ann Houser

The Southern Africa Project (originally named South Africa Legal Assistance Project) of the Lawyers' Committee for Civil Rights Under Law formed in 1967 as the US-based legal rights organization sought a means to become involved with anti-apartheid work. By the mid-1970s, this foray left the Lawyers' Committee vulnerable to criticism that it had transitioned away from its mission to change and challenge the US Bar. Once comprised primarily of liberal white lawyers, the Project soon became a space for increasing numbers of young African American attorneys to fight against continuing racial injustices following the mainstream civil rights movement.
Attorney Millard Arnold served as Project director, beginning in 1977. Within Southern Africa, Arnold committed the organization to addressing two key areas: lack of basic human rights and the practice of deviating from international jurists' definitions of rule of law. Protecting both, he argued, would legitimize not only governmental systems, but also the legal profession and "sanctity of the law."[1] His activism proved useful to public debates but not toward substantially changing US policy on South Africa. It did, however, help set a precedent for American citizens concerned about foreign policy. Ultimately,

1 Michael Schnehage: Upper Echelon: Millard Arnold. In: *Moneyweb*, 26.09.2012. http://www.moneyweb.co.za/moneyweb-upper-echelon/upper-echelon-millard-arnold--executive-director-m?sn=2009%20Detail (accessed 05.02.2015).

Arnold's intersection with South African Student Association (SASO) co-founder Steve Biko led the Project to a case that would resonate with justice seekers from around the world and increase the organization's prominence in an increasingly prominent movement.

I.

The Project's work with SASO and the Black Peoples Convention (BPC) led it to defend Sathasivan Cooper and eight others in the 1975–1976 Terrorism Trial, where Biko spoke on behalf of activists accused of distributing anti-government pamphlets and speaking out against the state at a 1974 rally celebrating South Africa's decision to recognize Samora Machel's Frelimo as the government of newly-independent neighboring Mozambique. Lasting seventeen months, the trial became the longest-running one to receive Project support. It also became the longest political trial of the era, with the extended time frame giving leaders such as Biko – called to the witness stand to explain the ideals of Black Consciousness – ample time to publicly expound upon their grievances with the state. That distinction is particularly weighty in a period that involved a veritable prosecuting frenzy. Relatively dormant since the mid-1960s, state prosecutors regained steam during the mid-1970s as they tried students and other young activists, beginning a cycle of violence that eventually spiraled during the 1980s into the detention, torture, and murder of tens of thousands of children. In an effort to prevent further martyrdom and deny activists the publicity they had gained during the 1975–1976 trial, the government soon sped up trials – making drawn-out ones like the SASO/BPC incident – all the more rare. This increasingly concerned the lawyers, who believed their clients had been further denied due process.[2]

The Project supported trialists through raising nearly $200,000 for their defense and providing support and American expert witnesses to attorneys.[3] In this context Millard Arnold had a phone conversation, initiated by SASO/BPC attorney Shun Chetty, with Biko. "We

2 Michael Lobban: *White Man's Justice: South African Political Trials in the Black Consciousness Era.* London: Clarendon 1996, p. 148.

3 Lawyers' Committee for Civil Rights Under Law: *Supplement to the Interim Report,* 1975. Personal Papers of Douglas Wachholz, pp. 64–65.

spoke very briefly; he was understandably guarded, although nothing of any great substance was discussed," Arnold said. "I was struck by his thoughtful and contemplative voice, and whilst we didn't speak for very long, I was impressed."[4] The moment passed quickly, and as the group went to trial, all nine defendants were eventually found guilty of treason and served sentences on Robben Island.

Despite this disappointing outcome, the trial had featured one silver lining, which was advocate David Soggot's intense questioning of the defendants and Biko. Soggot, an adviser for Project partner and funder, the Lutheran World Federation, had been initially barred from contact with Black Consciousness prisoners, a move he successfully appealed before also obtaining permission to put the banned Biko on the witness stand.[5] He then maximized the opportunity. "The lawyer's meticulous examination and his admiration for the charismatic leader offered Biko the chance to lay out as never before his political philosophy," Dennis Herbstein wrote.[6] Laying out that philosophy and highlighting the oppression it had grown from, however, did little to stop the inevitable verdict.

The SASO/BPC sentences came on December 16, 1976. Six months earlier – June 16 – South African police shot and killed at least 176 unarmed school children in Soweto. They injured scores more. Inspired largely by Black Consciousness philosophies, the teenagers had been marching in opposition to the Afrikaans Medium Decree and its mandate that Afrikaans and English become the medium of instruction in all schools, including those where the majority of students – and teachers – spoke an African language such as Zulu or Xhosa as mother tongue. The first student killed, thirteen-year-old Hector Pieterson, followed older children into the march even after his family forbade it; he was intensely curious about the exciting happenings. Sam Nzima's iconic photograph of the dying Pieterson

4 Millard Arnold: E-mail interview by Author, 30.03.2014.

5 David Beresford: David Soggot Obituary: Civil Rights Lawyer Connected with Several of South Africa's Most Famous Cases. In: *The Guardian*, 27.06.2010. http://www.theguardian.com/world/2010/jun/27/david-soggot-obituary (accessed 30.10.2013).

6 Dennis Herbstein: David Soggot: Lawyer Who Fought for Justice in Apartheid Era Namibia. In: *The Independent*, 17.06.2010. http://www.independent.co.uk/news/obituaries/david-soggot-lawyer-who-fought-for-justice-in-apartheidera-namibia-2002398.html (accessed 30.10.2013).

being cradled by Mbuyisa Makhuba while his seventeen-year-old sister Antoinette Sithole cries out in anguish became front-page fodder for newspapers around the world. Police rounded up Sowetan adolescents en masse, and state prosecutors charged them with incitement or treason. The Soweto Students Representative Council, the group that organized the March, found its leaders on trial in a case partially funded by the Southern Africa Project.[7] Their peers across the country launched similar uprisings with similar results. Around six hundred students died as protestors met with retribution across the country.

II.

Meanwhile, the still-banned Biko moved home to King Williamstown, where he and his comrades began transitioning from their activist student lives to ones more focused on community development and vocational-based community changes.[8] Biko, now banned, remained active in political work, finding his house searched often and himself detained just as much. Carefully remaining within the letter of the law, he nonetheless found himself tried five times on charges ranging from traffic violations to breaking his banning orders. These cases had the regime's desired effect of depleting BPC coffers. He remained committed to the struggle.

In 1977, Biko was arrested and detained in Port Elizabeth under the Terrorism Act. Police interrogated and beat him to the point of unconsciousness. During a four-day period, he demonstrated disruptions in speech and mobility and exhibited odd behaviors often associated with brain trauma. Fearing repercussions with their brutal methodology under close domestic and international scrutiny, officers drove the deteriorating, and by then comatose, leader to a hospital in Pretoria – naked and without cover in the back of a Land Rover. They dumped him on the floor of a cell upon arrival and shortly thereafter gave him an intravenous drip. He died alone and unattended during the wee hours of September 12.

7 Lawyers' Committee for Civil Rights Under Law: *Southern Africa Project Annual Report*, 1981, p. 2.

8 Mamphela Ramphele: *Across Boundaries: The Journey of a South African Woman Leader* New York: The Feminist Press at CUNY 1999, p. 94.

Though police initially attempted to refuse his family body visitation or burial rights, friends managed to disseminate photos of his bruised, bloody, and swollen face. Official reports claimed Biko died of a hunger strike, but the inquest into his death conclusively demonstrated that massive head trauma as a result of the beatings had killed him. He was the twentieth person to die under detention in as many months.[9] Prophetically, Biko spoke with an American reporter just three months before his death. His arguably most famous statement, published in *The New Republic* in 1978, revealed his attitude on detention, interrogation, and being roughed up during questioning:

> You are either alive and proud, or you are dead, and when you are dead, you don't care anyway. And your method of death itself can be a politicizing thing. So you die in the riots. For a hell of a lot of them, in fact, there's really nothing to lose—almost literally, given the kinds of situations they come from. So if you can overcome the personal fear of death, which is a highly irrational thing, you know, then you're on the way. And in interrogation the same sort of thing applies. [...] If they talk to me, well I'm bound to be affected by them as human beings. But the moment they adopt the rough stuff, they are imprinting in my minds that they are police. And I only understand one form of dealing with police, and that's to be as unhelpful as possible. So I button up. [...] If they beat me up, it's to my advantage. I can use it.[10]

Indeed, his brutal death and subsequent cover-up and falsification of medical records became an incredibly politicizing thing for black South Africans, and soon, to Africans and sympathizers throughout the Diaspora.

III.

The Southern Africa Project began lending assistance to Biko's family and legal representatives such as attorney Shun Chetty, eventually sending Louis H. Pollack to observe the death inquest. Sydney Kentridge, serving as the family's attorney, flew secretly to Washington, DC, in order to consult with Lawyers' Committee members such as

9 Dean Louis H. Pollack: *The Inquest into the Death of Stephen Bantu Biko.* A Report to the Lawyers' Committee for Civil rights Under Law, Prepared for the Southern Africa Project. February 24, 1978. University of Cape Town Archives, Biko Doctors Case Collection (BC 822), Folder B2 (Legal).

10 Donald Woods: *Biko: The True Story of the Young South African Martyr and His Struggle to Raise Black Consciousness.* New York: Henry Holt 1978, pp. ix–x. In Biko's writing, the reporter is named only as "an American businessman."

Peter J. Connell and Tyrone Brown and medical experts in order to help fine tune his case.[11] It helped him contact a Detroit neurosurgeon, who examined Biko's medical records and photographs of his body, helping Kentridge to craft a compelling case that he had been beaten and abused.[12]

This initial partnership resulted in some stress for Chetty, who may have initially indicated to Arnold that he believed Biko had been tortured but later recanted, following a *Washington Post* story highlighting that fact.[13] Chetty had worked with the Southern Africa Project for several years.[14] Arnold also told the newspaper that "there may well be a case to be made against the security forces for murder," noting the success a year before of the Mapetla Mohapi death suit against police that was ultimately dismissed but resulted in a judge's reprimand to officers.[15] In an attempt to deflect international criticism and pressure, the South African government eventually offered financial restitution to Biko's family.[16] The US$ 78,000 they received presented a record amount for a death in detention suit.[17] Along with his colleagues, Arnold maintained the pressure, publishing *Steve Biko: Black Consciousness in South Africa*, a testimony transcript from the SASO/BPC trial, as a means of introducing the martyr to Americans.[18]

Arnold's attempts to gain a visa to observe the inquest ultimately failed, as did efforts by some international journalists. Anthony Lewis of the *New York Times*, for example, could not obtain government

11 Joseph D. Whitaker: Lawyers' Group Here Works for Civil Rights in South Africa. In: *The Washington Post*, 19.12.1977, p. A6.

12 Sir Sydney Kentridge: E-mail correspondence with Author, 12.02.2014.

13 Comments Misunderstood, Biko Family's Lawyer Says. In: *The Washington Post*, 16.09.1977, p. A15; Jay Ross: Key S. African Black Dies in Custody: U.S. Officials Criticize Death in Custody of Moderate Black Leader in S. Africa. In: *The Washington Post*, 14.09.1977, p. A1.

14 Ray Alexander Simons: Interview with Shun Chetty, 16.08.1979, for SANA. University of Cape Town Special Collections, Ray and Jack Simons Collection (BC1081), Biographical Information: 1940s–1990s.

15 Ross: African Black Dies in Custody, p. A1.

16 Bill Branigin: Chetty Quits South Africa: Prominent Civil Rights Activist Fears Ban on Law Practice, Seeks British Asylum. In: *The Washington Post*, 11.08.1979, p. A12.

17 Caryle Murphy: Jesse Jackson's Tour Angers South African Government. In: *The Washington Post*, 29.07.1979, p. A27.

18 Millard Arnold (ed.): *Steve Biko: Black Consicousness in South Africa*. New York: Random House 1979.

permission to cover the story, though a handful of press corps members received access.[19] In conjunction with the Section of Individual Rights and Responsibilities of the American Bar Association, the Committee on International Human Rights, and the Bar Association of the City of New York, Arnold instead sent the University of Pennsylvania Law Dean to observe the tenth day of the official inquest into Biko's death, which commenced in November, 1978, fourteen months after the murder. Pollack joined about two-hundred other observers, most of them black South Africans, in a chilly Pretoria synagogue building-cum judicial space.[20]

Past President of the British Law Society David Napley, invited by the Law Societies of South Africa, joined Pollack as the inquest's other international observer.[21] Napley's final report expressed admiration for what he perceived as fair procedures following the rule of law. He did, however, add that, though structures of law enforcement and criminal procedure were fundamentally sound, the enforced laws were "of an extreme severity in that they provide for very heavy penalties."[22] In the Southern Africa Project's opinion, Biko's violent end had violated – in addition to compassionate human consciences – the two principles Arnold focused on protecting. His death was a brutal denial of his human right to life, and solitary confinement and indefinite incommunicado detention had not been consistent with the individual liberties that a rule of law sought to safeguard.[23]

Pollack's report to the Lawyers' Committee explained to Americans the implications of Biko's death, paying particular attention to the Terrorism Act and its definition of threats to the state.[24] Biko had been detained under Section Six of the Act, which preyed on white fears to consign people with "threatening" ideology to wearing the label of "terrorist." Under the act, someone who simply sought to "embarrass" the state (or any individual within it) could be considered

19 Pollack: *Inquest into Death*, p. 13.

20 Ibid., p. 12.

21 Ibid., p. 13.

22 Quoted in N. Barney Pityana: Revolution within the Law? In: Id. / Mamphela Ramphele / Malusi Mpumlwana / Lindy Wilson (eds): *Bounds of Possibility: The Legacy of Steve Biko and Black Consciousness.* Atlantic Highlands, NJ: Zed Books 1992, pp. 201–212, here p. 201.

23 Millard Arnold: Preface. In: Pollack: *Inquest into Death*, pp. i–ii, here p. i.

24 Pollack: *Inquest into Death*, pp. 2–4.

a terrorist. Biko fit the bill.[25] While the Terrorism Act put its violators outside of the law – and thus made them ineligible for any type of due process or representation – deaths in police custody brought with them opportunities for an inquest.

Along with advocates George Bizos and Ernie Wentzel and attorney Shun Chetty, Kentridge represented the Biko family, finding himself constrained to investigate only the martyr's death, rather than the related circumstances of his imprisonment and treatment.[26] He found his visit to the Lawyers' Committee exposed. Bizos recalled that "[t]he matter was not public knowledge. How could they have known? Sydney Kentridge leaped to his feet and objected to the question (about the trip). No explanation was given. We could only conclude our phones were bugged."[27] Kentridge then continued, unfazed, receiving a standing ovation from African attendees as he questioned witnesses in English, refusing the magistrate's demands to speak Afrikaans.[28] Security police responded only in Afrikaans, rendering their testimonies unintelligible to the mostly English-speaking international press corps.

As the inquest unfolded, Biko's comrades, many of whom had handled the mechanical and mundane details of medical examination, legal proceedings, and burial found themselves in the midst of a grief process that brought at first disbelief and then sadness. "It took three weeks for the story of a killing to unfold," journalist and Biko friend Donald Woods wrote:

> And during that time a strange sense of ordinariness overlaid the painful and shocking facts that came out. On the first day we heard about leg irons and then we actually saw them. They were brought into court and we heard the chains clanking and saw the heavy rings of iron that rubbed Steve's ankles until they bled.[29]

Though authorities undertook what Pollack called a "quasi inquest" in the interest of appearing concerned about Biko's treatment in

25 Pollack: *Inquest into Death*, p. 4.

26 Ibid., p. 17.

27 George Bizos: *No One to Blame: In Pursuit of Justice in South Africa.* Cape Town: David Phillip 1998, p. 52.

28 Ibid., p. 55.

29 Donald Woods: *Biko: The True Story of the Young South African Martyr and His Struggle to Raise Black Consciousness.* New York: Henry Holt 1978, pp. 226–227.

detention, they were not willing to carry that interest far enough into the public sphere to offer justification for what had happened. Just hours prior to the reading of the verdict, police officers arrested Biko's brother and cousin along with several associates.[30] Magistrate Prins told a reporter from the banned *New York Times* soon after reaching his conclusion that "To me, it was just another death. It was just another job, like any other."[31]

IV.

Its involvement with the inquest greatly raised the Project's profile in both South Africa and the United States. "During this period, and following Biko's death, the apartheid government's crackdown on the Black Consciousness Movement, became a major focus of the Project's activities," Arnold remembered. "Indeed, the Project received more requests for assistance between 1979–1980 than any other time in its sixteen-year history […] In that regard – it is still sad to say – Biko's death was a catalyst for elevating and escalating the awareness of Americans to the plight of black South Africans."[32] Indeed, Biko's death elevated him to the status of martyrdom, and came to symbolize and eventually eclipse his powerful, short life. In a *Daily Dispatch* piece eulogizing him, Trudi Thomas noted that:

> It has been suggested that only one in a hundred black people had heard of Steve Biko before he died. That makes about 160,000 people – not a bad tribute to a man who was prevented from meeting and speaking to people at twenty-six and died at thirty. However, even if the percentage of people who knew him was small, there are few who are unfamiliar with his ideas, which are now significantly and increasingly shaping a nation. I did think of him as indestructible. As it happens I was wrong about his body. I had obviously attributed to it the same qualities as his transcendent spirit. It lives on, setting alight thousands of hearts and minds.[33]

The Project's report played, according to Arnold, an important role in convincing US President Jimmy Carter of apartheid's horrors and aided his decision to not lift sanctions against Rhodesia.[34]

30 Pollack: *Inquest into Death*, p. 25.

31 Ibid.

32 Millard Arnold: E-mail interview by Author, 30.03.2014.

33 Woods: *Biko*, p. 80.

34 Millard Arnold: E-mail interview by Author, 30.03.2014.

Additionally, US Ambassador to the UN Human Rights Commission Jerome Shestack asked Arnold to present remarks at the UN Human Rights Convention session in Geneva, making him the main voice providing a US response to the tragedy.[35]

Pollack's and Napley's accounts of the trial, replete with shocking descriptions of Biko's brutal treatment, conveyed the absurdity of the inquest and its willingness to address his end of life care at face value only. Despite Magistrate Prins' expected ruling, the inquest and the attorney's continuing efforts to use Biko's death to draw attention to conditions in detention did do just that. Pollack's report was presented to the United States Congress, a body that had heard reports from both the South African regime's attorneys and Biko friend and journalist Donald Woods during the months prior. Prins' one decision favorable to Biko had been to refer the case to the Medical Association of South Africa (MASA), citing the Medical, Dental and Supplementary Health Services Act of 1974 that allowed referral "if it appears that there is a *prima facie* proof of improper or disgraceful conduct," leaving open the possibility that any number of Biko's doctors might indeed have been guilty of neglect.[36] Blame for Biko's death thus officially shifted from the thuggish Security Police to his attending physicians.

Though Americans knew little of Biko, Arnold had received several of his manuscripts from historian Gail Gerhart, with whom he had been consulting on Black Consciousness, and set out to disseminate them. Two books were subsequently published that would transform a generation of student activists – the transcript of Soggot's questioning of Biko in the SASO/BPC trial, printed in the United States; and from England the International Defence and Aid Fund for Southern Africa (IDAF) published the now-iconic *I Write What I Like*.[37] That work, of course, helped inspire workers in the continuing struggle for civil rights, bringing full-circle the work of the Lawyers' Committee.

35 Millard Arnold: E-mail interview by Author, 30.03.2014.

36 N. Barney Pityana: Medical Ethics and South Africa's Security Laws: A Sequel to the Death of Steve Biko. In: Id. / Ramphele / Mpumlwana / Wilson (eds): *Bounds of Possibility*, pp. 78–98, here p. 81.

37 Arnold (ed.): *Steve Biko: Black Consciousness in South Africa*; Steve Biko: *I Write What I Like: Steve Biko, a Selection of His Writings*, ed. by Aelred Stubbs. London: Heinemann 1987.

Biko's essays and legal testimonies jibed with the thoughts of Arnold and others working against a global color line. In his explanation of Black Consciousness, Biko wrote that the philosophy was

> in essence the realization by the black man of the need to rally together with his brothers around the cause of their operation – the blackness of their skin – and to operate as a group in order to rid themselves of the shackles that bind them to perpetual servitude.[38]

In South Africa, "Biko Lives!" would be painted across building walls in testament to the power of the ideals of a leader whose physical body had been killed but whose words would continue to inspire strugglers.[39] The words also resonated around the world, and Arnold notes being moved by students discussing their practice of wearing the book on chains around their necks for quick reference and quotation.[40] It also helped the Southern Africa Project's work to come full-circle, following critiques of its overseas work as a distraction from issues at home. "We've been under attack to a certain degree because there are those who believe the Lawyers' Committee ought to be concerned with civil rights only in this country," Arnold told *The Washington Post* shortly before the inquest into Biko's death began:

> The definition people tend to give to civil rights is a narrow one that has come up as a result of our own experiences in this country. The truth of the matter is that civil rights is really an end product of human rights and it transcends all borders.[41]

V.

The larger Lawyers' Committee had also come under criticism shortly before the inquest into Biko's death, as several prominent members believed it had turned from its original race-blind mission. Founding member Morris Abram recalled the tensions between black and white, mostly Jewish, members in both the Committee and the larger

38 Biko: *I Write What I Like*, p. 53.

39 Andile Mngxitama / Amanda Alexander / Nigel C. Gibson: Biko Lives. In: Id. (eds): *Biko Lives! Contesting the Legacies of Steve Biko.* New York: Palgrave Macmillan 2008, pp. 1–20, here p. 1.

40 Schnehage: Upper Echelon.

41 Millard Arnold, quoted in Joseph Whitaker: Lawyers' Group Here Works for Civil Rights in South Africa. In: *The Washington Post*, 19.12.1977, p. A6.

federal government following the election of Jimmy Carter.[42] Many black Americans felt that too few gains had been won since the 1960s and, echoing South African Black Consciousness leaders, conveyed their perceptions about white apathy toward the status quo. White Americans, meanwhile, often wondered if the multiracial coalitions within which they had worked in the decades prior were disappearing, feeling betrayed by the new color consciousness after working so hard to erode it.

Allegations of a secret nuclear relationship between Israel and South Africa had also fractured traditional Jewish-black coalitions in both Southern Africa and the United States. Many Jews remained staunch allies, remembering the sting of anti-immigrant discrimination against them, while others enjoyed the white privilege that allowed them to move, however precariously, up from the bottom of the ladder.[43] The Biko death inquest may have served to rebut to these feelings, as black American and white South African attorneys worked to get to the bottom of what had happened to the Black Consciousness leader. Biko's writings did indeed transcend borders at a time when South Africa's regime had tried to portray internal opposition as having vanished in the face of an allegedly more 'benign' apartheid system.[44] Additionally, Soweto and the death of Biko served to unite African-Americans, often divided on strategies toward South Africa.[45]

In 2013, US President Barrack Obama told students at the University of Cape Town that he had been politicized largely as a result of learning about the South African freedom struggle and studying "the words of Biko."[46] Like his compatriots coming of age in the late 1970s and 1980s, Obama the student:

42 Morris Abram: *The Day is Short: An Autobiography.* New York: Harcourt, Bruce, Jovanovich 1982, pp. 254–255.

43 Sasha Polakow-Suransky: *The Unspoken Alliance: Israel's Secret Relationship with Apartheid South Africa.* New York: Pantheon 2010, p. 20.

44 Manning Marable / Peniel Joseph: Series Editors' Preface: Steve Biko and the International Context of Black Consciousness. In: Mngxitama / Alexander / Gibson (eds): *Biko Lives!*, pp. vii–x, here p. vii.

45 Scott Thomas: *The Diplomacy of Liberation: The Foreign Relations of the ANC Since 1960.* New York: IB Tauris 1996, p. 196.

46 Barrack Obama: Remarks by President Obama at the University of Cape Town, 30.06.2013. http://www.whitehouse.gov/the-press-office/2013/06/30/remarks-president-obama-university-cape-town (accessed 10.07.2013).

> [H]ad never cared much for politics. I didn't think it mattered to me. I didn't think I could make a difference. And like many young people, I thought that cynicism – a certain ironic detachment – was a sign of wisdom and sophistication. But then I learned what was happening here in South Africa [...] It was the first time I ever attached myself to a cause.[47]

The American president entered politics due to the influence of young South African leaders. Biko had confided to Aelred Stubbs that he often felt guilty thinking of friends in detention who had been detained "for activities in something that I was most instrumental in starting" while he himself remained "not with them."[48] The publication of *I Write What I Like* ensured that he remained forever with the generations of activists whom he was instrumental in inspiring.
The success of *I Write What I Like* also earned Arnold accolades for his role in disseminating it, but the process of involvement with inquests and trials often necessitated mundane legal work. Arnold elicited widespread celebrity endorsements for *I Write What I Like* and reported to the United Nations on South Africa's detainees. Following a report about Biko's death, he authored a report for the Centre Against Apartheid in 1977. This document focused on the reality of torture and death for forty-one prisoners aged sixteen to sixty-two under detention between 1963 and 1977 and called for an international judicial inquiry into how so many young South Africans had had their lives taken, particularly since the number of deaths in detention had increased dramatically since early 1976.[49]

VI.

Apartheid posed a danger not only to South Africa and Namibia, Arnold believed, but to the greater international legal order. In the years following Biko's death and the internationalization of Black Consciousness, he made a number of public appearances arguing that point. In 1978, he brought together at the Association of the Bar of the City of New York's offices prominent legal scholars for a

47 Ibid.

48 Biko: *I Write What I Like*, p. 200.

49 Lawyers' Committee for Civil Rights Under Law: *Deaths in Detention in South Africa*. Prepared for the United Nations Centre Against Apartheid, December 1977. Deaths in Detention/Biko Folder, Brian Bunting Collection (MCH-07-114-1-4), Mayibuye Archives, University of the Western Cape.

two-day investigation into apartheid's international implications – the first major conference to do so. Among the issues the conference addressed were the erosion of self-determination policies outlined by the United Nations in South Africa's new Bantustan policy, the denial of principles of nationality and citizenship to black South Africans and Namibians, the creation of stateless peoples in violation of Hague Convention outlines, conflicting claims to the territorial sovereignty of Walvis Bay, and a disregard for human rights as understood by international law.[50]

The conference, which brought together American lawyers and South African exiles such as Joel Carlson, Michael Davis, and Peter Mutharika, led the lawyers to a consensus regarding their duty to uphold international law and thereby render apartheid illegitimate. Among the heated debates of the conference, one occurred surrounding why it had been held in the United States rather than Southern Africa, with the lawyers present ultimately concluding that their role would be in directing US and UN policy toward the region.[51]

Nigerian Ambassador to the UN Leslie O. Harriman concluded that a legal solidarity had become necessary, particularly in the wake of Biko's death and the sham inquest. He argued that those present could:

> […] therefore understand that the prominent political prisoners in Southern Africa are lawyers. I particularly refer to Nelson Mandela, who felt it is his duty to violate the unjust laws. To him the causes, the beginning and the end, and the sufferings are secondary; and yet we find some people telling us that there is hope because there is a process of law in South Africa and because that regime held an open inquest in the death of Steve Biko. The verdict was, of course, that no one was to blame for the death of Steve Biko. The verdict was the same as almost all of their inquests over the death of detainees, though we have proof of continuing torture in South African jails. Our conclusion is that we are dealing with a regime which has no parallel in the modern day world.[52]

50 Millard Arnold (ed.): *Apartheid: The International Legal Implications*. A Report of the November 1978 Conference on the International Legal Effects of South Africa's System of Apartheid. Washington D.C.: Southern Africa Project 1979.

51 Ibid., pp. i–iii.

52 Dinner Remarks of Ambassador Leslie O. Harriman, Nigerian Mission to the United Nations, quoted in Arnold: *Apartheid: The International Legal Implications*, pp. 99–100.

Though no direct action came out of the conference, the lawyers present ultimately decided on continued efforts at economic sanctions as the best course of action against South Africa and re-affirmed a desire to direct US policy in the direction of enforcing human rights and rule of law.[53]

The final outcome of Biko's inquest became a controversial meeting between South African members of Parliament and US congressmen. Arnold organized the event, attended by Senators George McGovern and Paul Tsongas, Representatives Peter McCloskey, Steve Solarz, and Howard Wolpe, and journalists Charles Cobb and Anthony Lewis. Ultimately, the meeting provided an early opportunity for influential American policymakers to directly pressure their South African counterparts, something that would occur increasingly as 1980s sanctions campaigns heated up.

In conclusion, the expertise, funding, and connections gave the Southern Africa Project of the Lawyers' Committee for Civil Rights Under Law the opportunity to engage a rare solidarity in its anti-apartheid group. This occurred particularly and prominently with the death of Steve Biko. The Project assisted in 'making' Biko, through providing financial aid and judicial moral support to his family's legal team and through publishing and disseminating his ideas to international audiences previously unfamiliar with his work. While Biko proved influential during his life, it was his death that brought Black Consciousness to the forefront of international consciousness regarding apartheid – a process that indelibly demonstrated the Project's influence.

53 Ibid., pp. 65–66.

Bwanamvinyo, Protean Nyerere, and the Battleground of Ideas

The Contribution of Swahili Novels to East African Intellectual History

Lutz Diegner*

In this article I will look into two fundamental questions of sources and methodology in doing research on African intellectual history. By taking East Africa as a case in point, I start with the assumption that (a), due to the language barrier, African-language intellectual literature, in this case Swahilophone[1] intellectual literature from Tanzania and Kenya, has not been given much attention in research in African intellectual history yet.[2] My second assumption is that (b), Swahili

* I wish to thank Miša Krenčeyová and Arno Sonderegger, and all the participants of the international symposium 'African Thoughts on (Neo-)Colonial Worlds: Steps towards an Intellectual History of Africa', held at the Department of African Studies, University of Vienna, 6–7 November 2014, for an inspiring exchange of ideas in an affectionate atmosphere. I especially thank Kai Kresse and Arno Sonderegger for their constructive comments on earlier drafts of this article. *Asanteni sana.*

1 Swahili, a Bantu language, and one of the most widely known among the approximately 2,000 African languages on the whole, is spoken by an estimated 80–100 million speakers, most of whom are not first-language speakers. I use the term 'Swahilophone' to denote the diverse linguistic and cultural background of Swahili speakers in East Africa and beyond.

2 For instance, Julius Nyerere, former Tanzanian president and political thinker, published many of his writings in Swahili as well, and, of course, gave many of his speeches in Swahili, but as his main works have been published in English, the Swahili texts remain largely neglected, at least on an international scale (Cf. e.g. Julius Nyerere: *Binadamu na Maendeleo.* Dar es Salaam: Oxford UP 1974; Julius Nyerere: *Man and Development.* Dar es Salaam et al.: Oxford UP 1974.) For non-fictional Swahili intellectual discourse, the wide and diverse range of Swahili newspapers

fictional texts, and I will concentrate here on novels, provide considerable insights into East African intellectual history. In engagement with the main topic of this volume, I have divided the main part of this article into three sections. The first two sections deal with the following questions: How are 'great' African/black thinkers re-/presented and discussed in Swahili novels? In how far can pronounced Swahili novelists themselves be regarded as 'great' or major thinkers? In the third section, I will concentrate on thoughts on (neo-)colonial worlds in Swahili novels, and mainly deal with the way (neo-)colonial history is conceptualized in these novels.

Swahili literature, different from many other African language literatures, has a long written tradition, while being rooted in oral tradition (as any literature in the world). The oldest manuscript known so far dates back to the 16th century.[3] The dominant overall genre of Swahili literature, both oral and written, has been poetry, with different forms of written prose only coming up in the 19th century.[4] While

provides a rich source, the most important titles being, from Tanzania: *Raia Mwema* ('Good Citizen'), http://www.raiamwema.co.tz/; *Mwananchi* ('Compatriot'), http://www.mwananchi.co.tz/; *Nipashe* ('Tell me [the news]'), http://www.ippmedia.com/frontend/index.php; *Rai* ('Opinion'), http://www.rai.co.tz/; *Mtanzania* ('The Tanzanian'), http://mtanzania.co.tz/; *Majira* ('Time'), http://majira.co.tz/; and from Kenya: *Taifa Leo* (Swahili offshoot of *Daily Nation*), http://digitaledition.nationmedia.com/?xml=TaifaLeo#folio=1; *Swahilihub*, http://www.swahilihub.com. For Swahili intellectual discourse in book form, see the collection of articles and essays by Jenerali Ulimwengu and Issa Shivji, which to my knowledge have not been reviewed or written about in any form yet; cf. Issa Shivji: *Insha za Mapambano ya Wanyonge.* Kimehaririwa na Bashiru Ally ['Essays on the Battle for the Poor, ed. by Bashiru Ally'; written 2003–2011]. Dar es Salaam: Taasisi ya Taaluma za Kiswahili, Chuo Kikuu cha Dar es Salaam 2012; Jenerali Ulimwengu: *Rai ya Jenerali* ['Jenerali's Viewpoint'; newspaper articles and essays, most of them written 1993–1995]. Dar es Salaam: E & D n.d. [2005]. More recent sources of importance are socio-political or culture-oriented blogs, for example *Jamii Forums* ('Society Forums'), with different sub-sections, including '*Jukwaa la Historia*' ('History Tribune'), http://www.jamiiforums.com/jukwaa-la-historia/), or Chambi Chachage's *Udadisi*, http://udadisi.blogspot.com (all accessed 23.02.2015).

3 See Mugyabuso M. Mulokozi (ed.): *Tenzi Tatu za Kale* ['Three Ancient Epic Poems']. Dar es Salaam: Taasisi ya Uchunguzi wa Kiswahili 1999, p. vii. For the history of Swahili poetry see Mugyabuso M. Mulokozi / Tigiti S. Y. Sengo: *History of Kiswahili Poetry, A. D. 1000–2000: A Report.* Dar es Salaam: Taasisi ya Uchunguzi wa Kiswahili, Chuo Kikuu cha Dar es Salaam 1995, and Naomi Shitemi: *Ushairi wa Kiswahili kabla ya Karne ya Ishirini* ['Swahili Poetry before the 20th Century']. Eldoret: Moi UP 2010.

4 For the history of Swahili prose see Jack Drake Rollins: *A History of Swahili Prose. Part I: From Earliest Times to the End of the Nineteenth Century.* Leiden: Brill 1983; Elena Bertoncini-Zúbková / Mikhail D. Gromov / Said A. M. Khamis / Kyallo W. Wamitila:

much of the written Swahili poetry evolved by involvement with and adaptation of Arabic poetry, the novel as a genre has been adopted from Western literature, and is a rather recent innovation in Swahili literary history. The exact beginnings of the Swahili novel itself are disputed; James Mbotela's *Uhuru wa Watumwa* ('The Freeing of the Slaves', 1934)[5], though mostly a biographical historical account which tends towards a eulogy on British colonialists, has certain traits of a novel.[6] Actually, the Swahili novel came into being simultaneously with the notion of 'modernity' (*usasa*) in Swahili literature.[7] The advent of modernity in Swahili literature is attributed to Shaaban Robert (1909–1962), whose prose texts also comprise two texts which are seen as transitional towards the modern novel, namely *Utubora Mkulima* ('Utubora the Farmer') and *Siku ya Watenzi Wote* ('The Day of all Doers'), both published posthumously in 1968.[8] His two parabolic narratives *Kufikirika* ('A Place to Imagine'; 1967 [1946]) and

Outline of Swahili Literature: Prose Fiction and Drama. Leiden / Boston: Brill 2009. Rollins analyses the different (sub-)genres of Swahili prose before the 'advent' and adaptation of the novel, such as *kisa*, *hadithi*, *hekaya*, *kioja*, *habari*, *wasifu*, *simo*, *masimulizi*, *neno la hekima*, and *ngano* (the dissociation and differentiation of these terms by ways of translating them into English is a complex endeavour). Cf. Rollins: *A History of Swahili Prose*, pp. 63–106.

5 James Mbotela: *Uhuru wa Watumwa.* London: Sheldon 1934. The English translation was published as: Id.: *The Freeing of the Slaves in East Africa.* London: Evans 1956.

6 Cf. Bertoncini-Zúbková et al.: *Outline of Swahili Literature*, p. 33; Said A. M. Khamis: *Uhuru wa Watumwa* de James Mbotela (Kiswahili, 1934): un premier roman politiquement trop correct. In: Xavier Garnier / Alain Ricard (eds): *L'effet roman. Arrivée du roman dans les langues d'Afrique.* Paris: L'Harmattan 2006, pp. 127–138.

7 For an introduction into the Swahili novel see Bertoncini-Zúbková et al.: *Outline of Swahili Literature*; Xavier Garnier: *Le roman Swahili. La notion de "littérature mineure" à l'épreuve.* Paris: Karthala 2006; Fikeni E. M. K. Senkoro: *Fasihi. Toleo Jipya* ['Literature. New Edition'; it only deals with prose, and concentrates on novels]. Dar es Salaam: KAUTTU 2011; Joshua S. Madumulla: *Riwaya ya Kiswahili. Nadharia, Historia na Misingi ya Uchambuzi* ['The Swahili Novel: Theory, History and Foundations of Analysis']. Dar es Salaam / Nairobi: Mture / Phoenix 2009.

8 Cf. Bertoncini-Zúbková et al.: *Outline of Swahili Literature*, pp. 40–42. Concerning the actual years of writing the works (which is crucial in understanding Shaaban's writing and publishing 'career' in late colonial and early independence times), I follow Mugyabuso M. Mulokozi who argues that *Utubora Mkulima* has most probably been written in 1946–1947, and *Siku ya Watenzi Wote* in 1960–1962. Cf. Mugyabuso M. Mulokozi: Utangulizi ['Introduction']. In: Shaaban Bin Robert: *Siku ya Watenzi Wote* ['The Day of All Doers']. Dar es Salaam: Taasisi ya Uchunguzi wa Kiswahili, Chuo Kikuu cha Dar es Salaam 2008, pp. iv–vii, here pp. iv; vi.

Kusadikika ('A Place to Believe In'; 1951)[9], though not to be classified as novels, definitely earn him a place in East African intellectual history, as he conceives them as utopias of equality and humanity. After Shaaban Robert, the advent of the 'modern' novel is commonly attributed to the beginning of the 1970s, with a new generation of mostly Tanzanian writers coming up.[10]

In this article, I will concentrate on post-colonial Swahili novels, with a special focus on recent ones published after 1990. I will start with readings of how particular thinkers of renown are (re-)presented and discussed in selected novels, and then argue for considering particular novelists as thinkers on their own terms. Further on, I will discuss thoughts on (neo-)colonial worlds in Swahili novels by both Tanzanian and Kenyan writers, and finally make a case for considering Swahili fiction as a rich source for East African intellectual history.

'Great Thinkers' in Swahili Novels

At the outset of this section, I will illustrate that the range of 'great thinkers' in Swahili novels is as wide, chronologically and regionally alike, as from Aristotle to Malcolm X. Further on, I will discuss what I call the 'omni-protean presence' of Julius Nyerere in these novels. After a long initial phase of 'writing self' in the contemporary Swahili novel – in a narrowly not quite East African, but Tanzanian sense – it

9 *Kusadikika* was published with the subtitle *Nchi iliyo angani* ('A Country in the Sky'). According to Bertoncini-Zúbková et al.: *Outline of Swahili Literature*, p. 38, David C. Sperling translated it into English in 1973. However, I could not trace the publication of this manuscript.

10 The most prominent Swahili novelists of the early/middle 1970s are Cuthbert Omari, Euphrase Kezilahabi, Ndyanao Balisidya (Tanzanian mainland), Mohamed Suleiman Mohamed (Zanzibar), and Katama Mkangi (Kenya). See Bertoncini-Zúbková et al.: *Outline of Swahili Literature*, pp. 82–83, 93–101, 90–92, 145–148, 50–51. For the dominance of Tanzanian Swahili writing until 2000, and Kenyan Swahili writing coming up strongly since the 2000s, see e.g. Kyallo W. Wamitila: Reading the Kenyan Swahili Prose Works: A Terra Incognita in Swahili Literature. In: *Afrikanistische Arbeitspapiere* (*AAP*) 51 – *Swahili Forum* IV (1997), pp. 117–125; Lutz Diegner: The Kenyan Challenge (?): Dis/Continuities in Swahili Novel Writing 50 Years after Independence. In: Hannelore Vögele / Uta Reuster-Jahn / Raimund Kastenholz / Lutz Diegner (eds): *From the Tana River to Lake Chad: Research in African Oratures and Literatures: In memoriam Thomas Geider*. Köln: Köppe 2014, pp. 341–356. For an outline of most recent developments in the Swahili novel, see Mikhail D. Gromov: Visions of the Future in the 'New' Swahili Novel: Hope in Desperation? In: *Tydskrif vir Letterkunde* 51,2 (2014), pp. 40–51.

was Euphrase Kezilahabi's novels *Nagona* ('Nagona', 1987/1990) and *Mzingile* ('Labyrinth', 1991) that opened up a Tanzanian perspective on globally influential ideas in intellectual history. Conceived as a 'classical' 'writing back' to dominant European discourses on the one hand, on the other hand it put the Swahili novel on the world literary map not only for its post-modern experimentation, but also for its philosophical sophistication. In the novel *Nagona*, note the irony of Socrates, Aristotle, Plato, Hegel, Marx, Darwin, Nietzsche, and Freud, appearing as literary characters with a quite unlucky fate.[11] They are told to sit in a circle, to retch and spit out their souls into their hands, and then to discuss with them in order to clean them, an endeavour which proves futile in the end. In another ironic turn, their souls are washed away by a river stream, and they cheer their freedom. This is how the narrator satirizes conflicts and debates in 2,500 years of intellectual history:

> "Sasa hivi wametulia kidogo. Zamani wakianza majadiliano yao na roho zao ilikuwa vurugu tupu. Na wakianza majadiliano wao kwa wao basi hapo duara iliwaka moto. Nietzsche akianza tu kuzungumza, Freud anachukua buku lake na kuanza kuandika. Nietzsche atalipiga teke buku hilo. Usiombe kusikiliza mjadala kati ya Marx na Hegel au kati ya Hegel na Nietzsche. Na ubahatike basi kuona jinsi Wayunani wanavyojikweza na kudai ubaba wa hawa wengine. Ndiyo maana kikundi hiki nimekitenga mbali kidogo na vikundi vingine. Wataalamu wa Kiafrika, walikuja katika kikundi hiki lakini waligombana na kila mtu hasa Darwin aliyewafuata kila mahali akichunguza mataya yao. Waliomba waanzishiwe kikundi chao. Niliwahamisha maana nao walikuwa wabishi. [...]"[12]

> "Right now they have calmed down a bit. In former times, when they began their discussion with their souls, there was pure disorder. And when they started discussing among themselves, well then, the circle was in flames. When Nietzsche just began to speak, Freud would take his book and begin to write. Nietzsche would kick that book. Don't ask to listen to the debate between Marx and Hegel or between Hegel and Nietzsche. And do happen to see how the Ancient Greek crow and claim fatherhood of the others. That is why I detached this group a little away from the other groups. The African scholars came to this group but they fought with everyone, especially Darwin who followed them everywhere, scrutinizing their jaws. They asked for a group of their own to be founded for them. I moved them elsewhere as they were quarrellers, too. [...]"

11 Cf. Euphrase Kezilahabi: *Nagona* ['Nagona']. Dar es Salaam: Dar es Salaam UP 1990 [1987], pp. 13–17.

12 Kezilahabi: *Nagona*, p. 15. All translations from Swahili, if not indicated otherwise, are mine.

The narrative voice humorously recounts intellectual history and its conflicts of ideas, for example between Nietzsche and Freud, as well as 'theories of descent', which all lead back to ancient Greece. In the last third of the text passage, the narrator indicates, though nameless, the African dimension of intellectual history, providing a parody of Charles Darwin's biologist racism.[13]

While Kezilahabi concentrates on satirically working through this list of intellectual giants in the European history of ideas as a means of subversion if not deconstruction, his contemporary Said Ahmed Mohamed opts for de-centering and de-colonizing this concept from the start. In his novels *Dunia Yao* ('Their World', 2006) and *Nyuso za Mwanamke* ('Faces of Woman', 2010), his 'pantheon' of great thinkers comprises Amilcar Cabral, Walter Rodney and Patrice Lumumba, as well as Frantz Fanon, W. E. B. DuBois and Malcolm X, and Mahatma Gandhi (who already appears in his *Babu Alipofufuka*, 'When Grandfather Came to Life Again', 2001).[14] These 'heroes' of black and/or 'people of colour' intellectual history and their writings mostly appear only briefly in the text; their writings are not discussed; they are invoked as intellectual role models to draw inspiration from. As becomes clear from the list above, Said Ahmed's 'pantheon', without exception, consists of thinkers with a strong political, and a strong activist character. In *Nyuso za Mwanamke*, the imaginary encounter of protagonist Nana with Mahatma Gandhi reads as follows:

> Basi, njia ikaenda mbele kwa kasi kutuhakikishia kwamba gari letu likirejea nyuma. Mbele ya nyuma alizuka Mahatma Gandhi. Alizuka akasimama kati-kati ya njia lakini tulimkwepa. Alikuwa kasimama kundini mwa watu akihutubia amani na utulivu, lakini aliowahubiria walitimua zogo na kupigana. […]

13 For a critical discussion of this particular – Eurocentric – choice of intellectual 'giants' and the 'namelessness' of African representatives see Lutz Diegner: *Die Ausweitung der Gesellschaftskritik in den swahilisprachigen Romanen von Euphrase Kezilahabi und Said Ahmed Mohamed* ['The Swahili Novel Beyond Criticizing Society: A Comparative Dialogical Reading of Euphrase Kezilahabi and Said Ahmed Mohamed', English and Swahili manuscripts in preparation]. Köln: Selbstverlag 2007, pp. 225–227.

14 See Said Ahmed Mohamed: *Babu Alipofufuka* ['When Grandfather Came to Life Again']. Nairobi: Jomo Kenyatta Foundation 2001, p. 121 (Mahatma Gandhi); id.: *Dunia Yao* ['Their World']. Nairobi: Oxford UP 2006, pp. 192–193 (Amilcar Cabral, Walter Rodney, Patrice Lumumba); id.: *Nyuso za Mwanamke* ['Faces of Woman']. Nairobi / Kampala / Dar es Salaam: Longhorn / Sasa Sema 2010, pp. 85–86 (the four mentioned, as well as Frantz Fanon, W. E. B. DuBois and Malcolm X), and ibid., p. 220, where all of them are listed, adding Ahmed Ben Bella, Kwame Nkrumah, Jomo Kenyatta, Julius Nyerere, and Nelson Mandela.

> Tulipompita Gandhi, alituona au pengine aliiona ile kasi ya gari letu. Akapiga kelele kutuasa twende polepole ili tufike salama. Tena akatuonya tuchunge amani tunakokwenda. Mimi nikampigia kelele: Hizi ni nyakati nyingine Gandhi. Serikali zetu hazina tena subira wala hazijali roho za watu wake. Hazina ustahamilivu wa kiasi kile cha Waingereza wale wa zamani. Ungedai hiki na hiki leo Waingereza wangekuua, kwa sababu unakwenda kinyume na maslahi yao. Wangekuekea *sanctions*. Ingawa walifanya hivyo zamani kwa siri. Sasa wanafanya dhahiri.[15]

> Well, the road moved forward fast and proved to us that our car was moving backwards. In front of behind Mahatma Gandhi emerged. He emerged and stood in the middle of the road, but we avoided him. He stood among a group of people preaching peace and tranquillity, but the ones he preached to began to quarrel and fight. […] When we passed by Gandhi he saw us, or perhaps he saw the speed of our car. He shouted at us to warn us we should drive slowly in order to reach our destination safely. Furthermore he warned us to safeguard peace where we went to. I shouted at him: These are different times, Gandhi. Our governments are neither patient nor do they care about their people's souls. They are not as tolerant as these British were in in the past. If you claimed this and that today the British would kill you, because you are going against their interests. They would impose *sanctions* on you. Though they did so in the past, secretly. Now they do it openly.

This text passage shows how in Said Ahmed's novels, intellectual history is intrinsically inter-twined with political history, in this case culminating in the comment that today's neo-colonialism is even worse than colonialism during Gandhi's era was. This goes in line with his general conceptualization of history from a Global Southern perspective, which I will deal with in the third section.

Despite the abovementioned processes of 'Africanizing', de-colonizing and thus 'internationalizing' the circle of 'great thinkers', there is first and foremost one East African thinker dealt with in the Swahili novel who goes about like a ghost of inspiration, but also of intimidation: '*Baba wa Taifa*', the 'Father of the Nation', '*Mwalimu*' ('Teacher') Julius Kambarage Nyerere (1922–1999). An otherwise poignantly critical intellectual, sociology professor Chachage Seithy L. Chachage (1955–2006) in his *Makuadi wa Huria* ('Pimps of the Free Market', 2002) not only dedicates the whole novel to "*Mwalimu*"[16], but (re-)constructs him as a charismatic leader who is regarded by

15 Mohamed: *Nyuso za Mwanamke*, p. 85. Typographical errors in the original text have been blue-pencilled by me.

16 Chachage Seithy L. Chachage: *Makuadi wa Soko Huria* ['The Pimps of the Free Market']. Dar es Salaam: E & D 2002, p. viii.

the people as standing in one ancestral line with the prominent hero of anti-colonial struggle, Kinjeketile, spiritual head of the Maji Maji war against German colonial rule (1905–1907). This virtually encyclopaedic novel recounts the history of today's *Tanzania Bara* (Tanzanian mainland) from the 1840s until today, with a special focus on its southern parts, and in particular the Rufiji delta region. Nyerere's 1955 travel to the region is narrated as follows:

> Nyerere alipopita sehemu za Rufiji kwa mara ya kwanza mwaka huo huo, watu wa huko wakasema; "Kinjikitile amerudi kumalizia kazi ambayo aliianza!" Wakaamini hivyo, wakasema: "Hatutakuwa watumwa tena. Saa imewadia siafu kuwa pamoja na kumtoa nyoka pangoni!"[17]

> When Nyerere passed by the Rufiji area for the first time in that very year, the people there said: "Kinjeketile has come back to finish the work he had started!" They believed so, and said: "We won't be slaves anymore. The time has come for the ants to be united and to get the snake out of the cave!"

Gabriel Ruhumbika, for his part, introduces Nyerere as a character in his novel *Miradi Bubu ya Wazalendo* ('Silent Projects of the Patriots', 1992) in order to illustrate how the dialogue between the socialist regime and the population in the last years of Nyerere's reign went astray. In the concluding passage of the novel[18], Nyerere, at a public meeting, is confronted with a poor retired former messenger of his, who desperately seeks his help, showing him the humble gifts he got when he was retired – a table clock, a small radio, and a walking stick – instead of a pension to live on. Nyerere, taken by surprise and rather unsettled first, enthusiastically mistakes these objects as presents by a decade-long supporter and cheeringly presents them to the crowd. This public misunderstanding has immediate repercussions in the media:

> Kamera za waandishi wa habari zikafanya kazi yake tena, na mtangazaji wa Radio Tanzania akapasha wananchi kote nchini hayo yaliyokuwa yanatokea hapo kwa lugha motomoto na bila ya kupumua, kama kwamba anatangaza mpira wa Simba na Yanga. [...] Kesho yake wananchi wa Tanzania, ambao hawakusikia kwenye radio wakati wa mkutano na kwenye taarifa ya habari ya jioni hiyo habari za Ndugu Saidi, wakatangaziwa tena na radio pamoja na magazeti yetu yote, la Chama na la Serikali, juu ya uzalendo wa Ndugu Mzee Saidi bin

17 Chachage: *Makuadi wa Soko Huria*, p. 213.

18 Cf. Gabriel Ruhumbika: *Miradi Bubu ya Wazalendo* ['The Silent Projects of the Patriots']. Dar es Salaam: Tanzania Publishing House 1995 [1992], pp. 162–166.

> Jabiri. Magazeti yote mawili, kwenye kurasa zake za mbele yalikuwa na picha ya Mwalimu amekubatiana bega kwa bega na Mzee mwenye mvi mwenzake, Saidi bin Jabiri, zenye vichwa vya maneno vikubwa visemavyo: "MWALIMU ASIFU UZALENDO WA MESENJA".[19]
>
> And the press photographers went to work with their cameras again, while the Radio Tanzania announcer informed the whole nation of what was happening there passionately and without pause as if he was announcing a soccer match between Yanga and Simba.[20] […] The following day *wananchi* of Tanzania who had not listened to the national radio at the time of the rally or during the evening news heard broadcast on Radio Tanzania and read in both the papers of our nation, the Party paper in Swahili and the Government one in English, the news of the patriotism of Ndugu Saidi son of Jabiri. The two papers had on the front page the photograph of Mwalimu linked shoulder to shoulder with another old man with grey hair like him, Saidi son of Jabiri, with the same title in huge bold letters saying: "MWALIMU PRAISES THE PATRIOTISM OF A MESSENGER".[21]

Finally, the 'presents' end up in a Nyerere Commemorial Museum in his home town Butiama in Northwestern Tanzania. The novel concludes:

> Hizo ndizo habari za nyongeza Watanzania walizoelezwa juu ya kuagana kwa huyo mwananchi mzalendo hasa na kiongozi wake mkuu, mwanga wa maisha yake, baba wa Taifa lake. Hivyo ndivyo shida za Ndugu Saidi bin Jabiri zilivyopokelewa na viongozi wa jamii yake ya kijamaa.[22]
>
> That was the additional news the people of Tanzania were told regarding how that *mwananchi* and *mzalendo* said good-bye to his great leader, the light of his life, the father of his Nation. That was how the difficulties facing the life of Ndugu Saidi son of Jabiri were addressed by the leaders of his *ujamaa* society.[23]

In his novel *Babu Alipofufuka* (2001), Said Ahmed Mohamed uses the 'Proteus' motif to create a personage representing ever-changing and ever-escaping omnipresence of political power on different levels. In a play on the typographic representation of the word 'Proteus', the narrator refers to the ever-changing nature of the ancient Greek

19 Ibid., pp. 164–165.

20 Ibid., endnote 56: "Simba: Swahili for 'Lion', the name of a famous soccer team in Dar es Salaam, the traditional rival of Yanga above"; Gabriel Ruhumbika: *Silent Empowerment of the Compatriots*, trans. from Kiswahili by the author. Dar es Salaam: E & D Vision 2009, p. 173.

21 Ruhumbika: *Silent Empowerment*, pp. 168–169.

22 Ruhumbika: *Miradi Bubu ya Wazalendo*, p. 166.

23 Ruhumbika: *Silent Empowerment*, p. 170.

god: The word appears in about a dozen of varieties of using different combinations of capital and bold letters, italics, and metathesis (changing the order of letters), for example as 'prO ***Teus***', '***PROtEus***', '***Porteus***', or '***Pr****o****t****e****us***'. According to the aesthetic agenda of this novel, omnipresent, but invisible and thus protean political power is frightening and disenfranchising on the national and the international level.[24]

> *Na K, zaidi ya wote, anaamini kwamba […] hakuna mbora mwengine zaidi ya* ***PROTEUS****. Hata* **Proteus** *akiingia gizani kujificha, akatafutwe kuombwa kuja kuleta uwokozi katika kila jambo. Na kwa kweli si amewasikia mara ngapi watu wakiungama kwamba hawajui watafanya nini iwapo* prO **Teus** *atakufa leo. Na yeye K hujibu moyoni mwake "Mimi nitakuwa* **pRoteus** *wa pili." Ingawa hata yeye K anajua kwamba* **Porteus** *hawezi kufa. Anaweza kujigeuzageuza tu. Kwa kweli, mara ngapi mwenyewe* **PROtEus** *amesema hafi?*[25]

> *And K, more than anyone, belives that […] there is no better guy than* ***PROTEUS****. Even if* **Proteus** *goes into hiding in the dark, he should be searched for and asked to come to bring salvation in any matter. And as a matter of fact didn't he hear people confess so many times that they didn't know what they should do if* prO **Teus** *died today. And K was used to answer by himself, "I will be the second* **pRoteus**.*" Though even K knew that* **Porteus** *cannot die. He can only transform himself repeatedly. Really, how many times* **PROtEus** *himself said he doesn't die?*

For the national level, the 'Proteus' motif in the text can arguably be read as a critique of Nyerere's omnipresence in Tanzanian politics playing a much more decisive role than just being a grey eminence well after he had stepped down in 1985, actually until his death in 1999. Reading the above quotation, Nyerere's influence even went on far beyond his death, and, as the novel was written around 1998/1999, can be seen as a prophecy of '*Mwalimu*''s 'long shadow' in Tanzanian politics, and a continued strand of socio-political hagiography around his person, as well in scholarship as in the general public.

Swahili Novelists as Thinkers

As will be shown, Euphrase Kezilahabi (born 1944) and Said Ahmed Mohamed (born 1947), can be regarded as distinguished 'thinkers' on

24 Said Ahmed Mohamed: *Babu Alipofufuka*, pp. 11, 18. For all the (typo-)graphic variations, and a thorough reading of the 'Proteus' motif in this novel, see Diegner: *Ausweitung der Gesellschaftskritik*, pp. 186–192, 214–215.

25 Mohamed: *Babu Alipofufuka*, p. 11.

their own terms.[26] In this section, I will read Kezilahabi's concepts of political and intellectual history as a 'battleground', and a 'dance of ideas', respectively. Further on, I will provide some insight into Said Ahmed's critique of Western-dominated academia ('Professor-Know-It-All'), and the cultural repercussions of globalization from an (East) African perspective, captured in the symbol of the carambola tree. Euphrase Kezilahabi's 'construct of ideas' is visible in his work as a creative writer who has written novels, short stories, a play, and poetry, and as an academic who in his PhD thesis discusses existentialism and different paradigms of African philosophy.[27] It is the intertwining of his fictional and his academic work that makes Kezilahabi a (re-)thinker of existentialism who consciously re-models it in an African/Tanzanian perspective, as well as he comes up with a whole epistemological critique of European-dominated intellectual history. A central argument of his is to render the world of wars and the world of thoughts as *dunia uwanja wa fujo*, 'the world is a battleground', 'the world is an arena of chaos'. From 'great thinkers' to prominent protagonists of world history to so-called ordinary people, the hypothesis in Kezilahabi's homonymic novel (1975) goes:

26 These are only two novelists as two cases in point. I have already mentioned Shaaban Robert's importance for East African intellectual history. Further good examples for case studies could be Katama Mkangi (1944–2004), whose science-fiction novel *Walenisi* ('They Are Us'. Nairobi / Kampala / Dar es Salaam: East African Educational Publishers 1995) develops Shaaban Robert's utopian writing further, combining it with a socio-political critique of postcolonial Kenya, and William Mkufya (born 1953), whose epic novel *Ziraili na Zirani* ('Asrael and Zirani'. Dar es Salaam: Hekima 1999) independently elaborates on Kezilahabi's epistemological critique of intellectual and religious history. – These five novelists are all male. In Swahili literature, there is a big gender inequality issue at stake. There a very few women novelists, and I think the major reason is that women find themselves in socio-economic (and family) structures which make it particularly difficult to engage in this 'long(est) form' of creative writing, on the one hand, and in patriarchal structures in the publishing industry, on the other. Interestingly, there is more and more published short story writing by women, there has always been female poetry (though often published under male pen names), and if we take the example of drama, two of the three most renowned Tanzanian Swahili playwrights are women: Amandina Lihamba and Penina Mlama Muhando. For a discussion of their works see Bertoncini-Zúbková et al.: *Outline of Swahili Literature*, pp. 205–210, 213–214, 218–220.

27 For an outline of his fictional works see Diegner: *Ausweitung der Gesellschaftskritik*, pp. 20–24; Bertoncini-Zúbková et al.: *Outline of Swahili Literature*, pp. 93–101, 125–128. His PhD thesis *African Philosophy and the Problem of Literary Interpretation* (Madison: University of Wisconsin 1985) remains unpublished.

> Kila mwanadamu ameumbwa kuja kufanya fujo yake halafu anajiondokea na kupotea.[28]
>
> Every human being has been created to come [to the world] to make her/his own mess, and then s/he betakes her/himself and gets lost.

In his ground-breaking novel *Nagona* (1987/1990), the image of a 'battleground of ideas' is further developed into the concept of *ngoma kuu*: the 'great dance' of ideas.[29] Drawing from the way the narrator depicts the 'illustrious' personages of intellectual history, he conceives a dance competition of ideas, where certain groups of dancers attempt to get into the 'navel of the circle'. All four groups, be it the 'philosophers', the 'psychologists', the 'revolutionaries', or the 'madmen', finally fail.[30] This imagery can be read as the endless, and in the end futile, search for insight and truth, a one and only truth which is not reachable. Though this appears to be a rather pessimistic view, Kezilahabi seems to be more interested in stressing the fact that searching for truth is a life-long process which should never end.[31]

Said Ahmed has authored a considerable number of novels, short stories, plays and poems. His 'construct of ideas' is marked by an engagement with undogmatic Marxism, combined with a relentless interrogation of East Africans' cultural and political identity in times of globalization. In *Babu Alipofufuka*, the narrator uses the image of the carambola (star fruit) tree to explain his scepticism about the effects of 'globalizing' East African identity. In *Babu Alipofufuka*, a grandfather-ghost constantly haunting the protagonist K, a decadent government official, says:

> Kila kitu kimeumbwa na kanuni zake K … na kwa hivyo huwezi kuung'oa mbirimbi Pemba kwenda kuupandikiza Montreal. Hauwi, ng'o hauwi! Na hata ukiduhushiwa na kudekezwa vipi kwenye vitalu, hauwezi kuja juu sawasawa na ule wa Pemba.[32]
>
> Everything has been created with its rule, K … and thence you cannot unroot a star fruit tree in Pemba, and go and plant it in Montreal. It will not grow, never

28 Euphrase Kezilahabi: *Dunia Uwanja wa Fujo* ['The World an Arena of Chaos']. Dar es Salaam / Nairobi / Kampala: East African Literature Bureau 1975, p. 92.

29 Cf. Diegner: *Ausweitung der Gesellschaftskritik*, pp. 227–229, 249–254.

30 Cf. Kezilahabi: *Nagona*, pp. 53–61.

31 Cf. Diegner: *Ausweitung der Gesellschaftskritik*, pp. 266–272.

32 Mohamed: *Babu Alipofufuka*, p. 50.

> will it grow! And even if it will be ever as much protected and indulged in patches, it cannot come up the same as the one in Pemba.

The image of the carambola tree, which can only fully flourish and grow fruits in Pemba, postulates a certain 'naturalness' of one's identity in relation to one's origin – by implying botanical arguments, though. This text passage can be read as an implicit plea for a world which maintains its distinct regional characteristics, as well as for an acknowledgement and preservation of diversity in the global context.[33]

In his novel *Nyuso za Mwanamke* ('Faces of Woman', 2010), Said Ahmed adds to this a critique of Western-dominated scholarship,[34] which is impersonated by an anthropology professor who interprets any cultural or societal phenomenon s/he encounters in a place resembling Zanzibar as part of an overall hypothesis of "chaos and invention in Africa", and is therefore given the name 'PKA', "Professor-Know-It-All". The way the professor talks to her/his informant, who is Nana, the presumably Zanzibari protagonist of the novel, is described like this:

> Mtu angesikia namna PKA alivyokuwa akimwambia Nana, angehisi kwamba binti huyo ndiye hasa bara la Afrika.[35]
>
> If somebody heard the manner how PKA was talking to Nana, he would feel that this young woman [i. e., Nana] was indeed the [entire] African continent.

Here, the narrator clearly exposes criticism of undifferentiated 'all-in-one' research on 'Africa' on the one hand, and the problem of pre-designed findings in research on the whole.

Thoughts on (Neo-)Colonial Worlds in Swahili Novels

Interestingly, colonialism features most prominently in Swahili novels from Kenya, and from Zanzibar, whereas the Tanzanian mainland writers have not dealt with colonialism that much, most of them consciously concentrating on a concomitant chronography of the post-colonial era they live in. First, I will provide the example of what I

33 For a more elaborate reading along these lines cf. Diegner: *Ausweitung der Gesellschaftskritik*, pp. 211–214.

34 Cf. Mohamed: *Nyuso za Mwanamke*, pp. 275–282.

35 Ibid., p. 276.

call 'de-centering Mau Mau'[36] in a Kenyan Swahili novel. Secondly, I will discuss the conceptualization of pre-colonial, colonial and post-colonial history in Zanzibari novels, before finally providing a brief example of how East African repercussions of global capitalism are dealt with in a Kenyan novel.

Whereas both the academic and the fictional engagement with Mau Mau seem to be dominated by anglophone discourse and writing on the one hand, and by dealing with the preeminent role of the Gĩkũyũ group, on the other, Swahili novels provide insights into rather under-represented dimensions of this widely known anti-colonial war. While the 'modern classic' of Kenyan Swahili writing immediately after independence, Peter Kareithi's *Kaburi Bila Msalaba* ('Grave without a Cross', 1969) concentrates in a conventionalised way on Gĩkũyũ characters, Mwenda Mbatiah's *Wimbo Mpya* ('New Song', 2004) highlights the Meru group's participation, commitment and perception of Mau Mau.[37] This agenda of remembering and discussing the contribution of smaller groups instead of the tendency to oversimplify Mau Mau as a rather homogeneous 'Gĩkũyũ affair' seems to me to be a remarkable addition to the study of perceptions of Mau Mau and some of its long-term consequences for Kenyan collective memory. It is something rather underrepresented in many conventional sources on Mau Mau; thus, taking a Swahili novel into account as a source of historiography can be instructive to get a more comprehensive picture of otherwise well-studied research topics. Of course, this is not to say that 'the Meru part' in historiography on Mau Mau was or is not present. However, it is interesting to note that as recently as in 2011, 'Field Marshal' Bairungi Marete, who was a deputy leader to Dedan Kimathi and was allegedly killed by order of Jomo Kenyatta in 1965, was still called an "Unsung Mau Mau Hero" in the Kenyan *Daily Nation*.[38] It is this Field Marshal Bairungi Marete, a member of

36 In a Pan-African perspective, Mau Mau, the anti-colonial war in Kenya (1952–1960), is one of the most prominent examples of an anti-colonial war – similar to the Maji Maji war in today's Tanzania (1905–1907) referred to above.

37 Cf. Peter Kareithi: *Kaburi Bila Msalaba* ['Grave without a Cross']. Nairobi: East African Publishing House 1969; Mwenda Mbatiah: *Wimbo Mpya* ['New Song']. Nairobi: Jomo Kenyatta Foundation 2004.

38 Charles Wanyoro: Unsung Mau Mau Hero Whose Family Cries Foul over Injustice. In: *Daily Nation*, 11.01.2011. http://www.nation.co.ke/News/regional/Unsung+Mau+Mau+hero+whose++family+cries+foul+over+injustice+/-/1070/1087940/-/114 brc5z/-/index.html. In July 2014, his wife Evangeline

the Meru group, who features as a protagonist in Mbatiah's novel published in 2004.

Taking the example of Said Ahmed's novels, pre-colonial, colonial *and* postcolonial times are presented and discussed as a continuum of exploitation and misery, starting with slavery until contemporary times. In his *Dunia Yao* (2006), the advent and sequence of colonialism are presented as follows:

> *[A]kaingia Bwanamvinyo na majahazi yake ya matanga mengi akisema kaja kudhibiti Uislamu usienee, lakini hasa, kaja kuteka eneo na njia ya biashara ya Bahari ya Hindi. Tena tukaimba wimbo wa "Kuku[!,] [S]imba karegea, karegea kongwe!" Bwanamvinyo akang'olewa. Tena akaja Bwanamkalimoto. Hakukaa sana. Alibadilishana na Bwanahimaya, kisiwa hiki kwa kisiwa kingine kilichokuwa na umuhimu na mwafaka wa kivita kwake.*[39]

> *[A]nd then Don Vinho came in with his vessels full of sails, saying he came to prevent Islam from spreading, but specifically, he came to seize the region and the trade route of the Indian Ocean. Again we sang the song of "[Listen, Little] Chick! The Lion has slackened, he has slackened, he's an old crock!" Don Vinho was rooted out. And then, Herr Fiercefire came. He didn't stay for long. He made a deal with Mister Empire, exchanging one island for another which was of military importance and suitability to him.*

As can be seen, the sequence of European colonialisms is metaphorically rendered as a *prosopoeia*, a personification, for each colonial power. The intertext of a children's song obviously popular in Zigua, Zaramo and Zanzibari traditions[40] is a humorous sarcasm which metatextually refers to the weakening and fading out of Portuguese rule in East Africa towards the end of the 17th century. In the following, the narrative voice likens the system of colonial rule to a sophisticatedly carved Makonde statue where different groups in society pile up in different layers, each group sitting on top of another. Then, in striking unambiguity, the narrator states that in postcolonial times, the Makonde statue, as a symbol for the hierarchical political structure, is still there, and the system of power has just changed in colour.[41]

Muthoni died, and Marete's fate featured again in the press. Cf. Kirimi Murithi: Widow of Field Marshall Baimungi Dies Aged 91. In: *The Star*, 24.07.2014. http://www.the-star.co.ke/news/article-179548/widow-field-marshall-baimungi-dies-aged-91 (both accessed 23.02.2015).

39 Mohamed: *Dunia Yao*, p. 147.

40 I owe this insight to Abela Mutembei, Bakari Baringo and William Mkufya. Thank you very much for enlightening me on that matter.

41 Cf. Mohamed: *Dunia Yao*, pp. 147–148.

In Said Ahmed's preceding novel *Babu Alipofufuka*, the already mentioned grandfather-ghost who haunts a decadent government official named 'K' says:

> "Tarikhi ya nchi hii ndivyo inavyokwenda K – si unajua?" [...] "dhuluma moja juu ya nyengine. Ikisha hii inakuja hii. Zinabadilishana rangi tu dhuluma. Na madhalimu wanabadilisha mafigu. [...]"[42]

> "This is how the chronicle of this country proceeds, K – don't you know?" [...] "one oppression on top of another. Once this is over comes that. The oppressions just interchange their colour. And the oppressors change their masks. [...]"

While this is a pointed statement on colonial/post-colonial continuities regarding the uneven distribution of power, in a second step, this conception or conceptualization of history also establishes a firm link to contemporary times of imbalanced 'globalization'.

> "[...] Nyuma ulikuweko utumwa na dhiki. Mbele itakuwa na dhiki na utumwa mkubwa zaidi. Kuna tofauti baina ya kutawaliwa na kununuliwa! Ukitawaliwa unaweza kupigana ukapata uhuru wako. Ukinunuliwa huwezi kujikomboa, kama huna pesa za kulipa kujikomboa, kama aliyekununua atataka kukurejesha ulivyokuwa. [...]"[43]

> "[...] Behind us there was slavery and misery. In front of us there will be even worse misery and slavery. There is a difference between being ruled and being bought! If you are ruled by someone you can fight and obtain your freedom. If you are bought you can't free yourself, if you don't have the money to pay for your freedom, if the one who bought you wants to take you back to the way you were before. [...]"

Basing my argument on a more detailed discussion elsewhere[44], this conceptualization of history leads to a cyclic succession of slavery as being deprived of freedom and forced to work leading to a slavery of 'being bought' by capitalistic globalization. This conceptualization of history in *Babu Alipofufuka* can be illustrated as follows:

42 Mohamed: *Babu Alipofufuka*, p. 101–102.

43 Ibid., p. 94.

44 Cf. Diegner: *Ausweitung der Gesellschaftskritik*, pp. 202–205, 285–288.

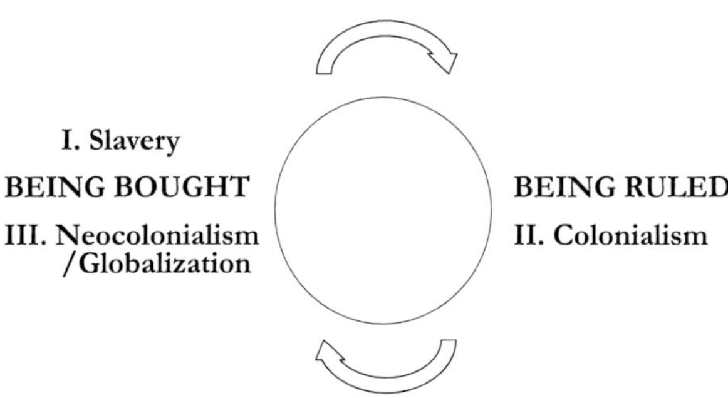

Abb. 1: The conceptualization of history in the novel *Babu Alipofufuka* (Diegner: *Ausweitung der Gesellschaftskritik*, p. 286, adapted version).

Coming back to the image of the Makonde statue in *Dunia Yao*, the link between criticizing the continuity of hierarchical power structures in colonial and postcolonial times, and a criticism of globalization, reads as follows:

> *Mnara wa kinyago cha Wamakonde haujabadilisha nidhamu na mpangilio wake. Zilizobadilishwa ni nafasi. […] Ukitazama harakaharaka utadhani huyu ndugu yetu ndiye aliye juu kabisa. Lakini kwa jicho kali la ndani na tulivu, juu kabisa utakuona kutupu. Nafasi hii imekaliwa na Majira, na juu zaidi ya Majira, dude linaloitwa utandawazi; watawala wa dunia walioko nje kabisa. Wasioonekana kwa macho!*[45]

> *The Makonde sculpture tower hasn't changed its rigour and regularity. What has changed are the positions. […] If you have a hasty look you will think it is indeed our brother who is on the very top. But with a sharp, intensive and calm eye on it, you will see that the position at the very top is empty. This position is inhabited by Time, and on top of Time, this monstrosity called globalization; the rulers of the world who are completely outside. Who are not visible for the eyes!*

The reign of '*ndugu yetu*', "our brother" – the African(s) – is not what it seems to be. It is *Majira* ('Time/s') with a capital 'M' which reigns, and these times are reigned by "a monstrosity called globalization", which is characterized as from "outside" and invisible.

Taking a look at further East African entanglements with Global Northern (neo-)colonialism there is an example of how capitalistic globalization works on the East African local level in Kyallo

45 Mohamed: *Dunia Yao*, p. 148.

Wamitila's novel *Msimu wa Vipepeo* ('Season of Butterflies', 2006). We read about a German investor who got insider information on which historical building to buy on a supposedly Kenyan island which resembles Lamu. When the national elite representatives from metropolitan '*Kitambaasie*', 'Boastaboutnothing' – seemingly a symbolic rendition of Nairobi – are confronted with criticism of selling historical heritage, this is their reply:

> "Ni la kihistoria ndiyo, lakini historia huandikwa na watu; watu kama wewe!" [...] "Historia haikuzuii kuliuza; wajua hiki ni kipindi cha utandawazi na soko huria; na tunahimizwa kuhimiza uwekezaji ili tuinue uchumi wa nchi [...] Unaweza kusema hiki ni kipindi cha kuifuta historia," [...].[46]

> "[The building] is historical, yes, but history is written by people; people like you!" [...] "History doesn't prevent you from selling it; you know this is the time of globalization and free market; and we are forced to force investment in order to uplift the economy of the country [...] You can say this is the period of wiping out history," [...].

Here, "we are forced to force" gives a clear-cut image of East Africans being deprived of their own will and agency; globalization in the end appears as a threat to history, as a threat to a balanced understanding of its importance in order to understand the past, and to draw conclusions for the future.

The examples discussed above show how in contemporary Swahili novel writing, conceptualizations of history seem to agree in constructing a continuum of slavery, colonialism, neo-colonialism, and globalization.

Conclusion

Contemporary Swahili novel writing from both Tanzania and Kenya contributes to East African intellectual history in various respects. Swahili novels recurrently involve references to 'great thinkers' – both European and African, as well as Asian – in a move to foster the social, political, and epistemological criticism expressed in these texts. In some instances, these references pay reverence, and seem to be mainly intended to serve as an inspiration to the reader. In other instances, however, these references do question, satirize, and thus

46 Kyallo W. Wamitila: *Msimu wa Vipepeo* ['Season of Butterflies']. Nairobi: Vide~Muwa 2006, p. 65.

subvert, the standing of the said intellectual 'giants' in a genuinely creative way. Moreover, renowned Swahilophone novelists can be considered as distinctive and innovative ('great') thinkers in their own right. They do not only offer complex and individualized political visions about (neo-)colonial worlds, establishing a dialogue with their Swahilophone readership, but they also provide epistemological criticism per se, which, among a wide range of repercussions, also leads to the question of 'Who defines what intellectual history is'?

By taking the contribution of Swahili novels to East African intellectual history as a case in point, I will conclude by outlining the desiderata I see for an advancement of trans-disciplinary research in African history: As part of the overall need to use African-language sources as sources of historiography in a more widespread, intensive and systematical way, *fictional literature* in African languages deserves a more prominent status in historiography. For instance, scholars intending to write an 'intellectual history' of *ujamaa*, the Tanzanian variant of African socialism, should not content themselves with their findings from conventional, non-fictional sources. Involving or putting a major focus on Swahili fiction as a source will provide them with insights into otherwise inaccessible intellectual discourse, and therefore significantly add to or redefine their overall assessment.

Near and Far

African Academic Literature in France and Germany

Ninja Steinbach-Hüther

African academic literature is said to be either non-existent or on the margins of global knowledge production, but French and German publishing houses provide more literature written by African authors than is generally expected. However, they are differently set and divers on differing levels with regard to their offering of African academic literature as part of global knowledge production. While global processes, according to literature on globalization, often theoretically suggest a worldwide linkage of knowledge and knowledge cultures, an exemplary look at French and German publishing houses and their publishing of African academic literature shows that strong national preferences and orientations remain in the transfer processes of literature. This paper contributes to the debate of African knowledge production and African intellectual history by means of quantitatively approaching the academic writing of the Social Sciences and the Humanities by Africans published in France and Germany since the 1960s. The results presented here are a first step towards a larger study.[1]

Research on Africa gained legitimacy in various disciplines worldwide since the 1950s and 1960s. The establishment of departments and distinct institutions of African Studies, courses and numerous journals

1 The research question of this paper is part of my larger PGD-project. Supervisors of the project are Matthias Middell at Leipzig University and Michel Espagne at the *École Normale Supérieure* in Paris. The research question is explained in detail at http://gesi.sozphil.uni-leipzig.de/staff/.

on Africa are indicators for an immensely growing academic interest in Africa.[2] In comparison to colonial times, the interest in African countries shifted from rather Eurocentric perspectives that had put great emphasis on European activities in Africa, towards efforts of bringing African perspectives into the picture as well. Going along with this idea, the International Congress of Africanists – held in Accra in 1962 and supported by UNESCO – recommended a push for the writing of African history by Africans themselves. Subsequently, various books indicative of this change of perspective were published; landmarks were the eight-volume *Cambridge History of Africa*, edited by Roland Oliver and John Fage (1975–1986), and the *UNESCO General History of Africa* (1981–1993). The latter was "edited by leading African pioneer scholars who all subsequently also made a name for themselves as administrators and/or politicians"[3].

At the same time, nationalist research and historiography within African countries experienced a considerable increase mainly pushed by two phenomena: first, a new emphasis on and esteem for oral traditions; second, at the institutional level rather than on the level of contents. The first sets of African universities were established after World War II and in independent Africa,[4] emanating in anglophone Africa from the late colonial university colleges (notably the universities of Ibadan in Nigeria, Legon in Ghana, Makarere in Uganda, Karthoum in the Sudan). In francophone Africa, early examples are the Catholic University in Belgian Congo and the University of Dakar in Senegal. Even though this growing nationalist production decreased during an era of crisis in the 1980s, the demand for indigenous knowledge increased in various disciplines. Area and Regional Studies increasingly moved towards research with scholars *from* the region rather than just working *on* the region.[5]

2 Felix Brahm: *Wissenschaft und Dekolonisation: Paradigmenwechsel und institutioneller Wandel in der akademischen Beschäftigung mit Afrika in Deutschland und Frankreich, 1930–1970*. Stuttgart: Steiner 2010.

3 Toyin Falola: African Historical Writing. In: Axerl Schneider / Daniel Woolf (eds): *The Oxford History of Historical Writing*, vol. 5: Historical Writing since 1945. Oxford: Oxford UP 2011, pp. 399–421, here p. 401.

4 Ibid., p. 406.

5 Matthias Middell: *Self-reflexive Area Studies*. Leipzig: Leipziger Universitätsverlag 2000; Cf. Wolf Lepenies (ed.): *Entangled Histories and Negotiated Universals*. Frankfurt am Main: Campus 2003.

Hence, if interest in a certain region grows significantly, we are most often confronted with the need for publications from and on this region. Nevertheless and in spite of the rather positive literary development until the 1980s years of crisis,[6] African academics from within Africa's different countries and from outside the continent in the academic spheres of the Global North deplore the global marginalization of African academic literature. Even worse, leading figures in the debate of African knowledge production argue that, if scholarly literature written by African academics is available at all on the markets of the Global North, it is likely to be ignored.[7] In that sense, African academic literary production and reception are often considered either to be comparatively marginalized on a global level or non-existent at all in the relevant communities that produce, receive, reproduce and distribute academic literature within different processes of knowledge transfers. This is confirmed by statistical facts: Africa's contribution to the global book production mounts up to 3 % only (its contribution to academic literature ranging on a lower level than that); and 60 % of all publications on the African continent are assigned to the production of scholarly literature.[8] Also, the amount of academic journals that are produced in Africa takes a back seat compared to journal editing in the US or in Europe.[9] Consequently,

6 Gudrun Honke: Verlagswesen und Buchhandel. In: Jacob Mabe (ed.): *Das Afrika Lexikon: Ein Kontinent in 1000 Stichwörtern.* Stuttgart: Hammer 2004, pp. 674–676; Philipp Altbach (ed.): *Publishing and Development in the Third World.* London: Zell 1992; James Gibbs / Jack Mapanje / Flora Rees (eds): *The African Writers' Handbook.* Oxford: African Books Collective 1999.

7 Walter Bgoya: Introduction – Scholarly Publishing: An Overview. In: Alois Mlambo (ed.): *African Scholarly Publishing: Essays.* Oxford: African Books Collective 2006, pp. 1–11, here pp. 5–7.

8 Solani Ngobeni: Scholarly Publishing in South Africa. In: Id. (ed.): *Scholarly Publishing in Africa: Opportunities & Impediments.* Pretoria: African Institute of South Africa 2010, pp.69–83. Statistics on the African part of the global book industry and on books that were published in African countries differ significantly. Ripken, for example, mentions that far less than 2.5 % of the books worldwide are printed on African soil; Peter Ripken: Traditionen und Gesellschaften im Spiegel der afrikanischen Literatur. Vortrag, Akademie für politische Bildung, Tutzing, 27.06.2008. http://www.petrakellystiftung.de/fileadmin/user_upload/newsartikel/PDF_Dokus/Ripken_Literatur.pdf (accessed 03.03.2013).

9 Mark Graham / Scott Hale / Monica Stephens: Die Orte akademischen Wissens. In: Corinne M. Flick (ed.): *Eine Geographie des Wissens der Welt.* Oxford: Oxford Internet Institute / University of Oxford 2011, pp. 14–16. www.oii.ox.ac.uk/publications/convoco_geographies_de.pdf (accessed 20.02.2015).

these blank spots on the maps of knowledge[10] seem to affirm factually what can be found in the relevant literature: that African academic debates in various subjects comparatively barely reach out into global academic communities and their production chains, however much interconnected and networked the debaters actually might be.[11]

However, in contrast to the opinion that African authors and their books are rarely present in the global editorial world, the data of two national libraries of countries that belong to the global players in that field – France and Germany – initially seems to proof the opposite. At least in their national reference collections, there exist far more entries for people with African country codes than one would expect under the circumstances mentioned before. More than 8,000 registered authority notes of the *Deutsche Nationalbibliothek* (DNB) are assigned with an African country code, and almost six times more are registered with an African country or language code in the reference system of the *Bibliothèque nationale de France* (BnF). Such labeled book publications range well into the thousands. Of course, not all of these books were written by Africans.

Albeit, at first glance and given the facts mentioned above, these numbers seem to be surprisingly high, and they already suggest remarkable differences between France and Germany and the global setting of French and German publishing houses. It is therefore worthwhile to consider the presence of African academic literature in Germany and France in more detail, especially because German and French publishing houses have been, apart from the British and US-American publishing industries, among the more prominent destinations for African literature since the 1960s. As African literature has been and still is published – if not produced in the first place – to a large amount on and for the markets of the Global North, it might not be found in the statistics referring to the African continent but rather belonging to the knowledge contribution that is attributed to other

10 Christoph G. Paulus: Die Handhabung von Wissen im Recht. In: Corinne M. Flick (ed.): *Wem gehört das Wissen der Welt*. Frankfurt am Main: Frankfurter Verlagsanstalt 2011, pp. 151–163, here p. 162.

11 Manuel Castells: *The Information Age: Economy, Society and Culture*, vol. 1: The Rise of the Network Society. Oxford: Wiley Blackwell 2010. Cf. Arjun Appadurai: Globale kulturelle Flüsse. In: Fernand Kreff / Eva-Maria Knoll / Andre Gingrich (eds): *Lexikon der Globalisierung*. Bielefeld: Transcript 2011, pp. 111–113; Gayatri Spivak: *Other Asias*. Oxford: Blackwell 2008.

countries.[12] Both France and Germany have long experienced economic, political and cultural entanglements with African states and also register a considerable number of 'all or partly' emigrated African academics. In Germany, they presumably constitute the comparable majority of emigrants who produce (and later publish) academic literature; in the USA, according to Paul T. Zeleza, who did extensive research on African academics in the diaspora, they represent the best educated and most productive immigrants in continental comparison.[13]

Confronting the common allusion that African academic literature is either non-existent or insufficiently available, I am retracing one part of African intellectual history through the lens of quantitative methods. I will proceed from the basis of the whole of African authors and literature listed in the reference collections of the national libraries of Germany and France. The scope of the analysis is restricted to authors and editors of books and monographs from the Social Sciences and the Humanities published in France and Germany since the mid-20th century. Giving a first overview rather than a detailed description of the data, I aim at testing where the authors of this literature and the literature itself have actually come from to show how far 'Academic Africa' has reached French and German publishing houses in the defined period of time. This provides insights into only a small section of the whole amount of possibilities that quantitative analyses can offer to contribute to the debate of African knowledge production.

12 Evidently, institutions such as the African Books Collective (Oxford) or the Dakar-based Council for the Development of Social Science Research as well as the Africana Librarians Council in the USA or SCOLMA in Great Britain have been and still are committed to indigenous African publishing by counter-reacting to non-indigenous publishing tendencies (cf. Hans Zell: Professional Reading, Review of *African Scholarly Publishing*. In: *The African Book Publishing Record* 33,2 (2007), pp. 106–110). However, non-indigenous publication is still widely spread and therefore needs to be taken into account if judging the position of African scholarly publishing worldwide. Cf. R. W. Tijssen: Africa's Contribution to the Worldwide Research Literature: New Analytical Perspectives, Trends and Performance Indicators. In: *Scientometrics* 71,2 (2007), pp. 303–327.

13 Paul Tiyambe Zeleza: The African Academic Diaspora in the United States and Africa: The Challenges of Productive Engagement. In: *Comparative Studies of South Asia, Africa and the Middle East* 24,1 (2004), pp. 261–275. For further information see Id.: *In Search of African Diasporas: Testimonies and Encounters*. Durham: Carolina Academic Press 2012.

Shedding Light on African Academic Literature in Germany and France

As already mentioned, the amount of people with African country code is unexpectedly high in both data sets.[14] For the German case, out of the initially offered 8,000 authority codes with African country codes, only 2,781 were linked to at least one book title. Out of this amount, authors coming from Egypt (27.1 %), South Africa (16.5 %), Nigeria (5 %), Cameroon (5 %), Algeria (4.5 %), Ethopia (4.4 %), Morocco (4.2 %), Kenia (4.2 %), Tunisia (2.4 %) and Libya (2.3 %) were

14 The rather complex datasets were compiled by the BnF (2014) and the DNB (2012) from their catalogue repositories ("*catalogue général*" http://catalogue.bnf.fr; "Katalog der *Deutschen Nationalbibliothek*" https://portal.dnb.de) and according to different criteria: At least one of the authors of a publication has to be somehow connected to the African cultural region according to the denoted country code (or, in the case of the BnF data, according to an African language code alternatively); the publications linked with these people became relevant only if published in the form of books/monographs; the publications had to be published after 1950; the publications had to be published in France and Germany respectively. Excluded are books which are not published in France and Germany but that were bought by the BnF or the DNB for their collection. Furthermore excluded are books that were published in francophone or germanophone countries other than France and Germany but which therefore also fall under the National Library's collective order (e.g. some African countries, (francophone) Canada and Switzerland as well as Austria). While the BnF provided data for both authors and books, the DNB provided data for authors only. Those book entries were later checked manually according to the defined research criteria. In addition to that, by including relevant authors that were found in the DNB reference system according to their African language code, the DNB data was complemented manually by the author as well. Therefore, the research criteria were identical but acquired differently.
The data of the BnF was processed in a first step within an interdisciplinary project, together with the Natural Language Processing group of the local Computer Science department (Leipzig University), in order to filter out irrelevant records. In the following step, I analysed the remaining entries manually in the same way as with the DNB data before counter-checking whether the authors and their book publications fit the defined criteria. For instance, neither had the whole group of people written books that belong to the Social Sciences and Humanities nor had the persons been affiliated with an African language or country code in each case just because of their origin. To the contrary, many of the authors that were found in that first sample had an educational or thematic relation to the country or language they were assigned with. For more information on the first step of the methodological approach of the BnF data see Thomas Efer / Ninja Steinbach-Hüther: Quantitative Analyses in Global and Area Studies using Graph-based Filtering of Heterogeneous Catalogue Data. In: Lars Grunske / Erhard Plöderer / Eric Schneider / Dominik Ull (eds): *Proceedings of INFORMATIK 2014*. Bonn: Gesellschaft für Informatik 2014, pp. 1027–1037. Parts of this footnote have appeared verbatim before in the specified publication.

most dominant in the DNB data (sample A.1).[15] In the French data – by taking into account 38,705 country code entries of an amount of 45,285 distinct authority entries (25,694 male, 6,334 female, 13,257 undetermined) – the following countries of origin were mainly dominant with regard to the authors' geographic backgrounds: Algeria (8.3%), Morocco (8.2%), Egypt (6.4%), South Africa (5%), Tunisia (4.4%), [France] (4.4%), Cameroon (4.1%), [Israel] (4%), Senegal (3.2%) and Democratic Republic of the Congo (2.6%) (sample B.1).[16]

Both cases cannot be compared yet as the DNB, until recently, only provided data for authority notes with African country codes rather than language codes. Even if it was already possible to further pursue this analysis by manually including relevant authors that were acquired from the DNB reference system due to their African language code, this methodological step is still active and therefore only offers preliminary results. Including the African language codes as one of the research criteria for acquiring the library datasets was especially important for the French data to also get the authority notes of those African academics that had been only assigned France as country code – for example because of their French citizenship etc. The country codes, on the other hand, do not imply that the relevant people automatically are Africans but might have been chosen only because of their professional backgrounds that could be geographically, linguistically or in content linked to the African continent.

It is quite obvious then that the notion of 'Africa' and 'African' is problematic and its definition for analytical purposes is crucial. First of all, some of the people (both within and outside African countries) might not define themselves within a schematic frame of being 'African' as they identify themselves far more in accordance with their intellectual production rather than according to geographic dispositions. Secondly, changing places of living and working might

15 For matters of practicability and readability, the results of the different analyses are named as samples (sample A for the DNB data, sample B for the BnF data). This calculation is based on the 2,827 country codes that the 2,781 authority entries were linked with. This shows that some of the authority entries were assigned more than one country code.

16 The 45,285 authority notes were compiled by the BnF according to their African language or country codes. The non-African countries in square brackets appear because of authors with African language codes rather than an African country code.

influence the ways of researching and writing, for example to become better or easier understood and received.[17] Three common notions of 'Africa/n' are available. In *the continental discourse*, 'Africa' is seen as a homogeneous total in which pan-African elements are integrated and diasporic groups included. This contrasts with *the national discourse* that defines 'Africa' as the sum of the single political states to be found on the continent, as well as with the proponents of *the ethnic discourse*, who refer to common language and culture on local and regional levels. Following the argument of Benin's philosopher Paulin Hountondji – who thought it necessary to de-mystify 'Africanity' and to reduce it to "simply the fact, and, in itself, perfectly neutral, of belonging to Africa – by removing the mystic halo of values arbitrarily grafted upon this fact by ideologists of African identity"[18] – and for reasons of clarity, I handle these different aspects pragmatically as I do not aim to propagate a peculiar concept of 'Africa' nor a specific reality of 'Africanity'. Correspondingly, my pragmatic definition includes both African academics within the African continent and intellectuals from Africa who are situated outside the continent. This implies that also agents of the diaspora are included, and it applies to agents of both the earlier, more politically minded pan-Africanist diaspora and to the contemporary, more economically entailed diaspora.

If we consider the thematic scope of the analysis more closely and only take into account relevant authors (geographically and on the level of contents according to the criteria mentioned above), we can see that, in the German case, the data is already reduced heavily to less than 350 relevant authors (90 % male, 10 % female) with less than 900 books from the Social Sciences and the Humanities. Including those thematically relevant authors found according to their African language code, we advance one preliminary result: books in the Social Sciences and the Humanities were published mainly by authors coming from Egypt (19.6 %), South Africa (18 %), Nigeria (11.3 %), Cameroon (7 %), Kenia (5.5 %), Ethiopia (4.6 %), Algeria (4 %),

17 See Ninja Steinbach-Hüther / Matthias Middell: Zur Präsenz akademischer Literatur aus Afrika in Deutschland – eine Bestandsaufnahme. In: Steffi Marung / Matthias Middell (eds): *Transnational Actors – Crossing Borders: Transnational History Studies*. Leipzig: Leipziger Universitätsverlag 2015, pp. 243–261.

18 Paulin J. Hountondji: *African Philosophy, Myth and Reality*. Bloomington: Indiana UP 2002 [1976], p. vii–xxviii, here pp. xi–xii.

Morocco (4 %), Democratic Republic of the Congo (3.1 %), Tunisia (2.5 %) (sample A.2a).[19] Thus, when concentrating on the Social Sciences and the Humanities only, we find again – and in a similar hierarchical order – in sample A.2a most of the countries that have already been listed in the higher ranks in sample A.1 which did not have particular thematic restrictions. But when relating the main authors' books to their country codes to show which authors have been most productive in German publishing houses in the Social Sciences and Humanities, only the top 4 remain the same (but with different results on the percentile level) and other countries like Burkina Faso and Mali that are not present in sample A.2a become more relevant here: Egypt (23.9 %), South Africa (23 %), Nigeria (7.9 %), Cameroon (7 %), Morocco (5.3 %), Ethiopia (3.3 %), Burkina Faso (2.7 %), Algeria (2.6 %), Mali (2.5 %) and Kenia (2.3 %) (sample A.2b).

At the current point of analysis, the French data was analysed only according to authors with relevant books from the Social Sciences and the Humanities that have a Dewey-classification.[20] Searching for a most practical and manageable way of handling the huge amount of data, the Dewey classification system of classifying books and other works based on their subjects into different categories of knowledge was helpful as a first step to reduce the data source to get thematically seizable results. Taking into account 3,805 country codes of 3,806 remaining authors with at least one book with Dewey classification, mainly authors coming from Cameroon (13.4 %), Democratic Republic of the Congo (8.9 %), Algeria (8.5 %), Senegal (7.5 %), Morocco (7.3 %), Republic of the Congo (6.4 %), Tunisia (6.1 %),

19 Preliminary results of the analysis in which only the numbers of the African country code entries were taken into account are offered in Steinbach-Hüther / Middell: Präsenz akademischer Literatur.

20 For further information on Dewey classification and its usage in the *Bibliothèque Nationale de France*, see: http://www.bnf.fr. At this stage of analysis, the initially presented 45,285 authority notes were reduced to 6,169 authority entries according to the research criteria as presented above. Excluded were authority notes with unspecific language codes (like "i.", "eg.", "mul" for "multilingual"), which means, consequently, that authors with an African country code and an unspecific language code are excluded here as well. This was the case for 206 authors. Until now, only those books were taken into account which were linked with these 6,169 remaining authority entries and have a Dewey-classification. I manually counter-checked all of their books in accordance with the research criteria. It will be necessary also to follow this procedure for the remaining books and also include the rest of the authors with African country code and unspecific language code in a further research step.

Ivory Coast (5.7 %), [France] (3.4 %) and Egypt (3.2 %) published books in the Social Sciences and the Humanities (sample B.2a). In contrast to the DNB data with similar results in the first sample and in the second, the results for the French data are quite differently distributed in the first sample B.1 and the second sample B.2a. With regard to the remaining 5,673 thematically relevant books with 6,075 country code entries and affiliated Dewey classification, we can see that authors from Cameroon (12.8 %), Democratic Republic of the Congo (9.2 %), Algeria (8.8 %), Republic of the Congo (7.2 %), [France] (7 %), Senegal (6.8 %), Morocco (6.6 %), Tunisia (6.6 %), Ivory Coast (4.8 %) and Egypt (4.4 %) have been most productive in French publishing houses in the Social Sciences and Humanities (B.2b).[21]

Even though the analyses have not been terminated neither for the DNB data (that should be counter-checked and further completed for the language codes) nor for the BnF data (that needs to be further developed for the considerable amount of almost two thirds of the remaining books without Dewey classification): these preliminary results show, on the one hand, particular geographic orientations in both cases. On the other hand, it is obvious that the number of published books do not forcibly correlate with the number of authors from a certain country (see comparison of samples A.2a and A.2b and B.2a and B.2b) which suggests a certain productivity of authors (from the samples a) which influences the results for the hierarchical ranking of countries (from the samples b).

Both for French and German data, significant tendencies of concentration with regard to the countries of origin of the authors can be observed. While the interest in some regions was relatively constant during the whole time span, the interest in authors from other regions increased significantly at certain times and decreased at others.[22] Obviously, we cannot automatically conclude that there

21 In comparison to how the DNB data could be methodologically approached, in the case of the BnF data, the country codes of the books were calculated by including the country codes of all of the people that were indicated in the library catalogue data as being relevant for the publication (in general: authors, secondary authors and translators).

22 This indicates the more qualitative research part of the PhD project. For further information and visual representation of the results, please contact the author: Ninja.Steinbach-Huether@uni-leipzig.de.

exist correlations between book publications and the interest of the German and French public in a specific African country, but the quantifying approach allows us to assume that the frequency of book publications from a certain country or at least from an author of a certain country also testifies a particular political or intellectual reference to this country within France or Germany. Let us just think about postgraduate programs or invitations for guest scholarships that is the context of numerous cases in which the elevated publications and contacts to publishers materialized.[23] The connection between country of origin and interest in the country presupposes a correlation that still needs to be counter-checked. I follow the assumption that the majority of authors wrote about social practices in their countries and the region where they came from. This could be the nation state but also a region or city. For the German case, this could already be observed by authors coming from countries listed in the lower ranks in terms of numbers. By contrast, authors with country codes that were listed in the higher ranks in terms of numbers seem to have written thematically more independently.[24]

With regard to the publishing houses, the data show significant tendencies of concentration. A small number of publishing houses dominate the whole domain of publishing African academics in the Social Sciences and the Humanities. For now, *Peter Lang Verlag*, *Theorie und Praxis Verlag*, *Verlag Herder*, *LIT Verlag* and *Beck und Glückler* are most dominant in the German case, whereas according to the French data, the most prominent publishing houses are *Éditions L'Harmattan*, *Éditions Edilivre*, *Éditions Gallimard* and *Présence Africaine*. The national

23 For instance, more than one quarter of all of the relevant authors of the DNB data have direct educational connections to Germany (stays for graduation, dissertation or habilitation). Apart from university partnership programs, exchange possibilities as offered by the Alexander von Humboldt Foundation or the German Academic Exchange Service testify recent tendencies: www.humoldt-foundation.de; www.daad.de. For educational exchange programs between African and French academics cf. http://www.ladocumentationfrancaise.fr/var/storage/rapports-publics/074000601/0000.pdf; Antoine Grassin (ed.): La mobilité des étudiants d'Afrique sub-saharienne et du Maghreb. In: *Les notes du Campus France*, Hors-série numéro 7, June 2013. http://www.campusfrance.org/sites/default/files/note_07_hs_Afrique.pdf (both accessed 13.02.2015). Cf. Andreas Eckert: Universitäten und die Politik des Exils. Afrikanische Studenten und antikoloniale Politik in Europa, 1900–1960. In: Rüdiger vom Bruch, Rainer C. Schwinges (eds): *Universitäten und Kolonialismus*. Stuttgart: Steiner 2004, pp. 129–145.

24 Steinbach-Hüther / Middell: Präsenz akademischer Literatur.

publishing houses in each case differ in thematic preferences and (economic and thematic) editorial policy so that there are publishing houses that contribute quantitatively and others contributing rather qualitatively to the presence of African academic literature on the German and the French book market. A first impression is that we find a combination of both in France rather than in Germany.

Conclusion: Approaching African Intellectual History Quantitatively

Whereas a worldwide linkage of knowledge and knowledge cultures is often assumed in academic theories, this exemplary look at African academic literature in French and German libraries shows that strong national preferences and geographical orientations remain in the transfer process of literature. Regarding the unfiltered records, the difference between the French and the German data concerning geographical preferences is quite striking. Apparently, French and German publishing houses are differently set with regard to their offering of African academic literature as part of global knowledge production. There seem to exist different geographical academic 'Africas' in both national editorial worlds, even though the BnF data is more equally and vastly distributed than the German data which is characterized by higher concentrations: With regard to the BnF data taken altogether, the top 10 of the countries of origin only account for around 50 % of the whole data whereas, in the case of the DNB, the top 10 of the countries of origin account for approximately 76 % (see samples A.1 and B.1).

In general, French publishing houses seem to be much more oriented to countries that used to fall under French colonial rule than German publishing houses which do not seem to have particular interest in authors from former German colonies. This is probably due to the fact that Germany lost its status as colonizer more than four decades earlier than France and Germany's relation to African countries is characterized by more ruptures than France's relation to African countries. France held up stronger African connections, and remained deeply involved especially with its former colonies.[25] Not surprisingly

25 For further reading see Pascale Blanchard / Sandrine Lemaire (eds): *Culture Coloniale: La France conquise par son empire, 1871–1931*. Paris: Éditions Autrement 2003;

then, there are far more publishing houses that are specialized in the publishing of African literature in France than in Germany. Since 1949 when *Présence Africaine* set out to become a publishing house, and the 1970s when *Éditions L'Harmattan* and *Éditions Karthala* came to the fore, African and French publishers organized themselves to particularly publish African academic literature. More recently, plenty of other French publishing houses such as *Éditions Gallimard*, *Albin Michel*, *Éditions Silex* and *Éditions du Seuil* became important for the publishing of African authors who increasingly belong to what might be called the postcolonial generation of African authors.[26] These examples show that the interest in African literary transfer started earlier in France than in Germany.

However, the current state of analysis does not yet allow too many comparisons between France and Germany, because the data has not been wholly taken into account. Therefore, with regard to African literature from the Social Sciences and the Humanities, only tentative concluding observations are possible for now: it seems that academic literature from that field was published more often in France and Germany during the last six decades than one would probably assume bearing in mind its marginal status on a global level. We are confronted with an amount of books in French publishing houses that is many times higher than what is to be found in German publishing houses. There apparently exists a much bigger key market for literature that is written by Africans in France than in Germany. Looking at the particular geographical background of its authors, the quantitative methodology proposed here is an effective way to retrace one part of African intellectual history to provide a peculiar frame for qualitative interpretation. It allows a better understanding of the manifold dimensions of academic flows from Africa to two

id.: *Culture Coloniale: Les colonies au cœur de la République, 1931–1961*. Paris: Éditions Autrement 2004; Felix Brahm: 40 Jahre Vereinigung für Afrikawissenschaften in Deutschland (VAD), 1969–2009. VAD-Online-Paper, 2009. http://www.vad-ev.de/fileadmin/user_upload/pdf/FelixBrahm-40JahreVAD.pdf (accessed 14.02.2015); Brahm: *Wissenschaft und Dekoloniasation*; Christophe Charle: *La crise des sociétés impériales. Allemagne, France, Grande-Bretagne (1900–1945): Essai d'histoire sociale comparée*. Paris: Éditions du nouveau monde 2001; Frederick Cooper: *Citizenship between Empire and Nation: Remaking France and French Africa, 1945–1960*. Princeton: Princeton UP 2014.

26 Bennetta Jules-Rosette: *Black Paris: The African Writers' Landscape*. Urbana / Chicago: University of Illinois Press 2000, p. 129.

European countries that have been dedicated to the publication of African literature for many decades but with differing geographic and thematic orientations. The question therefore remains how contents that, according to theory, shall be globally accessible are received, made available and/or taken into account in various national contexts. Notwithstanding the increasing international entanglement and transnational transfer relations that go with globalization, France and Germany apparently have different national approaches to African knowledge that we do not know much about yet.

Knowledge Production about the Cameroonian State in Urban Intellectual Discourse

Janine Kläge

> All typifications of common-sense thinking are themselves integral elements of the concrete historical social-cultural *Lebenswelt* within which they prevail as taken for granted and as socially approved. Their structure determines among other things the social distribution of knowledge and its relativity and relevance to the concrete social environment of a concrete group in a concrete historical situation.[1]

According to this quote from German sociologist Alfred Schütz, knowledge is always produced, reproduced and institutionalized as a product of society and constitutes the basis for identification. Expanding on that, Michel Foucault argued that systems of thought and knowledge (*discursive formations*) are ordered by rules that were unconsciously achieved, and determine conceptual premises creating boundaries of knowledge relations of power. Language therefore is not only describing but also prescribing, constituting reality.[2]

As a result from the long history of colonial domination, knowledge production regarding Africa exists mainly in European-centered terminology and is shaped by institutionalized descriptions produced in non-African contexts. Early on, some African thinkers challenged this state of affairs critically, and set out to produce knowledge about Africa in the realms of decolonization and post-colony. Already in the 1950s, Cheikh Anta Diop asked provoking questions about how

1 Alfred Schütz: Husserls Importance for the Social Science. In: Id.: *Collected Papers*, vol. I: The Problem of Social Reality, ed. by Maurice Natanson. The Hague: Nijhoff 1962, pp. 140–149, here p. 149.

2 Michel Foucault: *The Archaeology of Knowledge*. London / New York: Routledge 2002.

truly 'African' African history can be when she is based on European models about the African past.[3] Wole Soyinka's neologism *tigritude* – meaning the essence of being a Tiger – ridiculed the attempt of the *négritude* movement to define the nature of Africa and Africans in culturalist terms, while still arguing for Africans to be proud of themselves – but on their own terms.[4] The Congolese linguist and novelist, philosopher and anthropologist-historian V. Y. Mudimbe pointed out that "History is a legend, an invention of the present. It is both a memory and a reflection of our present."[5] Mudimbe showed in his book *The Invention of Africa* that 'Africa', understood as a constructed image or a specific idea, was formed from outside the continent, and basically does not exist. 'Africa' is an imagination, a pall that changed steadily over the last 200 years.[6] This evidence led some African writers to strive for an African epistemology. Cameroonian writer and prominent 'post-colonialist' thinker Achille Mbembe, for instance, encourages African intellectuals to produce knowledge and discourses *from* Africa and not *about* Africa. For him the sole knowledge about Africa we currently have is the knowledge about how Africa ought to be.[7] To develop a postcolonial identity of Africa, it is required to overcome external tools and thoughts linked to deficiency and needs, and to produce knowledge about what is Africa today.[8]

3 Cheikh Anta Diop: *Nations nègres et culture*. Paris: Présence Africaine 1954.

4 Wole Soyinka: *Myth, Literature and the African World*. Cambridge: Cambridge UP 1978; Janheinz Jahn: *A History of Neo-African Literature*. London: Faber 1968; David Simo: Was ist Afrika? Postkoloniale Konstruktionen von Afrikabildern. In: Aïssatou Bouba / Detlev Quintern (eds): *Das Bild von Afrika. Von kolonialer Einbildung zu transkultureller Verständigung*. Berlin: Weißensee 2010, pp. 75–88.

5 V. Y. Mudimbe: *The Invention of Africa: Gnosis, Philosophy, and the Order of Knowledge*. Bloomington: Indiana UP 1988, p. 195.

6 Ibid. Cf. Christiane Reichart-Burikukiye: Erinnerungsräume und Wissenschaftstransfer. Die Erfindung Afrikas. In: Winfried Speitkamp (ed.): *Erinnerungsräume und Wissenstransfer: Beiträge zur afrikanischen Geschichte*. Göttingen: V&R unipress 2008, pp. 11–34; Winfried Speitkamp: Erinnerungsorte und Erinnerungskulturen in Afrika. In: Sonja Klein / Vivian Liska / Karl Solibakke / Bernd Witte (eds): *Gedächtnisstrategien und Medien im interkulturellen Dialog*. Würzburg: Königshausen & Neumann 2011, pp. 273–282.

7 Achille Mbembe: African Modes of Self-Writing. In: *Public Culture* 14,1 (2002), pp. 239–273.

8 Achille Mbembe: *On the Postcolony*. Berkeley: University of California Press 2001, pp. 1–23.

This affects also the description and evaluation of African states. Various actors within and beyond Africa such as the donor community, international organizations and former colonial powers define the 'nature' of the African state. Most commonly, the state in Africa is measured in terms of deviations from an idealized model of the 'modern state'. The academic discussions offer a multifarious repertoire of metaphors and abusive terms such as 'peripheral state', 'quasi state', 'fictive state' or 'developmentalist state'.[9] In this paper I am looking at what knowledge about the Cameroonian state is produced and how it circulates among people who live within this *discursive formation*. It is based on 47 interviews conducted in three Cameroonian urban areas – Yaoundé, Douala, and Bamenda – with 60 intellectually engaged activists in the years 2011 and 2012. My guiding question is: 'How is the Cameroonian state perceived by its subjects and represented by its political class?' The interviews allow for the revision of recent depictions of African states through the lens of urban Cameroonian people who are working in various artistic fields and middle class professions (lawyers, journalists), shaping the knowledge production about the Cameroonian State. Within Cameroon it is not only the ruling elites shaping the appearance of the state, but ordinary citizens as well. The language split between French and English speakers in Cameroon makes for a further layer of difference in the ways the Cameroonian state is imagined and treated. They all are involved in discursive practices and negotiate and push for particular ideas of how the Cameroonian state ought to be.

In academic discussions on the Cameroonian state, explicit and implied reflections of its structure and function or dysfunction were differently accentuated. In the 1960s and 1970s considerations were given to the issue of political integration and nation-building. Political science perspectives were dominant, as was modernization theory. The state in Cameroon, understood as an autonomous entity with full authority, was held responsible for the implementation of political

9 Rainer Tetzlaff / Cord Jakobeit: *Das nachkoloniale Afrika. Politik, Wirtschaft, Gesellschaft.* Wiesbaden: VS 2005, p. 77 ('peripheral'); Robert Jackson: *Quasi-States: International Relations, Sovereignty and the Third World.* Cambridge: Cambridge UP 1990; Richard Sandbrook: *The Politics of Africa's Economic Stagnation.* Cambridge: Cambridge UP 1985 ('fictive'); Kevin R. Cox / Rohit Negi: The State and the Question of Development in Sub-Saharan Africa. In: *Review of African Political Economy* 37,123 (2010), pp. 71–85 ('developmentalist').

integration.[10] French political scientist Jean-François Bayart was one of the first to explicitly analyze the state in Cameroon in more historical terms. He focused on the interests and political actions of the ruling class, its reproduction and its power relations.[11] Luc Sindjoun proposed an explicit analysis of the Cameroonian state.[12] Starting from Bertrand Badie's concept of the *Etat importé*, he described its genesis in order to expose the complicated processes 'behind' the category *state*. Badie defined the state as an "acclimatation locale ou culturelle nourrice de l'exceptionnalité de chaque expérience"[13] which creates what he called *État caméléon*. The Cameroonian state, fluid in its complexity, must be considered in its distinctive cultural and historical context.

Recent research emphasizes in particular the restraining factors for democratization and questions, at least implicitly, the function of the state.[14] Observations shift to questions of decentralization[15] and emphasize the interaction between government and political opposition as well as with traditional authorities. Considering the apparently incomplete process of the introduction of democratic practices and

10 Victor LeVine: *The Cameroons from Mandate to Independence*. Westport: Greenwood 1964; Michel Prouzet: *Le Cameroun*. Paris: Librairie générale de droit et de jurisprudence 1974; Jean-Francois Médard: L'État sous-développé au Cameroun. In: *Année africaine*, June 1977, pp. 33–84; Hans Illy: *Politik und Wirtschaft in Kamerun: Bedingungen, Ziele und Strategien der staatlichen Entwicklungspolitik*. München: Weltforum 1976.

11 Jean-Francois Bayart: *L'État au Cameroun*. Paris: Presses de la Fondation nationale des sciences politiques 1979.

12 Luc Sindjoun: *L'État ailleurs: Entre noyau dur et case vide*. Paris: Agence intergouvernementale de la francophonie / Economica 2002.

13 Bertrand Badie: *L'Etat importé: Essai sur l'occidentalisation de l'ordre politique*. Paris: Fayard 1992, p. 14.

14 Jean-Germaine Gros (ed.): *Cameroon: Politics and Society in Critical Perspective*. Lanham: UP of America 2003; John Mukum Mbaku / Joseph Takougang: *The Leadership Challenge in Africa: Cameroon under Paul Biya*. Trenton: Africa World Press 2004; Emmanuel Fru Doh: *Africa's Political Wastelands: The Bastardization of Cameroon*. Bamenda / Mankon: Langaa 2008; Emmanuel Yenshu Vubo: *Civil Society and the Search for Development Alternatives in Cameroon*. Dakar: CODESRIA 2008; Tangie Nsoh Fonchingong: *Cameroon: The Stakes and Challenges of Governance and Development*. Bamenda / Mankon: Langaa 2009; Timothy Mbuagbo / Robert Mbe Akoko: Roll-Back: Democratization and Social Fragmentation in Cameroon. In: *Nordic Journal of African Studies* 13,1 (2004), pp. 1–12.

15 Cosmas Cheka: The State of the Process of Decentralisation in Cameroon. In: *Africa Development* XXXII,2 (2007), pp. 181–196; Jean Claude Eko'o Akouafane: *La décentralisation administratives au Cameroun*. Paris: L'Harmattan 2009.

institutions, it was stressed again and again that the democratic process has been blocked in various ways. Academic discourse claims commonly that democratization is a pre-requisite for development. The view that democracy and development depend upon each other is also found among Cameroonians. Discussions about the state in Cameroon most often culminate in the central issues: What is wrong in the Cameroonian state, and how can it regenerate to assert itself as a 'modern state'? Against the backdrop of these globally circulating academic narratives, I look at the image and imaginations of the Cameroonian state among intellectually engaged activists. How do they talk about the Cameroonian state and which knowledge about it is circulating and reproduced? For the purpose of this paper all interviewees are categorized as *intellectuals* according to the understanding of Rainer Lepsius who wrote that "Intellectuals are, sociologically, not persons with any personal characteristics, but persons who do something particular"[16] and who do so in public. The data stems from interviews made in the capital Yaoundé and in Douala, both French-speaking areas, as well as in the principle town of anglophone Cameroon, Bamenda.

Cameroonian Discourses on the State

The interviews allow for the identification of specific expectations and functions of the state. The Cameroonian state was perceived and imagined in terms of particular social and political issues such as (1) the current economic situation and development, (2) the democratic process and governance, (3) the international context, (4) the public social services, corruption and embezzlement of public funds. The interviewees draw attention to the state by criticizing the Cameroonian state. They imagine the state through claims. State deliveries are considered the main task and function of the state. Their critique points at the health and educational system, at infrastructure, security as well as at basic needs such as electricity and water. In the following, the general scope of the intellectuals' claims to the Cameroonian state will be illustratively demonstrated. Most statements of the

16 Rainer M. Lepsius: Kritik als Beruf. Zur Soziologie der Intellektuellen. In: Id.: *Interessen, Ideen und Institutionen*. Opladen: Westdeutscher Verlag 1990, pp. 270–285, here p. 277, my translation.

interviewees reveal the image of a state whose core tasks are health and education. This corresponds to the state's official rhetoric, but is contradicted by its actual practice which favors the military sector. Regarding budget, internal security was perceived as the most important function of the state:

> L'Etat c'est une machine. L'Etat c'est pas un département ministériel. Tout doit être important mais sauf que maintenant, dans le Cameroun, ils ont fait un peu l'inverse parce-que le ministère qui a le budget au Cameroun c'est l´armée. Maintenant il y a après les forces armée, la santé et l´éducation.[17]

> The state is a machine. The state is not a government department. Everything must be important, but presently in Cameroon, they are doing little against it, because the ministry which has the budget in Cameroon is the army. Today, health and education come after the armed forces.

Again, in the context of the educational system, the interviewees stress that there is a gap between the obligatory school attendance and the real political action to enforce it:

> C'est difficile de voir un enfant qui ne va pas à l'école, sauf vraiment les enfants qui sont à l'abandon dans la rue, et c'est vraiment une infirme partie, c'est vraiment signifiant. Chaque parent se bât pour que son enfant aille à l'école. Officiellement c'est gratuit mais c'est pas obligatoire. Si tu t'envoies pas ton enfant à l'école, on ne va pas te forcer. Mais les gens se sentent vraiment obligés parce que si tu n'envoies pas ton enfant à l'école, toi même tu te sens qu'il y a un problème.[18]

> It is difficult to see a child who does not go to school unless the children who are really abandoned in the street, and it's really a falsified part, it is really significant. Every parent contests for their child to go to school. Officially it's free but it is not compulsive. If you're not sending your child to school, you will not be forced. But people really feel obliged because if you do not send your child to school, yourself, you feel that there is a problem.

The relatively high rate of school enrollment is constructed as a result of the Cameroonian social system. Children are part of the retirement arrangement, and parents pursue to send them into school and are voluntarily engaging staff (teachers) and organizing fundraising events.

Another gap between official policy and reality is considered in the declaration of access to education without charge. The interviewees

17 Interview Yaoundé 09.10.2011. All translations from French interviews are mine.

18 Interview Yaoundé 07.10.2011.

articulate the obligation to pay informal fees raised by the authorities of the institutions. The parents ensure the inscription of their children in educational institutions by pay for these informal fees. The payments are perceived as governmental school fee, which would be charged hidden fees. In one case an interviewee argued that public school fees appear in the membership contributions of the parents' association. Becoming a member in this association was not optional, and consequently he had to raise a large sum to participate. Consequently, he would not speak of free education.[19] In addition, not only the collection of informal fees, but also incurred costs contradicts the image of free education. Thus, the interviewees referenced school uniforms, books and school meals as public fees.[20] Free education was therefore interpreted as official rhetoric only, not actual practice.

The same appears in statements made about the difference between public and private schools.[21] The main inequalities are seen in financial terms. Thus, private schools are much more expensive and contribute to social injustice since the low-income segment of the population is excluded from access to them. Not only the different financial endeavor between the state and private schools is significant, but also differences in quality of teaching. These differences were characterized in terms of class size. Attending a public school class with an average of 100 children was contrasted with only 20 children in a private school class that exposed the indication for low and high quality of education. Therefore, the educational system is in fact not free of charge; it comes as no surprise that claims for compensation were

19 See Interview Yaoundé 29.09.2011.

20 For instance: "L'école n'est pas obligatoire malheureusement, l'école n'est pas obligatoire. Elle est gratuite, officiellement gratuite, sauf que les enfants ne vont toujours pas; tout le monde ne va pas à l'école parce qu'on dit qu'elle est gratuite mais quand vous vous rendez compte qu'il faut acheter toutes les fournitures, les cahiers, les livres, vous vous rendez compte en réalité n'est pas, elle n'est pas si gratuite qu'on l'a dit. L'école n'est pas obligatoire chez nous, normalement." (Interview Douala 27.09.2011). There are many similar cases; cf. Interview Douala 19.09.2011; Bamenda 15.09.2012; Yaoundé 23.09.2011, 03.10.2011.

21 For instance: "L'école privée coûte généralement plus chère. Il y a généralement moins d'élèves, les professeurs sont beaucoup sérieux [on suit mieux les élèves], ça coûte plus chère" (Interview Douala 19.09.2011). Cf. Interview Douala 20.09.2011; Yaoundé 29.09.2011, 02.10.2011.

made by my interview partners.[22] In addition, there is also the claim to adjust the quality of public schools and private schools.[23]

The sample data of my interviews yields several significant differences in francophone and anglophone attitudes towards the Cameroonian state. The free school attendance and the gap between imagined state delivery and reality were the general claim among francophone intellectuals. In contrast, anglophone intellectuals living in the western region of Cameroon focused on the structure of the educational system, seen through a predominantly economic perspective. It might well be that the regional disparity is a result of experiencing different colonial administrations, French and British, and their survival into post-colonial times. The structure of the present Cameroonian central government, which largely follows the French (colonial) model, was taken over and implemented in many anglophone parts of Cameroon after the reunification in 1962. Consequently, the reorganized levels of government and the role of state officials and civil servants in this region are not traditionally anchored, as is the case in the French-speaking regions.[24]

> There is a cry for the reformulation of the educational system of Cameroon. The educational system in Cameroon is old and needs to be reformulated. We need a system in a direction where people will be trained in the needs of the environment. They should be trained to be job-creators, not job-seekers, because in the whole of Cameroon, people are being trained for job-seekers. It's the same system we have since 1960 and we've recycled it over the years. The government cannot recruit not longer everybody."[25]

22 Interview Bamenda 15.09.2012, 17.09.2012, 19.09.2012; Yaoundé 15.09.2011, 13.09.2011, 03.10.2011; Douala 19.09.2011, 27.09.2011.

23 For instance: "In the government school, you know that the teachers there sometimes they have a carefree attitude that teaching it's not very, very efficient." (Interview Bamenda 07.09.2012). Cf. Interview Yaoundé 03.10.2011; Douala 19.09.2011.

24 Tata Simon Ngenge: The Institutional Roots of the "Anglophone Problem" in Cameroon. In: Jean-Germain Gros (ed.): *Cameroon: Politics and Society in Critical Perspective*. Lanham: UP of America 2003, pp. 61–86; Victor Julius Ngoh: *Constitutional Developments in Southern Cameroons 1946–1961*. Yaoundé: Pioneer 1990; Bouopda Pierre Kamé: *Cameroun du protectorat vers la Démocratie 1884–1992*. Paris: L'Harmattan 2008, pp. 37–43, 156–171; Lotsmart Fonjong: *The Challenges of Nongovernmental Organisations in Anglophone Cameroon*. New York: Nova Science Publishers 2007, pp. 15–24; Milton Krieger: *Cameroon`s Social Democratic Front: Its History & Prospects as an Oppostion Politcal Party (1990–2011)*. Bamenda / Mankon: Langaa 2008, pp. 22–50; Engelbert Mveng: *Histoire du Cameroun*. Paris: Présence Africaine 1963; Ambe J. Njoh: *Plannig Rules in Post-Colonial States: The Political Economy of Urban and Regional Planning in Cameroon*. New York: Nova Science 2001, pp. 51–72.

25 Interview Bamenda 14.09.2012.

The claim on the state is to restructure the educational system and to develop the private sector, so that Cameroonians will be transformed from job-seekers into job-creators.

The perception of the state as biggest employer is also emphasized by francophone intellectuals. They consider it a profitable institution that promises a regular salary and health insurance. Furthermore, the civil service is perceived as the avenue for access to profitable incomes, often related to corruption. While the civil servants are imagined in the context of enrichment, the state is seen as a source of money.[26] As for the administration, the educational and health system and the security sectors are often related to corruption. The state is described as the main factor that causes corruption; it is seen as the responsibility of the state to correct this situation. For instance,

> It should be the responsibility of the state. That is the task of the state. Do you ensure that that is done, but, they don´t give that. So the parents, they want their children to have good education, they go into that. So that the parents keep on removing money from their pockets to pay for the education of their children, which is supposed to be the responsibility of the state.[27]

While francophone intellectuals focus on the corruption of everyday life, which is caused by low salaries of the civil services since the 1980s, the anglophone intellectuals direct their critique of corruption at the political class; they talk about "embezzlement".[28] The perspective of the anglophone interviewees has once more an economic angle. Through corruption, they argue, it will be difficult to find investments, and this is blocking Cameroonian economic development.[29]

> Government should rather encourage the private sector than the civil service. Instead of using that money to recruit the people who have no duty and are doing nothing, give this money to the private sector. The civil servant is minimal to develop a nation to go."[30]

26 Interview Douala 20.09.2011, 06.10.2011; Yaoundé 13.09.2011, 14.09.2011, 03.10.2011, 09.10.2011, 29.09.2011; Bamenda 18.09.2012, 20.09.12.

27 Interview Bamenda 21.09.2012.

28 One quote may serve as typical example: "High functionaries do a lot of things that are not good. For instance, embezzlement. People publicly embezzle public funds. You find a minister or a general manager are becoming all too rich, embezzling billions of money." (Interview Bamenda 19.09.2012). Cf. Interview Bamenda 15.09.2012.

29 Interview Bamenda 14.09.2012, 15.09.2012, 18.09.2012.

30 Interview Bamenda 17.09.2012.

By contrast, according to francophone interviewees, corruption has a stronger impact on every-day life, because it interferes with the delivery of public goods.[31] However, corruption of both ordinary people and the political elite is described as an ordering function. As one journalist put it,

> There [in Cameroon] is a whole system, a system that survives on corruption. If you fight corruption, generally the system will collapse. It is very risky to engage fully in the fight against corruption because it will mean the collapse of the entire system.[32]

For all the interviewees, the Cameroonian state is present in every-day life, particularly through the presence of the military and police, the political class and the civil service. The interviewees encounter the state during primary school (where there is a subject called "citizenship/civics") as well as in family discussions, and through personal experiences. To some extent all interviewees referred to their own personal experiences with the state. Their claims partly correspond to the self-conception of official state declarations that reinforce this perspective. Some, who already experienced the state regime of the first president Ahmadou Ahidjo (1960–1982), compared it favorably to the state under the second president, Paul Biya. For example,

> Yeah, when all that happened [the collapse of social deliveries] when Biya came in. Ahidjo was relatively more patriot. He thinks of this country more. But Biya is just working for the French just wanting himself to be maintain in office, and it is said, that's why Ahidjo was dethroned, why Ahidjo was removed from power, Ahidjo was tricked out of power.[33]

In doing so, the interviewees constructed the state since Paul Biya's inauguration in 1982 as 'tribal' and, concerning state deliveries, dysfunctional. One told me

> It was a farmer's hospital; it was functionally in those days of Ahidjo, because the road was maintained. There were people on the route maintaining the route,

31 For instance: "Maintenant c'est comme le cancer dans ce pays. Ça a en grainé tout le corps, tout le corps. On trouve la corruption à tous les niveaux, même dans le privé. C'est à dire tout le monde donne l'argent pour obtenir tel service." (Interview Yaoundé 29.09.2011). Cf. Interview Yaoundé 14.09.2011, 29.09.2011, 16.09.2011, 02.10.2011; Douala 19.09.2011, 20.09.2011, 23.09.2011.

32 Interview Bamenda 14.09.2012.

33 Interview Bamenda 21.09.2012. Cf. Interview Bamenda 19.09.2012; Yaoundé 06.10.2011, 09.10.2011.

> paid by government. But today, after Biya took up, those things are collapsed. The routes are not being maintained, the hospitals broken down.[34]

Another one declared

> Aujourd'hui, l'Etat camerounais a un problème, c'est un problème de déficit. Il y a un déficit de gouvernance au Cameroun. Ça dire l'état existe, le chef de l'état est très fort mais l'état ne marche pas. Ça veut dire que l'état est incapable de mettre de l'ordre, l'état est incapable de construire, l'état est incapable de faire quoi que ce soit pour le bien être des populations.[35]

> Today, the Cameroon government has a problem of deficits. There is a lack of governance in Cameroon. That implies that the state exists and the head of state is very strong but the state is not working. It means that the state is unable to establish order, the state is unable to build up, and the state is unable to do anything for the well-being of the population.

Moreover, the imagination of the Cameroonian state provides comparisons with other African and or Western states.

> Look at the whole neighbors: Nigeria. Nigeria is advanced! It would take Cameroon 100 years to attend the level Nigeria is today. Now that's a country colonized by the British! Look at Ghana: Advancing! Look at Zimbabwe: It's going! Look at South Africa: It's going. And when you turn around: look at Cameroon, Gabon, Congo, Equatorial Guinea, Madagascar: those are French companies. [...] Compare any French colony and English colony. The difference is clear. It's like day and night.[36]

Thus, African countries such as Ghana, Nigeria, Mali and Benin serve as reference points for political systems where the state allegedly provides for the separation of powers and democracy, guarantees respect for human rights and secures a peaceful alternation of government.[37]

> For example we had one president for the last almost 30 years. In other countries it's not the same – they are changing. We take the example of Ghana, even Nigeria, here. They are changing. Even though Cameroon is more politically

34 Interview Bamenda 21.09.2012.

35 Interview Yaoundé 06.10.2011.

36 Interview Bamenda 21.09.2012. Cf. Interview Yaoundé 30.09.2011, 15.09.2011; Douala 20.09.2011, 07.10.2011.

37 For instance: "Quand vous prenez un petit pays comme le Mali, vous voyez comment les choses fonctionnent là-bas. Là-bas aussi, les choses auraient pu être là-bas comme le Cameroun sauf que les trois forces qui se sont succédées là-bas, bien qu'ils soient arrivés par la force, étaient des démocrates; et ils ont donc travaillé pour instituer un système démocratique." (Interview Douala 06.10.2011).

> stable than Nigeria; the intense of leadership, Nigeria has had more leaders. I think we are not progressing, we are not. We have the same leaders, the same people over 30 years.[38]

The imagination of the Cameroonian state is also influenced by comparison with Europe and the US. Whereas the francophone Cameroonians I talked to strongly referred to Europe (France and Germany in particular) concerning the quality of the social system,[39] the anglophone interviewees made only little reference to Europe. Their imaginations were strongly orientated to the US state model. Particularly, on the issue of economic development they drew on the notion of a less influential state and emphasized how the economy is regulated by a strong private sector.[40]

Conclusion

The interviews with urban Cameroonians of their views on their state lead to the insight that imaginations and (re-)production of knowledge about the state differ according to the linguistic and cultural shift that pervades the country since colonial times. Among the French speaking intellectuals the dominant frame of reference is a version of a Western 'welfare state', with particular reference to education and health systems as well as infrastructure and security. To some extent this is matched by the self-conception of representatives of the state in Cameroon who reinforce this perspective.[41] Regarding the English speaking intellectuals the frame of reference is a 'liberal state' model, where market processes are less regulated by the state. This is often combined with reference to the US. This difference in the imagination

38 Interview Bamenda 18.09.2012.

39 See Interview Yaoundé 30.09.2011, 29.09.2011, 15.09.2011; Douala 20.09.2011, 07.10.2011, 23.09.2011.

40 For instance: "If you charge fees, you pay and of course it will be reflected in the salary of the workers. So I think that, like it's obtained in other economies, like the privately sector. The US economy for example. The Nigerian economy, because we are talking about Africa. So this has to do with the system. The system! Nigeria is English-speaking. And the orientation they had is kind of more liberal. There is more liberal and they have a liberal economy." (Interview Bamenda 21.09.2012). See also Interview Bamenda 14.09.2012, 15.09.2012, 17.09.2012.

41 See official declarations and speeches of representatives of the Cameroonian Government, presented and published by the Prime Minister: http://www.spm.gov.cm/fr/documentation.html?no_cache=1 (accessed 11.02.2015).

of an appropriate state model directly has an implication on how interviewees look at the role of administration in Cameroon. While the francophone intellectuals imagine a bureaucratic state and call for more public investment, the anglophone intellectuals see bureaucracy as an economic blockade that needs to be rigorously reduced. In the context of present economic crisis, the narratives get an explicit historical dimension, when referring to a past state regime that is unduly romanticized and favorably compared in favor of the current government and state bureaucracy. The expectation of the intellectuals is clearly to produce a usable Cameroonian state.

The configuration of core state tasks are reflected and produced in relation to globally common state models. In contrast to the general categorizations and interpretations of *weak* and *failing states* which dominate Western discourses on Africa, the Cameroonian government is perceived by Cameroonian urban intellectual discourse as being in need of reforms, but not as being illegitimate, weak or failed. The critical perception about the political elite, the lack of social benefits and the gap between political rhetoric and social reality provoke the idea of certain state models and their implementation. The construction of knowledge of how the Cameroonian state is and ought to be, is influenced, on the one hand, by state models circulating on a global scale. On the other hand, the perceptions of Cameroonians follow a particular logic in combining personal experiences with elements of external reference systems. Thus, the perception of the Cameroonian state is deeply affected by the subjective *Lebenswelt*. It is embedded in a particular *discursive formation*, which highlights the (re-)production of this particular knowledge.

Ethiopian and Ghanaian Thoughts on Asia's Rise

Development Strategies in Question

Felix Müller

The economic rise of several Asian countries since the 1960s has attracted attention all around the world, not least in Africa. Focusing on Ethiopia and Ghana in particular, I argue that in this process a social technology usually referred to as *developmental state*[1] has become an influential source of inspiration for intellectuals and policy makers looking for development strategies that might be applicable to their domestic context. Contrary to the assumption of a diffusion of ideas from powerful areas to less powerful ones, the developmental state model has made its way to Ethiopia and Ghana due to the deliberate considerations of policy makers and intellectuals. Its journey can be grasped most adequately if it is understood as processes of cultural transfers.[2] The central assumptions of the cultural transfer approach are that strategic groups identify certain deficits in their

1 The concept of the developmental state was coined with regard to Japan, cf. Chalmers Johnson: *Miti and the Japanese Miracle: The Growth of Industrial Policy, 1925–1975*. Stanford: Stanford UP 1982. However, in its rise to prominence in development discourse, the concept was increasingly associated with the so-called tiger states; see UNECA: The Developmental State: What Options for Africa? An Issues Paper, 2013. http://www.uneca.org/sites/default/files/uploaded-documents/CGPP/cgpp-3_issues-paper-english_final_160113.pdf (accessed 30.05.2014). For further information, and for a critique of pessimistic arguments regarding the transferability of the model to African settings, see Thandika Mkandawire: Thinking about Developmental States in Africa. In: *Cambridge Journal of Economics* 25,3 (2001), pp. 289–313.

2 Michel Espagne: *Les transferts culturels Franco-Allemands*. Paris: PUF 1999; Matthias Middell: Kulturtransfer und historische Komparatistik: Thesen zu ihrem Verhältnis. In: *Comparativ* 10,1 (2000), pp. 7–41.

society and make use of intermediaries who actively search for ideas or models in other cultures. Some of these ideas or models are then identified as appropriate problem solving devices (social technologies), followed by key actors' attempts to integrate them into the domestic realm, either by hiding their external origin or by making it explicit. Undoubtedly, a dimension of external agency and attempts at enforcement must be considered in the African context. Furthermore, the findings presented here suggest that orientation towards models developed elsewhere is facilitated if actors in the domain of origin are willing to engage in, and actively support, a process of transfer.

In this paper I examine how the success of Asian economies has been interpreted among Ghanaian and Ethiopian intellectuals and state representatives, and how these perceptions have influenced their policy choices and expectations toward the state. I am interested in a) key actors' analyses of internal challenges and their incentives to orientate themselves towards East Asian state models, b) the interaction with the role model countries, and c) the relevance of the compatibility of new models with already familiar ones. This examination will also widen our understanding of the role which other development paradigms play today in policy making and imagining an ideal state in the two countries. The case studies presented here are based on interviews carried out in Ethiopia and Ghana in the years 2013 and 2014.[3] They suggest that socialist and capitalist orthodoxies (or the interviewees' perceptions of these, for that matter) are currently being challenged by various actors in Ethiopia and Ghana. Growing orientation towards the developmental state model should be interpreted against the background of earlier experiences with stateness and ideologies without which this model would be less easy to relate to. In the Ethiopian case, the adaptation of the developmental state

3 The interviews were conducted within my work at Leipzig University's Centre for Area Studies in the project *Changing Stateness in Africa: Cameroon, Ethiopia and Ghana Compared*. This project is part of the DFG-funded SPP 1448 on *Adaptation and Creativity in Africa: Technologies and Significations in the Production of Order and Disorder*. I would like to thank my colleagues in the sub-project *Changing Stateness in Africa* (Ulf Engel, Matthias Middell, Janine Kläge and Lena Dallywater) for their constructive comments on earlier drafts of this paper. All errors are of course my own. Also, I am very grateful to everyone who supported the organization of the interviews, and to all the people who participated in them.

model cannot be fully understood without taking into account the ideological roots of the current leaders. In Ghana, the widespread sympathy for developmental governance is connected to the nostalgia for Jerry J. Rawlings' authoritarian military government (1981–1993) and the Nkrumah period (1957–1966).

Case Study: Ethiopia

After more than a decade of civil war of various insurgency forces against the *Derg* regime, the Ethiopian People's Revolutionary Democratic Front (EPRDF), led by the Tigrayan People's Liberation Front (TPLF), managed to seize control over Addis Ababa in May 1991.[4] From the beginning of its rule, and despite its own Marxist-Leninist roots, the EPRDF argued that socialism, which had been the former official state doctrine, was no longer a viable option. Against the background of the demise of the Soviet Union, and probably due to the necessity to offer something other than the former leaders, there was lots of talk about the introduction of free market policies in the government newspaper *Ethiopian Herald* in the second half of 1991. Nevertheless, representatives of the transitional government simultaneously stressed the need for state involvement in the economy.[5] Even though policies of market liberalization were adopted within the framework of structural adjustment, "power, policy-making, and resources [have been] controlled by, and in the direct interests of, the TPLF".[6]

According to Sebhat Nega, who has been with the TPLF since it was established, the essential elements of a developmental state were discussed within the EPRDF already before its successful grip on power in 1991 (even though the term itself may not have been used at that time). When I met Sebhat in November 2013, he directed the Ethiopian International Institute for Peace and Development (EIIPD), a training facility for diplomats of the Ministry of Foreign

4 Richard Pankhurst: *The Ethiopians: A History*. Oxford: Blackwell 2001, pp. 276–277.

5 *Ethiopian Herald*, 09.07.1991; *Ethiopian Herald*, 13.09.1991.

6 Alemayehu Geda: The Political Economy of Growth in Ethiopia. In: Jean-Paul Azam / Robert H. Bates / Stephen A. O'Connell / Augustin K. Fosu / Jan Willem Gunning / Benno J. Ndulu / Dominique Nijinkeu (eds): *The Political Economy of Economic Growth in Africa, 1960–2000*, vol. 2: Country Case Studies. Cambridge: Cambridge UP 2008, pp. 116–142, here p. 119.

Affairs (MoFA). He argued that there had been plans to establish a free market economy, but since there was no capitalist or middle class in Ethiopia, the EPRDF had to step in: "The free market economy cannot function by itself, especially under Ethiopian condition. Therefore, there must be a developmental state which intervenes selectively, whenever the market fails".[7] He pointed out that "from day one, before we entered Addis, we were talking about what should be the role of the government in a free […] market economy",[8] and that it was common sense that the government would have to play a role. Thus, even though Ethiopia's political leaders initially spoke in the neoliberal jargon of the early 1990s, their conviction that the state needs to guide the economy had remained strong.

A senior researcher of the EIIPD stated that "in 2010 EPRDF declared that it is the dominant party in Ethiopia, and its political economy doctrine is [the] democratic developmental state model".[9] Like Sebhat Nega, he emphasized that Ethiopia had been implementing the vision of a *democratic* developmental state, making it "different from authoritarian type of the Far East, and from state capitalism type of the West".[10] These statements should be read against the background of a scholarly debate on the compatibility or incompatibility of democratic and developmental governance.[11] As the developmental state model is commonly associated with authoritarian governance, it seems that Ethiopian state representatives feel they need to justify their version of the model by emphasizing its democratic nature.

7 Interview 18, 10.11.2013. A similar argument has been made comprehensively by Ethiopia's former Prime Minister Meles Zenawi, cf. Meles Zenawi: States and Markets: Neoliberal Limitations and the Case for a Developmental State. In: Akbar Norman / Kwesi Botchwey / Howard Stein / Joseph E. Stiglitz (eds): *Good Growth and Governance in Africa: Rethinking Development Strategies*. Oxford: Oxford UP 2011, pp. 140–174. Many interviewees described Meles as a very well-read leader exerting strong influence on the EPRDF government's policy decisions before his death in August 2012.

8 Interview 18, 10.11.2013.

9 Interview 2, 16.10.2013.

10 Interview 2, 16.10.2013. It seems that the interviewee did not use the term *state capitalism* to mean, for example, a state owning enterprises and making a profit from them, but rather a state whose policies are informed by capitalist ideology.

11 Adrian Leftwich: Democracy and Development: Is there Institutional Incompatibility? In: *Democratization* 12,5 (2005), pp. 686–703; UNECA: Developmental State; on related issues see Dani Rodrik: Political Economy and Development Policy. In: *European Economic Review* 36 (1992), pp. 329–336.

Elaborating what he understands by democracy in the Ethiopian context, the state-affiliated researcher argued that Ethiopia's multicultural and multiethnic nature make the country different from Asian ones; therefore, "the principle of democracy" in Ethiopia is to address linguistic, cultural, and religious diversity, and to distribute resources equitably.[12] This view is connected to a specific reading of nations going back to Stalin's understanding of the concept, based on which Ethiopia was redefined and restructured from a centralized to a federal multinational state under EPRDF rule.[13] Furthermore, it is reminiscent of notions of *good governance* put forward by influential development agencies, such as the World Bank, the International Monetary Fund (IMF), and the United Nations Development Programme (UNDP).[14]

In a similar fashion, an official document on *Foreign Affairs and National Security Policy and Strategy* states that "[d]emocracy guarantees that the members of the various nations, nationalities and religions in Ethiopia live in an atmosphere of tolerance. In the absence of a democratic order, national and religious divisions will invariably intensify [...]".[15] On a related note, the late Ethiopian Prime Minister Meles Zenawi (1955–2012) argued in a scholarly article that a developmental state "must achieve broad support for its development agenda"[16], but "[w]hether it builds such a consensus in the context of a fully democratic order or not does not determine its characteristics as a developmental state"[17]. In other words, Meles was convinced that a

12 Interview 2, 16.10.2013.

13 Jon Abbink: Ethnicity and Conflict Generation in Ethiopia: Some Problems and Prospects of Ethno-Regional Federalism. In: *Journal of Contemporary African Studies* 24,3 (2006), pp. 389–413; Christopher Clapham: Controlling Space in Ethiopia. In: Wendy James / Donald L. Donham / Eisei Kurimoto / Alessandro Triulzi (eds): *Remapping Ethiopia: Socialism & After*. Oxford: Currey 2002, pp. 9–30; Dereje Feyissa: The Ethnic Self and the National Other: Anywaa Identity Politics in Reference to the Ethiopian State System. In: Bahru Zewde (ed.): *Society, State, and Identity in African History*. Addis Ababa: Forum for Social Studies 2008, pp. 123–153.

14 See Ulf Engel / Gorm Rye Olsen: Introduction: The African Exception: Conceptual Notes on Governance in Africa in the New Millennium. In: Iid. (eds): *The African Exception*. Aldershot: Ashgate 2005, pp.1–13, here pp. 3–4.

15 FDRE: Foreign Affairs and National Security Policy and Strategy. 2002, p. 6. http://www.mfa.gov.et/docs/Foreign%20Policy%20English.pdf (accessed 20.11.2014).

16 Meles: States and Markets, p. 168.

17 Ibid., pp. 168–169.

developmental state (i. e. the Ethiopian state) does not have to be democratic (in the liberal sense) in order to achieve its goals.

Which particular countries do actually serve as developmental role models to the Ethiopian state? According to a senior official from the MoFA, inspiration for policy making comes primarily from South Korea, Taiwan, China, India, and Vietnam, and there is direct exchange with representatives of the Asian role models among the ministries, the EPRDF, in businesses, and also among NGO workers. "We are following [South Korea's] path. From the ministries of trade, investment, technology, development, tourism, and agriculture, people go to South Korea and China, mainly, and are trained there",[18] mainly regarding institutional empowerment and work efficiency.

A high-ranking EPRDF representative who has been to China himself explained that the orientation towards China had increased over the 2000s, following a split within the ruling party which strengthened the position of the "modernizers" vis-à-vis the proponents of more classical socialism.[19] In early 2001, the combination of long-established personal rivalries, differing approaches to the war with Eritrea (1998–2000), and ideological disagreements caused a split within the TPLF leadership which in the long run strengthened the position of Meles Zenawi.[20] Several government members resigned. The interviewee used the term "modernizers" to refer to those within the party who argued in favor of developmentalism. Considering the interview with Sebhat Nega mentioned above, it seems clear that the relationship between the state and the economy has for a long time been discussed within the EPRDF. After the split at the turn of the century, the specific idea of the Ethiopian democratic developmental state took shape, which according to the EPRDF representative implied the necessity to increase exchange with those countries that had "miraculously" developed their economies through developmentalist policies. The stated intention has been to learn from their experiences in order to address internal challenges.[21] By and large, this strategy of cultural transfer had been laid out officially in 2002:

18 Interview 3, 21.10.2013.

19 Interview 13, 28.10.2013.

20 Christopher Clapham: Post-war Ethiopia: The Trajectories of Crisis. In: *Review of African Political Economy* 36,120 (2009), pp. 181–192, here p. 184.

21 Interview 13, 28.10.2013.

> Asia could play a very important role in our development. It provides the main example of successful development. In addition it is from Asia that we can get highly trained manpower and technical assistance inexpensively. We also need to take advantage of the remarkably growing Asian economy.[22]

Mutual visits of Chinese and Ethiopian officials have played an important role in shaping Ethiopians' perceptions of the Chinese state model, and these perceptions have in turn shaped certain features of the Ethiopian developmental state. For example, according to the EPRDF representative, the China Executive Leadership Academy Pudong in Shanghai served as a role model for Ethiopia's Meles Zenawi Leadership Academy, which is most of all involved in the training of civil servants. Ethiopian experts and five high officials had been sent to Shanghai for two weeks to observe how the Pudong Academy works. The team also included one member of the EPRDF executive committee, which makes the final decision on any proposal developed through a delegation's experience abroad.[23] In November 2014, representatives of Meles Zenawi Leadership Academy and Beijing Administrative College discussed in Addis Ababa how to strengthen their cooperation. As stated on the EPRDF's online presence, the Ethiopian Academy "wants to draw lessons in the areas of Curriculum Development, Teaching Methodology and Research from the best experiences of Beijing Administrative College".[24]

Another measure which has been directly influenced (and in fact made possible) by the Chinese experience is the establishment of a Special Economic Zone (SEZ) in Ethiopia.[25] The interviewed EPRDF

22 FDRE: Foreign Affairs, p. 149. In this document, Japan is emphasized as a source of financial assistance (ibid., pp. 149–151). Even though the "Japanization" of Ethiopia in the first half of the 20th century is not mentioned (Bahru Zewde: The Concept of Japanization in the Intellectual History of Modern Ethiopia. In: Id.: *Society, State and History: Selected Essays*. Addis Ababa: Addis Ababa UP 2008, pp. 198–214), the text presents Japan as a development role model. During the interviews, however, Japan was rarely mentioned in this regard.

23 Interview 13, 28.10.2013.

24 EPRDF: Meles Zenawi Leadership Academy and Beijing Administrative College Officials Held Talks. 2014. http://www.eprdf.org.et/web/guest/news/-/asset_publisher/c0F7/content/melse-academy-and-beijing-academy-news-27-nov-2014 (accessed 15.01.2015).

25 The Ethiopia Oriental Industrial Park, which has been developed by the private Qiyuan Group, is situated about 30 km outside of Addis Ababa and mainly produces "steel and other construction materials for Ethiopia's booming construction industry" (Deborah Bräutigam / Tang Xiaoyang: African Shenzhen: China's Special Economic Zones in Africa." In: *Journal of Modern African Studies* 49,1 (2011), pp. 27–54, here p. 36.

representative associated SEZs directly with China and stressed that "[w]e believe that we need to have these zones".[26] Ethiopia's ruling party has established an agency for the development of SEZs, which according to this interviewee is in direct contact with the China Association of Development Zones. So far, Chinese experts have been leading the Ethiopian agency for SEZs, which in his view is due to their experience in implementing policies that are likely to attract foreign investment. He added that the long-term goal was to learn how Ethiopians themselves could take care of zone development and attract investors.[27]

Apart from China, the interviewee emphasized Ethiopia's strong relations with South Korea and the historical ties between the two countries. During the Korean War (1950–1953), Ethiopian troops fought on the side of South Korea, which in the view of the EPRDF representative is one of the reasons why the Korean government today feels it has the responsibility to assist the Ethiopian development effort. Even though China is the primary role model in terms of leadership and leadership training, South Korea was described as most important regarding economic development: "Even though we have a lot of experiences even from China, we feel that the economic model that we are adhering is much more resemble [sic] the South Korean, the economic model".[28] Thus, the EPRDF representative shares the view of the MoFA official cited above, who stated that Ethiopia was most of all following the South Korean development path.

In more concrete terms, the party representative referred to *Saemaul Undong*, South Korea's *New Village Movement* introduced in the 1970s commonly described as President Park's self-help based rural development strategy that complemented the state's focus on export-oriented industrialization.[29] According to the interviewee, many in

26 Interview 13, 28.10.2013. Even though such zones are of course not a Chinese invention, Ethiopian policy makers nowadays relate development zones almost exclusively with China.

27 Ibid.

28 Ibid.

29 See Jemal Abafita / Fikadu Mitiku / Kim Kyung Ryang: Korea's Saemaul Undong (New Village Movement): A Model for Rural Development in Ethiopia? In: *Journal of the Korean Society of International Agriculture* 25,3 (2013), pp. 217–230; Casper Hendrik Claassen: The Spread of Saemaul Undong: Overcoming the Bane of

the EPRDF think that due to South Korea's development progress, the concept is going to be obsolete there soon, but that Ethiopia can still benefit significantly from the idea. In 2012, South Koreans and Ethiopians agreed in Addis Ababa to set up a *Saemaul Undong*-related research center in which initially South Koreans will be involved, with the long-term goal of handing over the center entirely to Ethiopian leadership. The interviewee stated that the contract for this center had already been signed with the Ethiopian Ministry of Finance and Economic Development.[30]

An Ethiopian expert on NGO affairs experienced the transfer of development ideas between Ethiopia and South Korea personally. Accepting an invitation of the Korean embassy in Ethiopia, the activist and other Ethiopians went to Korea for a two weeks stay some years ago.[31] At the Korea Saemaul Undong Center, the Ethiopian delegation was joined by around fifty people from Asia, Africa, and Latin America, who all participated in the training on how to make developmental states work, with a particular focus on how to mobilize the masses for the developmental cause. According to the activist, this training is primarily aimed at government advisers, and felt to him like training in a military camp. The participants regularly had to get up early, do sports, sing a *Saemaul Undong* song, and (apart from planned trips) were not supposed to leave the "camp", which is situated in Yeongdong-daero, Gangnam-gu, around 75 km southwest of Seoul. Lectures on the history of *Saemaul Undong* in Korea were followed by field tours to villages in rural areas and to industrial sites, after which the participants discussed and presented on how to adapt *Saemaul Undong* to their respective countries of origin. In the Ethiopian case, emphasis was put on making more use of the country's own natural, human, and social resources, and the need for improved mass mobilization tools as well as a development

Pessimism. 2011. http://www.consultancyafrica.com/index.php?option=com_content&view=article&id=738:the-spread-of-saemaul-undong-overcoming-the-bane-of-pessimism-&catid=90:optimistic-africa&Itemid=295 (accessed 06.08.2014); Korea Saemaul Undong Center: Introduction. 2014. http://www.saemaul.com/english/ti_introduction.asp (accessed 05.05.2014).

30 Interview 13, 28.10.2013.

31 In order to guarantee the interviewee's anonymity, certain information has to remain rather vague here.

song.[32] Furthermore, the Ethiopian delegation highlighted that the competitive element of South Korea's village-based development program should be introduced in Ethiopia. The NGO worker presented the experience in a highly positive light and claimed that the Korea Saemaul Undong Center was where he understood the true meaning of the developmental state concept.[33]

Even though the official introduction of the developmental state model has provoked diverse criticism on the part of intellectuals not affiliated with the Ethiopian government, it has by no means been entirely rejected. In fact, Ethiopian intellectuals have also found inspiration in East Asian state models. For example, a researcher of the rather independent Ethiopian Economics Association was convinced that laissez-faire existed only in textbooks, and that even though President Park of South Korea was a ruthless dictator, he had developed the country very well. The economist approved of the introduction of the developmental approach in Ethiopia, but added that the Ethiopian version should be complemented by the Western system of checks and balances. Ethiopia's political development should follow the example of Brazil and South Africa, where in his view the developmental state model (which he associated with South Korea, Malaysia, China, and authoritarianism) and the principle of separation of powers (which he associated with western European democracies) had been combined successfully.[34]

A professor of political science at Addis Ababa University also approved in principal of the idea to introduce the developmental state model in Ethiopia. However, he emphasized that the government's role models – China, Taiwan, South Korea – have been able to make developmental policies work due to characteristics which Ethiopia lacks: widespread nationalism, a capable bureaucracy which sticks to the rule of law, and a political elite free from parochial and partisan influences. He described China and South Korea as places where all these things are intact: even though the laws there may be harsh, they apply left and right, making China and Korea role models

32 Meles Zenawi also emphasized the importance of broad support for the development agenda, referring to hegemony in the Gramscian sense (Meles: States and Markets, pp. 167–168).

33 Interview 6, 23.10.2013.

34 Interview 8, 23.10.2013.

for the adherence to the rule of law. Contrary to Ethiopia, China and South Korea were also serious about insulating the professional bureaucracy and fighting corruption in his view.[35] Measuring a developmental state by the autonomy of its bureaucracy was also suggested by Meles Zenawi. However, contrary to the professor who problematized parochial and partisan influences, Meles stressed that a state needs to be shielded from the interests of the private sector in order to implement developmental policies effectively.[36]

The crucial point here is that the interviewee's criticism, like that of many others, is most of all informed by his positive conception of what developmental states are really about. This conception has strongly influenced his expectations towards the Ethiopian state. He expected Ethiopia's leaders to have a clear direction, to come up with viable policies, and to be able to convince the people that government acted in their best interest – thus, to really live up to the label "developmental state". He added that he is "not very much a fan of democracy", for democracy is mainly about "pretensions and posturing" in his view.[37]

Case Study: Ghana

During interviews conducted in the Greater Accra Region and Akosombo in February and March 2014, a majority of intellectuals and state officials advocated the view that the kind of politics they associated with Ghana's Fourth Republic had significant strengths, but also weaknesses. Established political liberties like the freedom of speech were unanimously seen as important achievements that need to be preserved; also, peaceful and orderly changes of government constitute important elements of a sense of regional and continental superiority – most commonly, Nigeria was mentioned as a negative contrast.

Simultaneously, however, the democratic cycle of holding elections every four years is experienced as a serious obstacle to long-term planning and focused project implementation free of party politics. Many intellectuals and state representatives argued that Ghana would

35 Interview 7, 23.10.2013.

36 Meles: States and Markets, pp. 166–168.

37 Interview 7, 23.10.2013.

profit from a stronger orientation towards Asian developmental states, of which China and Malaysia were mentioned most prominently. In more concrete terms, this usually meant a demand for stronger, more assertive leadership, and for more long-term development commitment, yet in a continued context of political pluralism. Suggestions as to how to bring about the desired changes ranged from calls for a change in attitude,[38] to constitutional changes,[39] to the view that it is unfortunately too late for a democratic country like Ghana to incorporate elements of developmental states, except for institution building. Partly, these views are reminiscent of the debate on the compatibility or incompatibility of democratic and developmental governance mentioned above.

A civil servant in favor of the latter view stated that instead of rushing into democracy, the skilled leaders of South-East Asian countries had organized everything before they joined the "world of democracy". Ghana had not had leaders like Malaysia in his view, and since democracy had already been established in Ghana, the only thing left to be learned was "how to run businesses", meaning institution building. In the future, Ghana will most likely (and hopefully, in his view) move towards the US system of non-partisan institutions.[40] Dr. Nana Yaw Boampong Sapong from the Department of History of the University of Ghana shared this view in principal, in which democratic and developmental governance seem to constitute incompatible opposites.[41]

Other interviewees put less emphasis on institution building and argued instead for the need for more determined leadership in Ghana. Without making reference to a particular foreign country, a professor of development economics said that in Ghana

> there's lack of political will in the continuation of policies and programs. So we are in a country where there is a change of government, programs change, strategy change, while we all know the ultimate goal is the same. […] We all know that we want to educate every young person in this country, which is good. And every government that comes in tries to do that, the only difference is the approach. And one government comes and stops this approach and starts

38 Interview 26, 11.02.2014.

39 Interview 50, 08.03.2014.

40 Interview 43, 03.03.2014.

41 Interview 45, 04.03.2014.

> another. […] I think we've been talking about a long-term development policy for the country for a long time, and we need a government that will push for that. […] I can say that yes, democracy is good, but I think we need a dictator who is democratic, 'cause we cannot continue to allow discussions to go on, go on, go on – it has to stop somewhere.[42]

In this economist's view, the leader should listen to what other people have to say, but he should be able to reject everything if he is fully convinced of his plan.[43] At the same time, "going democratic, I think that is the best thing Ghana had done. I mean, nobody's even thinking of going military rule or having a coup attempt – it will not be feasible". The downside of "going democratic" is, in his opinion, that it is expensive in terms of time: decision-making in a parliamentary system takes too long.[44]

Another professor of economics put forward similar views. Following the shift towards the World Bank and the IMF in the 1980s, which in his view had led to the stabilization of Ghana's economy,

> we went into this political pluralism, ok, party politics. Now the idea was because the economy was in good shape, and hard decisions were taken, you know under Jerry Rawlings,[45] when the party system, that political pluralism comes in, it will be easier for the people to use their influence to dictate what type of policies and programs are implemented. But unfortunately, with the political pluralism, things rather degenerated. […] I have everything for political pluralism, democracy, etcetera. But you must have a developmental state, a government that is focused enough to know what must be done. And that was what Jerry Rawlings stood for, and that was why he was able to change the system from 1983 until 1992. […] In fact, even in [Rawlings' first term as elected president (1993–97)] … things were quite better, because he could exert discipline, call for compliance.[46]

42 Interview 32, 21.02.2014.

43 The male form is used here because the interview partner used it.

44 Interview 32, 21.02.2014.

45 Jerry John Rawlings, born 1947, first seized power in Ghana in a military coup in June 1979, and handed it over to a civilian government in the same year. He staged a second coup in December 1981, after which he ruled Ghana as a military dictator until he became the first elected president of the Fourth Republic in January 1993. His second and final term as president ended in 2001. In 1982, Rawlings had turned to the International Monetary Fund (IMF) for financial assistance, embarking on a path of structural adjustment that has strongly shaped Ghana's economic policy up to the present; cf. Roger S. Gocking: *The History of Ghana*. Westport: Greenwood 2005, chapters 10–12. He is still an active public figure and regularly comments on Ghanaian politics.

46 Interview 33, 21.02.2014.

Thus, this intellectual (like many others) established a causal link between political pluralism, party politics, and the stagnation of Ghana's development, and suggested a restructuring of Ghana along developmental lines as the solution of the problem. Comparing China's and Russia's recent economic history, he found that in Russia, similar to Ghana, the introduction of political pluralism had caused economic development to decline. In China, however, "[t]hey have liberalized the economic foundation, but the political structure, you see that it's still strong, making sure that the right decisions are taken".[47] But the Ghanaian developmental state which he desires should differ from China's in terms of respecting the needs of laborers more. A challenge to the introduction of the developmental state model in Ghana could be that "The East Asian countries are, are good examples to, to pick up from, but again unfortunately their cultural characteristics and work ethics are grossly different from, you know, ours".[48]

A sympathetic view of developmental governance is not confined to economists. A professor of history of the University of Ghana was also convinced that Ghana would profit if it were to orientate itself more towards China. However, in order to really make this happen, Ghanaians would have to "change their attitude" in his view, because they had become too used to consuming foreign goods – a complaint also mentioned in other interviews. But since people were unlikely to change their attitudes themselves, it was the state's responsibility to reduce reliance on imports, even if confronted with significant resistance: "For me, governance is all about leadership […]. As far as I'm concerned, a leader must lead. Everywhere people are shouting and crying, you still lead. […] People will protest, people will dislike you, but you must lead".[49]

State representatives also raised considerable criticism towards the Ghanaian state, and found inspiration in Asian examples in their quest for solution strategies. One senior civil servant stated that he sees "Ghana to be like an East Asian country, but in an African way. We don't say Germany, US, or Japan. Malaysia, South Korea,

47 Interview 33, 21.02.2014.

48 Ibid.

49 Interview 41, 28.02.2014.

Indonesia – the South-East Asian. They are our mentors, we look at their transformation".[50] In practical terms, this meant to him to attempt to create a skyline similar to that of Seoul. But it was Malaysia which this civil servant was most strongly inspired by. Contrary to the Ghanaian state, he explained, the Malaysian one had secured land ownership, and had intervened to provide cooking gas to common households, making charcoal obsolete. Responsible leaders had brought the country on a sustainable way of economic growth in his view.

His positive understanding of the Malaysian state is connected to a personal stay. For one month, he was trained on economic planning in a Malaysian technical cooperation training center; the trip was paid for by the Malaysian government. As in the South Korean training described above, participants came from Africa, Asia, and Latin America. The program consisted of lectures, discussions, and presentations given by each delegation. The training group also traveled Malaysia by bus and visited "district assemblies" in order to share ideas with their members. According to his own statement, the most important thing which the civil servant had learned during the training was that Malaysia's long-term plan of 25 years was better than Ghana's three years medium-term planning model. After his return, he had started to work towards convincing others of this perspective, wishing that "Ghana could be more like Malaysia".[51]

A Member of Parliament representing the current ruling party complained that Ghana lacked a leader who can enforce what is necessary. Today, it would not be possible anymore to implement, for example, the structural adjustment programs of the 1980s – instead, any attempt to introduce far-reaching reforms nowadays would only lead to a never-ending dispute in court. Thus, similar to the intellectuals not affiliated with the state, the Honorable saw a link between democratic decision-making processes and stagnating development in Ghana's Fourth Republic. He stated that Ghana wanted "to marry" China just as much as the West, because China treated Ghana like an adult and provided more money. However, despite his nostalgia for the effective decision-making under Rawlings' *Provisional National*

50 Interview 39, 26.02.2014.

51 Ibid.; cf. Interview 42, 03.03.2014.

Defence Council (PNDC, 1981–1993), the Honorable said he considered democracy – which had been perfected in the USA in his view – worthy of preservation, and did not want "marrying" China to translate into emulating China's style of governance.[52]

Conclusions

African intellectuals and state actors are increasingly inspired by East Asian development role models. Under different circumstances, intellectuals and policy makers in both Ghana and Ethiopia have arrived at the conclusion that their respective country would profit from a more pronounced orientation towards East Asian states, whose material success is seen as the outcome of strong and assertive, yet benevolent leaders being heavily and continuously involved in economic affairs. In both countries under review, key actors' perceptions of, and also interactions with, role model states have played a significant role in the formulation of policy choices (on the part of state officials) and expectations towards the state (on the part of intellectuals not affiliated with the state).

Most of the Ethiopian interviewees saw their perception of Asian developmentalism as a modern alternative to socialism, capable of preventing market failure, which was associated with neoliberalism. The developmental state model can be linked up with already existing imaginations of stateness within the ruling party EPRDF, and within Ethiopia at large. The adaptation of a development model focused not only on market, but more so on state power, is facilitated by the Ethiopian leaders' background in socialist ideology. What is more, the dominant party approach, which characterizes the Ethiopian developmental state, ties in well with earlier concepts of authoritarian rule in the country, which despite all attempts to get rid of them have had a long-term impact. This is also noticeable in the criticism of intellectuals, which is often aimed at the way *how* the developmental state model is implemented in Ethiopia, rather than at the model and its implications for state control per se.

In Ghana, most of the interviewees interpreted the developmental state concept as a governance model capable of overcoming political dead ends. The latter were usually traced back to a hasty, or not yet

52 Interview 37, 22.02.2014.

fully matured process of democratization. As in the Ethiopian case, the idea of the developmental state can be linked to already existing perceptions and experiences of stateness. The nostalgia for Rawlings' PNDC military government associated with quick and effective decision-making often serves as a reference point when the belief that Ghana would profit from a reorientation to China or Malaysia is explained. This should not be understood to imply that mainly NDC supporters (the party which Rawlings belongs to) argue in favor of more orientation towards Asian developmental states. Interviewees with a critical view of Rawlings also held that Ghana had rushed into democracy, and that they would have appreciated a slower transition organized by a leader comparable to Malaysia's.[53] Widespread worship for the authoritarian leadership of Ghana's first president, Kwame Nkrumah, also provides fertile ground for positive interpretations of developmental governance in East Asia and elsewhere.

During the interviews, talking about 'the state' quickly led to discussions about economic policy, and in this regard, most interviewees in both countries distinguished – sometimes implicitly – two extreme forms: command, or planned economy, which they associated with socialism; and competition-oriented market economy, which was associated with capitalism. Virtually all interviewees agreed that 'pure' capitalism does not fit Africa, and that socialism was outdated, even though it was considered better by some. The developmental state model was usually seen as some kind of a third way in between, combining significant state control of the economy with partial competition and market forces. In a similar vein, Meles Zenawi wrote that "state direction has been much more intrusive and comprehensive [in East Asia] than was the case in Europe"[54] and contrasted the "theory of the developmental state" with the "neoliberal paradigm".[55]

Of course, African intellectuals and policy makers have paid attention to Asia's rise at least since the early 1980s. However, until the 1990s, financial support could mainly be obtained from the Western and Eastern blocs. Initially after the end of the Cold War, the rules of the game were determined by Western donors making democratization

53 Interview 43, 03.03.2014.

54 Meles: States and Markets, p. 165.

55 Ibid., p. 170.

and liberalization a condition for development money.[56] What has changed since then is that several Asian (and other 'developing') countries have emerged as financially strong development partners of African governments, resulting from the formers' consistently high rates of economic growth. Between 1990 and 2000, China's GDP grew by an annual average of 10.6 %; South Korea's GDP grew by 5.8 %. The East Asian region altogether grew by 8.5 % in that period, and continued to grow at comparable rates in the subsequent decade.[57] This has increased and restructured the range of donors from which African policy makers can choose,[58] and this process comprises more than the usual suspects, like IBSA (India, Brazil, South Africa) or the BRICS (Brazil, Russia, India, China, South Africa).

With the ability and willingness of China and South Korea, the Ethiopian state has been able to implement its vision of a developmental state, challenging (neo-)liberal and socialist development orthodoxies in the process. While the Ghanaian state has maintained closer relations with Western donors, enthusiasm for Asian partners and state models has gained substantial ground there as well. Whether this will translate into a restructuring of the Ghanaian state and increase cooperation with Asian partners even more remains to be seen. The classification of Ghana as a lower middle income country has already made it more difficult for it to secure financial support from the IMF and the World Bank,[59] making a strengthening of the ties with

56 Leonardo A. Villalón: The African State at the End of the Twentieth Century: Parameters of the Critical Juncture. In: Id. / Phillip A. Huxtable (eds): *The African State at a Critical Juncture: Between Disintegration and Reconfiguration.* Boulder / London: Lynne Rienner 1998, pp. 3–25.

57 Manmohan Agarwal: South-South Economic Cooperation for a Better Future. In: Sachin Chaturvedi / Thomas Fues / Elizabeth Sidiropoulos (eds): *Development Cooperation and Emerging Powers: New Partners or Old Patterns?* London: Zed 2012, pp. 37–63, here p. 39.

58 Philippe Hugon: Cooperation: New Players in Africa. In: *International Development Policy* 1 (2010), pp. 95–113. http://poldev.revues.org/138 (accessed 19.11.2014); Dana D. La Fontaine: *Neue Dynamiken in der Süd-Süd-Kooperation: Indien, Brasilien und Südafrika als Emerging Donors.* Wiesbaden: Springer VS 2013, pp. 25–26; Sachin Chaturvedi / Thomas Fues / Elizabeth Sidiropoulos: Introduction. In: Id. (eds): *Development Cooperation and Emerging Powers*, pp. 1–10.

59 Todd Moss / Stephanie Majerowicz: No Longer Poor: Ghana's New Income Status and Implications of Graduation from IDA. Center for Global Development: Working Paper 300, 2012. http://www.cgdev.org/files/1426321_file_Moss_Majerowicz_Ghana_FINAL.pdf (accessed 12.06.2014).

Asian actors rather likely. What seems relevant for Western donors in particular is that a majority of the interviewed Ghanaians and Ethiopians does not share the widespread assumption that democracy fosters development, the latter of which was usually understood as economic growth with widely shared benefits. On the contrary, democracy is often seen and experienced as a development obstacle. These concerns should be taken seriously by the donor community, and they should be met with respect.

Rebel against Colonial Ties

Chinweizu, Radical Interpreter of Black Condition and Liberation

Joanna Tegnerowicz

The scholar, critic and poet Chinweizu, born in 1943, is not a well-known thinker outside his native Nigeria, even though his book *The West and the Rest of Us: White Predators, Black Slavers and the African Elite*, originally published in 1975, has been compared by some authors to such famous and seminal works on colonialism and neocolonialism as Frantz Fanon's *The Wretched of the Earth* and Walter Rodney's *How Europe Underdeveloped Africa.*[1] Chinweizu has never attained such international renown as, say, the Cameroonian philosopher Achille Mbembe, the author of, among others, *On the Postcolony*.[2]

One is led to wonder why Chinweizu's thought remains so little known in the world. Several factors may play a role. Is it partly because of the general disregard of the West for Black African intellectual production, unless a Black African scholar has achieved a high status inside the Western academic world? This is the case with the famous African writer and Chinweizu's compatriot, Wole Soyinka, who taught at many internationally renowned universities of the Western world.[3] It also applies to Achille Mbembe, who taught,

1 Chinweizu: *The West and the Rest of Us: White Predators, Black Slavers and the African Elite.* Lagos: Pero 1987; Frantz Fanon: *The Wretched of the Earth*, transl. from the French by Richard Philcox. New York: Grove 2004; Walter Rodney: *How Europe Underdeveloped Africa.* Abuja: Panaf 2009.

2 Achille Mbembe: *On the Postcolony*. Berkeley: University of California Press 2001.

3 See the entry on Wole Soyinka in: *The Oxford Companion to Modern Poetry in English*, ed. by Ian Hamilton / Jeremy Noel-Todd. Oxford: Oxford UP 2013, p. 582.

among others, at Columbia and Yale Universities, or to the Congolese scholar and writer V.Y. Mudimbe, the author of the very influential *The Invention of Africa*,[4] who taught, among others, at Stanford and Duke Universities. In contrast, Chinweizu is definitely not part of this world, the world of the most prestigious Western universities; he belongs to the Nigerian intellectual world. He publishes articles in Nigerian newspapers and on Nigerian websites, and last year he was honoured with a Lifetime Achievement Award by the large Nigerian multi-media company Silverbird.[5]

It is also tempting to suspect that Chinweizu's fiercely radical Afrocentric views and his crushing and virulent critique of the white world are somehow unpalatable for many Western intellectuals. Leading and highly significant American Afrocentric intellectuals such as Leonard Jeffries, Molefi Kete Asante and Frances Cress Welsing are highly controversial figures and have never been embraced by the US white-dominated liberal establishment which heavily influences the liberal public opinion in the rest of the Western world. According to Cedric J. Robinson, *The West and the Rest of Us* "received almost no notice or reviews"[6] when it was first published by the internationally renowned Random House, and one may wonder if it was at least partly due to Chinweizu's Afrocentric views.

One should also remember the immense popularity of postmodern approaches and postmodern academic jargon in today's Western academic world; Chinweizu is so unenthusiastic about postmodern thought and language that he has even devoted a satirical poem to "Professor Derrida Eshu" who pompously declares "If you, or just anybody can understand it, / It isn't a poem at all".[7] This wholly

4 V.Y. Mudimbe: *The Invention of Africa: Gnosis, Philosophy, and the Order of Knowledge*. Bloomington: Indiana UP 1988.

5 See the post by Hakeem Bello, dated 04.03.2014. http://www.lagosstate.gov.ng/news2.php?k=3315 (accessed 16.02.2015).

6 Cedric J. Robinson: *Black Marxism: The Making of the Black Radical Tradition*. Chapel Hill: University of North Carolina Press 2000, p. xxiv, fn. 10.

7 Quoted in R. Victoria Arana: Professor Derrida Eshu. In: *The Facts on File Companion to World Poetry, 1900 to Present*. New York: Facts on File 2008, p. 365. Eshu is one of the most important Yoruba deities. Ulli Beier, a scholar very familiar with Yoruba mythology, describes him in these words: "He appears as the divine trickster in Yoruba mythology; his delight is 'to turn right into wrong; wrong into right'. He revels in the absurd: 'he hits a stone until it bleeds' or 'he sits on the skin of an ant'" (Ulli Beier: *Yoruba Myths*. Cambridge: Cambridge UP 1980, p. 82).

irreverent and even sarcastic attitude towards postmodernism and its founding fathers might, too, have an impact on the reception of Chinweizu's works in Western academia.

In the eyes of those who have fully embraced the Western liberal interpretation of the world, this thinker is highly likely to appear as completely unpalatable, perhaps even shockingly so. In a lecture held in Lagos in 2006, Chinweizu denounced AIDS as the "New World Order bioweapon for global genocide" and claimed that the virus had been invented by the American government "for the declared purpose of global depopulation".[8] According to him, the World Health Organization vaccinated 97 million Africans with smallpox vaccines which had been deliberately infected with the HIV virus. Obviously this view goes completely against the opinion embraced by the mainstream academic establishment and many would dismiss it as a "conspiracy theory". It is, however, undeniable that the Polish-American scientist Hilary Koprowski, whose polio vaccine trials in the Belgian Congo are often linked with the emergence of AIDS by those who question the mainstream view on the genesis of this disease, was highly unethical in his approach,[9] and it cannot be ruled out that infected monkey kidneys were used to produce Koprowski's polio vaccine tested on Congolese children in the 1950s.[10]

Chinweizu is certainly not the only eminent African intellectual convinced that the West or the Global North is pursuing a hidden agenda which aims to reduce Africa's population: another too little known African intellectual, the late Cameroonian sociologist, philosopher and theologian Jean-Marc Ela (1936–2008), believed that the Global North is eagerly promoting the use of contraceptives in Africa in order to decrease African population, while at the same time trying hard to stimulate the birth rate in its own countries and worrying about the fate of its old people:

8 Chinweizu: Lugardism, UN Imperialism and the Prospect of African Power. A public lecture delivered at the Agip Recital Hall, Muson Centre, Onikan, Lagos, 18.02.2006. http://www.thepatrioticvanguard.com/lugardism-un-imperialism-and-the-prospect-of-african-power (accessed 16.02.2015).

9 David M. Oshinsky: *Polio: an American Story: The Crusade that Mobilized the Nation Against the 20th Century's Most Feared Disease.* Oxford: Oxford UP 2005, pp. 135–136.

10 Gareth Williams: *Paralysed with Fear: The Story of Polio.* Basingstoke: Palgrave 2013, pp. 258–259.

> Pendant qu'on s'interroge au Nord sur ce qu'il faut faire des vieux en même temps que les gouvernements s'efforcent de promouvoir des politiques natalistes en soutenant à grands frais la recherche de nouvelles technologies de reproduction, il faut larguer de millions de contraceptifs en Afrique pour diminuer la fécondité en vue d'endiguer l'explosion démographique du monde.[11]

> While the North is wondering what to do with its old people and its governments are trying to promote natalist policies, heavily investing in research on new reproduction technologies, millions of contraceptives have to be dumped to Africa in order to decrease fertility and thus stop the demographic explosion.

I.

There is another, probably much more widely known aspect of Chinweizu's thought which would be totally unacceptable to many liberal Western readers. In 1990, he published a treatise titled *Anatomy of Female Power: A Masculinist Dissection of Matriarchy*, a book where he advances the claim that women are not at all the oppressed sex, but, on the contrary, are able to control men and gain access to the latters' material resources. One can even read on the cover of the book that it is dedicated to "all men who have been confused, misused and abused by women, particularly since the coming of feminism" and that it is "definitely not for women".[12]

Chinweizu claims in this provocative book that women use, among others, men's desire to reproduce and strong sexual desire to manipulate them. He portrays the womb as the "female power's ultimate base":[13] in order to reproduce, a man has to access a woman's womb and, according to the Nigerian author, would be ready even to "conquer the whole world and lay it at a woman's feet."[14] At the same time, however, women's ability to manipulate and control men is not due only to natural differences: women can use access to sex as an instrument of ruthless control over men because as girls they are taught by their mothers to restrain their own libido and to narcissistically worship themselves. Interestingly, Chinweizu views clitoridectomy as an

11 Jean-Marc Ela / Marie-Sidonie Zoa: *Fécondité et migrations africaines: les nouveaux enjeux*. Paris: L'Harmattan 2006, p. 75, my translation.

12 Chinweizu: *Anatomy of Female Power: A Masculinist Dissection of Matriarchy*. Lagos: Pero 1990, front cover.

13 Ibid., p. 16.

14 Ibid., p. 18.

integral part of such process of social conditioning in some cultures: by reducing women's sexual excitability, it increases their sexual power over men. Boys, on the other hand, are taught by their mothers and other women to hunger for female kisses and caresses, and to believe that they should be self-sacrificing and heroic in order to conquer women's hearts.[15]

Chinweizu is merciless in his critique of feminism, but, importantly and interestingly, aware of its diversity. He reserves his kindest words for those feminists who are, as he puts it, "frustrated tomboys"[16] and mentions French pioneer feminist Simone de Beauvoir as an excellent example of such a "tomboy". In Chinweizu's opinion, the demands of such "tomboy feminism" for equal rights and opportunities with men are fully understandable, but he somewhat spitefully remarks that "tomboys" do not seem eager to "be drafted into infantry platoons or coal pits".[17] Despite this suggestion that such feminists are slightly hypocritical, the author of *Anatomy of Female Patriarchy* views the "tomboy" as the most desirable partner for the masculinist, the man who is not ready to surrender to female power, because "she is like a buddy with whom he could have sex and children"[18] and an ally (though only a partial one) in the masculinist's fight against the power of typical, calculating and manipulative women.

One of the founding mothers of liberal feminism, American journalist Betty Friedan, is portrayed by Chinweizu as an example of a wealthy "matriarchist", bored with her domestic paradise. As to the American radical feminist Andrea Dworkin, he views her as an example of a "termagant" – a woman who hates men and is ready to accept them only if they become "lobotomized robots and enervated poodles, all at her beck and call."[19] The "termagant's" hatred and contempt for men and their sexuality is so intense that "if she flirts and teases and leads an adolescent boy on, well beyond the limits of his self-control, and he rapes her, she would demand that he be hanged."[20] Many a reader used to the current mainstream Western

15 Ibid., pp. 30–34.

16 Ibid., p. 118.

17 Ibid., p. 128.

18 Ibid., p. 129.

19 Ibid., p. 120.

20 Ibid.

liberal discourse on the relations between men and women is likely to view this passage as a typical example of the patriarchal tendency to blame rape on women. Few, however, realize that, in her denunciation of all sexual violence against women, one of the most influential white American feminists, Susan Brownmiller, went so far as to portray Emmett Till – the 14-year-old Black boy who supposedly whistled at a white female shopkeeper, and was later tortured and murdered by the woman's husband and his half-brother – as a sexually aggressive male who insulted the white woman.[21] Brownmiller's book *Against Our Will: Men, Women and Rape*, where she writes about Emmett Till, was first published in 1975 and it is highly likely that Chinweizu has at least heard about her views, though – interestingly – he does not devote any attention to the demonization, bestialization and hyper-sexualization of Black men in his book on the dangers of matriarchy; it is probably at least partly due to the fact that he wrote this treatise with the Nigerian reader in mind, for *Anatomy of Female Power* was published by the Nigerian publisher Pero Press. Chinweizu's furious attack on "termagants" is, therefore, definitely not only a product of his own fears and anxieties but a polemical response to certain American discourses with hegemonic pretensions.

It should also be underscored that there are many African and Afro-descendant women who do not think fondly of white-dominated Western feminism. Chinweizu's compatriot, Osonye Tess Onwueme, mocks and denounces such feminism in her play *Tell it to Women: An Epic Drama for Women*.[22] The famous Ghanaian writer Ama Ata Aidoo believes that "Africa has produced a much more concrete tradition of women fighters than most other societies".[23] One of the best known African American critics of white-dominated feminism is the feminist bell hooks, and the African American writer Alice Walker even coined the term "womanist" to emphasize, among others, that Black feminists should be "committed to survival and wholeness of entire people, male and female".[24]

21 Susan Brownmiller: *Against Our Will: Men, Women and Rape*. New York: Fawcett 1993.

22 Osonye Tess Onwueme: *Tell it to Women: An Epic Drama for Women*. Detroit: Wayne State UP 1994.

23 Quoted in Ketu H. Katrak: *Politics of the Female Body: Postcolonial Women Writers of the Third World*. New Brunswick / London: Rutgers UP 2006, p. 17.

24 Alice Walker: *In Search of Our Mothers' Gardens: Womanist Prose*. Boston: Mariner 2003, p. xi.

Chinweizu's book on "matriarchy" should therefore not lightly be dismissed as a misogynist treatise. In a very provocative manner, he presents a vision of men, women and the relationships between them which completely contradicts the current dominant Western discourse. One may find many of his claims utterly unconvincing and unfair to women, but his whole analysis is undoubtedly refreshing and thought-provoking, and challenges the reader to question the orthodoxy of mainstream, white-dominated Western feminism.

II.

No less controversial was Chinweizu's ferocious attack on Wole Soyinka. In *What the Nobel Is Not*, an article published shortly after the latter was awarded the Nobel Prize in Literature, his much less famous compatriot denounced him in a derogatory manner. In an obvious allusion to postcolonial interpretations of Shakespeare's *The Tempest* which portray Ariel as the submissive servant of the colonial invader, Prospero, and in contrast to Caliban, the rebel against colonial rule and oppression, Chinweizu called Soyinka one of the "African Ariels". He denounced him as the Eliza Doolittle of the white Professor Higgins, and even as "Nigger Tom". Asking rhetorically and vitriolically, "Can one really expect a Nigger Tom to spurn a gift of laurels and bags of gold from the White Massa in the Big Baas house?"[25], he attacked Soyinka for what seemed to Chinweizu collaboration with the neo-colonial establishment.

Very significantly, Chinweizu alludes here to a famous speech by Malcolm X, the 1963 *Message to the Grass Roots*,[26] where the radical Black leader talked about "Uncle Tom" Blacks who were and are used by their white masters to control and contain other Black people. The Nigerian author quotes a part of the passage about "Tom" from this speech in his best known work, *The West and the Rest of Us*.[27] In his unforgiving attack on global white supremacy and oppression, both past and present, Chinweizu stands very close to Malcolm X. As to

25 Chinweizu: *Decolonising the African Mind*. Lagos: Pero 1987, p. 186.

26 Malcolm X: Message to the Grass Roots. In: Marcus D. Pohlmann (ed.): *African American Political Thought: Confrontation vs. Compromise, from 1945 to the Present*. London / New York: Taylor & Francis 2003, p. 125.

27 Chinweizu: *The West and the Rest of Us*, pp. 440–441.

Martin Luther King, fully embraced by white Western liberal opinion, the author of *The West and the Rest of Us* even views him as one of those Blacks who "had rendered a crucial service to Western hegemony by containing those insurrections by the oppressed which could have smashed Western power".[28] In fact, in *What the Nobel Is Not* Chinweizu makes it very clear that he thinks that all the Black Nobel Prize winners are, so to speak, Blacks who are in some way useful for the global white establishment. One may, of course, wonder if he changed his opinion after the African Caribbean poet Derek Walcott was awarded the Nobel Prize in Literature in 1992; or if he gave it a second thought after Nelson Mandela and the African American writer Toni Morrison – who was responsible for the publication of *The West and the Rest of Us* as an editor at Random House[29] – were respectively awarded the Peace Nobel Prize and the Nobel Prize in Literature in 1993. But to return to the attack on Soyinka, it is necessary to understand why Chinweizu once wrote about him with such blatant contempt and why he portrayed Soyinka as an "Uncle Tom" serving the interests of the white hegemony.

He even presents a list of accusations against his compatriot: first, he claims that Soyinka struck a harsh blow to the idea of *négritude*, the proud celebration of Blackness and Africanity associated mainly with the trio of seminal Black francophone writers: Aimé Césaire, Léopold Sédar Senghor and Léon-Gontran Damas. It is true that Soyinka is famous for his quip about the tiger who does not have to proclaim his "tigritude" and that he described *négritude* as an "inherently invalid doctrine" in his 1960 essay *The Future of West African Writing*,[30] but it was definitely not due to Soyinka's unwillingness to celebrate "the dignity of ancient Africa", as Chinweizu claims in his article. On the contrary, in the 1960 essay Soyinka portrayed Chinua Achebe as a more "African" writer than Senghor and added, "The less self-conscious the African is, and the more innately his individual qualities appear in his writing, the more seriously he will be taken as

28 Chinweizu: *Decolonising the African Mind*, p. 191.

29 Cf. Robinson: *Black Marxism*, p. xxiv, fn. 10; Doreatha Drummond Mbalia: *Toni Morrison's Developing Class Consciousness*. Cranbury: Rosemont 2004, pp. 167–168.

30 Quoted in Bernth Lindfors: The Early Writings of Wole Soyinka. In: James Gibbs (ed.): *Critical Perspectives on Wole Soyinka*. Washington, DC: Three Continents 1980, p. 43.

an artist of exciting dignity."[31] Chinweizu prefers, however, to see a blatant manifestation of Black self-hatred in Soyinka's poem *To My First White Hairs* because the Nobel-Prize winning poet compared his abundant hair to "hirsute hell chimney-spouts" and his head to a "scourbrush in bitumen".[32] Chinweizu also denounces Soyinka for propagating the "Euro-modernist" idea that poetry must be obscure, and for infecting African writers with the "Euro-Romantic" idea that writers have the right to feel superior to their readers and critics.

It seems that no other intellectual has attacked Soyinka as vehemently and contemptuously as Chinweizu. Timothy J. Reiss even described the latter's approach as "seemingly pathological demonization".[33] Of course, it is tempting to speculate why the author of *The West and the Rest of Us* felt so much anger towards Soyinka. Chinweizu, who himself published two collections of poetry in 1978 and in 1986[34] may have felt bitter because of Soyinka's fame. One should also take into account the possible influence of the ethnic divisions existing in Nigeria:[35] Soyinka is the most famous Yoruba writer and intellectual, whereas Chinweizu is Igbo.

It seems, however, that his merciless attack on Soyinka in *What the Nobel Is Not* was largely an act of revenge and personal bitterness. In fact, in *Pan-Africanism and the Nobel Prize*, an article published in 1985, before Soyinka was awarded the Nobel Prize, Chinweizu wrote about him with obvious sarcasm – but without the later furious contempt: "In my view, the Nobel prize and Soyinka's literary works deserve each other. It would have been an excellent example of the undesirable honouring the unreadable."[36] Then, he did not yet accuse Soyinka of being a self-hating Black man. In order to understand the change

31 Quoted in ibid.

32 Chinweizu: *Decolonising the African Mind*, p. 193.

33 Timothy J. Reiss: *Against Autonomy: Global Dialectics of Cultural Exchange*. Stanford: Stanford UP 2002, p. 448, fn. 18.

34 Chinweizu: *Energy Crisis and Other Poems*. New York / London / Lagos: NOK 1978; Chinweizu: *Invocations and Admonitions: 49 Poems and a Triptych of Parables*. Lagos: Pero 1986.

35 I am deeply grateful to Tunde Adeleke for his comments on the changing reception of Chinweizu in his native Nigeria, made at the Conference *African Thoughts and (Neo-)Colonial Worlds: Steps towards an Intellectual History of Africa*, Department of African Studies, Vienna, 07.11.2014.

36 Chinweizu: *Decolonising the African Mind*, p. 175.

in his attitude, it is necessary to know about an earlier venomous attack launched by Soyinka on Chinweizu. In his response to an essay published by another writer and a supporter of Chinweizu, Naiwu Osahon, Soyinka described Chinweizu as "a human incarnation of the bird Chichidodo" which "screams out loud its hatred of excrement but loves to feed on the worms that breed in it."[37] It should be added that the chichidodo metaphor earlier appeared in one of the most influential African novels, Ayi Kwei Armah's *The Beautyful Ones Are Not Yet Born* (1968)[38] showing the disillusion with post-colonial 'independence'.[39] In this context, the intensity of Chinweizu's anger is much easier to understand. Of course, this story is an excellent illustration of the importance of personal animosities for intellectual history. It should be added that Soyinka is not the only famous intellectual whom Chinweizu has accused of being an alienated African: one of the best known African historians, the Guinean Djibril Tamsir Niane (born in 1932), is presented as an "assiduous" propagandist for Arab imperialism in one of the articles from the collection *Decolonising the African Mind* called *Seasons of White Invaders.*[40]

III.

Chinweizu may easily appear as the enfant terrible among Nigerian intellectuals and probably seem unpalatable to many Western readers because of the polemic views he expressed in *Anatomy of Female Power*, his belief that the West created the HIV virus as a weapon of genocide against Black Africans, and his guess that the Nobel Prize is awarded only to those Blacks who in one way or another serve the interests of the global white hegemony, as well as because of his attitude towards Soyinka, one of the very few African authors who are admired by many in the West. It would be particularly easy to label and dismiss him as 'sexist' or 'anti-feminist', but it would only prove

37 Quoted in Bernth Lindfors: Beating the White Man at His Own Game: Nigerian Reactions to the 1986 Nobel Prize in Literature. In: James Gibbs / Bernth Lindfors (eds): *Research on Wole Soyinka.* Trenton, NJ: Africa World Press 1993, p. 344.

38 Ayi Kwei Armah: *The Beautyful Ones Are Not Yet Born: A Novel.* Boston: Houghton Mifflin 1968.

39 Lindfors: Beating White Man, p. 344. Interestingly, Lindfors does not mention the ferocity of Chinweizu's attack on Soyinka in *What the Nobel Is Not.*

40 Chinweizu: *Decolonising the African Mind*, p. 135; see also fn. 63.

the absurdity and dangers of labeling. One should remember that even Fanon has been crudely dismissed as "a hater of women" by the already mentioned Susan Brownmiller.[41] There might be something more and different to find in Chinweizu, perhaps even something to learn from. Such easy labeling may discourage some people from discovering and exploring the thought and works of those who have been negatively labeled by influential white Western intellectuals and other opinion leaders. It is of crucial importance to be able to look beyond the dogmas of the 'politically correct' Western liberal public opinion.

Chinweizu himself puts an enormous emphasis on the necessity to learn to think critically, to free one's mind from the damaging influence of educational institutions, to overcome the consequences of colonial "miseducation"[42]. With poignant sincerity and humility, he describes the process of his own intellectual liberation in the foreword to the African edition of *The West and the Rest of Us*:

> In my pain I began to suspect that my mind had been, over the years, held prisoner in a den where intellectual opiates were served me by official schools, by approved lists of books, by the blatant as well as subliminal propaganda of films, and by an overwhelming assortment of media controlled by interests inimical to, and justifiably scared of a true and thoroughgoing African nationalism.[43]

As he recalls, he realized that he had learnt to see the world in an imperialist way and to trust Western specialists and experts. This realization was the beginning of a painful process of unlearning much of what he had imbibed during his colonial "miseducation", and above all a process of getting rid of "negative attitudes towards things African"[44] and the resulting inferiority complex. In fact, Chinweizu presents himself as one of the victims of the alienating colonial conditioning which aims to perpetuate white control over Africa through teaching young Africans to despise their own culture, to be ashamed of African history – without being aware that they are learning not the real African history, but its white travesty which serves the

41 Brownmiller: *Against Our Will*, p. 250.

42 Chinweizu: *The West and the Rest of Us*, p. xii. The term used is most probably an allusion to Carter G. Woodson's seminal book *The Miseducation of the Negro*. Washington: Associated Publishers 1933.

43 Chinweizu: *The West and the Rest of Us*, p. xiii.

44 Ibid., p. xii.

interests of the West – and to associate the white world with civilization, rationality, humanism and universality.

According to Chinweizu, Christian religion was and continues to be a priceless instrument in this process of colonial conditioning. Colonial schools used various cunning methods to teach Africans to be uncritically submissive to whites: they "stuffed the heads of their victims with church devotional hymns, filled their psyches with submissive Christian attitudes, and undermined their attachment to the culture of their ancestors."[45] One may suspect that Chinweizu might have overestimated the power of Christian education. For instance, in Mongo Beti's novel *The Poor Christ of Bomba* (1956), the white Catholic priest becomes painfully aware of the futility of his efforts to truly Christianize rural Africans who stubbornly hold to their culture;[46] but it is necessary to emphasize that the Nigerian thinker believes that the most educated Africans are the most vulnerable to colonial lies, distortions and manipulations. They undergo a process of thorough "miseducation" and are made into "African Ariels"[47] whom the West cleverly uses to perpetuate its exploitation of Africa's resources.

One of the most interesting passages in *The West and the Rest of Us* is devoted to those Nigerian artists who escaped the alienating influence of universities: Chinweizu calls them "un-universitied" artists,[48] and mentions such examples of eminent artists as Nigerian writer Amos Tutuola, the author of the novel *The Palm-Wine Drinkard*,[49] and the painters Jimoh Buraimoh and Twins Seven-Seven alias Taiwo Oleniyi. Chinweizu's very negative view of university education recalls the words of one of the most famous Bob Marley's songs, *Babylon System*:

> Me say: de Babylon system is the vampire, falling empire,
> Suckin' the blood of the sufferers,
> Building church and university,
> Deceiving the people continually.
> Me say them graduatin' thieves and murderers;
> Look out now: they suckin' the blood of the sufferers.[50]

45 Chinweizu: *The West and the Rest of Us*, p. 76.

46 Mongo Beti: *Le pauvre Christ de Bomba*. Paris: Laffont 1956. English translation: *The Poor Christ of Bomba*. London: Heinemann 1971.

47 Chinweizu: *Decolonising the African Mind*, p. 2.

48 Chinweizu: *The West and the Rest of Us*, pp. 306–307.

49 Amos Tutuola: *The Palm-Wine Drinkard*. London: Faber & Faber 1952.

50 Bob Marley and the Wailers: Babylon System. On: *Survival*. Island Records 1979.

One is struck by a certain similarity between Chinweizu's theory of colonial and neocolonial exploitation and his (probably at least somewhat tongue-in-cheek) theory of the female exploitation of men: just like colonial educators condition their pupils, mothers condition boys to obey women and to crave their approval and affection; and this process of conditioning ensures women's continued access to men's material resources. Obviously it proves that he attached a great importance to psychological aspects of power and exploitation, and especially to the fact that the exploiters can induce the exploited to internalize values and attitudes which facilitate and perpetuate the exploitation. One of the distinctive features of Chinweizu's thought is his strong interest both in the economic and in the psychological aspects of colonialism and neocolonialism, as well as the way in which he links together these two kinds of aspects. Not only in this respect but in many others, his approach betrays an undeniable and strong affinity with the Fanonian one; unsurprisingly, the Nigerian thinker mentions Fanon, alongside Césaire, Malcolm X, Amilcar Cabral, Julius Nyerere, Hamidou Kane (the Senegalese writer), Mbonu Ojike (a Nigerian intellectual and politician), and the Chilean poet Pablo Neruda, as one of those who brought "a head-clearing gust of fresh, crisp air"[51] into his life when he became aware of the devastation caused in his mind by colonial "miseducation".

Those who do not see any reason to cleanse their minds from the effects of the alienating conditioning – the "African Ariels", those well-educated Africans who eagerly serve the interests of white supremacy – are those whom the author of *The West and the Rest of Us* largely blames for Africa's plight. He admits that no African is free from the "Ariel tendencies": "bits of Ariel and Caliban exist within each of us".[52] But he spares no harsh words for such alienated Africans as Kofi Busia, who became Prime Minister of Ghana after Kwame Nkrumah's overthrow in 1966, and Colonel Afrifa, who was one of the leaders of that coup d'état which overthrew Nkrumah and even published a book about the events, *The Ghana Coup*. Chinweizu comments with great sarcasm on some passages from that book,[53] as

51 Chinweizu: *The West and the Rest of Us*, p. xv.

52 Chinweizu: *Decolonising the African Mind*, p. 9.

53 Akwasi Amankwaa Afrifa: *The Ghana Coup, 24 February 1966*. London: Cass 1966.

well as on Busia's preface: he views these quotes from both Ghanaian politicians as blatant illustrations of their alienation. To take just one example, Afrifa claims in his book that the British military academy at Sandhurst gave him "independent thinking, tolerance, and a liberal outlook" and criticizes Nkrumah for paying "only lip-service to our [i. e., Ghana's] membership of the (British) Commonwealth of Nations" and for undermining "the bonds that bind us in this great union of people of all races, colours and creeds; an institution which is one of the surest hopes for the attainment of world peace which we all desire in this age."[54]

Chinweizu's devastating criticism of the alienated African elites bears a very strong affinity to the Fanonian criticism of the African bourgeoisie in *The Wretched of the Earth*. Fanon believes that this bourgeoisie "is not geared to production, invention, creation, or work"[55] and thus is only a caricature of its European equivalent – a "petty caste" which blindly imitates European models.[56] Fanon mentions, too, a "deeply cosmopolitan mentality"[57] as one of the features of African bourgeoisie, and mocks its fascination with Western luxury consumer goods and services such as "chromium-plated American cars" or "vacations on the French Riviera".[58] The Nigerian thinker, too, underscores that "African Ariels" are interested only in consumption and therefore useless and harmful to the economies of their countries. When speaking of the deeply alienated and parasitic elite, Chinweizu uses the Marxian term "petite bourgeoisie". In Chinweizu's view, the petit-bourgeois elite ruthlessly exploits the peasants, using the foreign exchange coming from the sale of export crops to fulfill its consumerist dreams. In consequence of this parasitic exploitation, African countries have become "poorfare states" because the stagnant productivity makes it increasingly difficult to satisfy the elite's consumerist appetite: the "poorfare state" is, as one can easily guess, the opposite of the welfare state existing in the West.[59]

54 Quoted in Chinweizu: *The West and the Rest of Us*, pp. 359–360.

55 Fanon: *The Wretched of the Earth*, p. 98.

56 Ibid., p. 119.

57 Ibid., p. 98.

58 Ibid., p. 120.

59 Chinweizu: *The West and the Rest of Us*, pp. 345–346.

It is worth paying particular attention to the fact that Chinweizu believes that this phenomenon of "poorfare states" explains the exploitation of ethnic divisions and loyalties in Africa: the "national cake" is not large enough, and the frenzied competition "for the little there is" opposes rival factions which may obviously be organized along ethnic lines. Of course, this explanation completely counters the very widespread Western myth of 'tribalism' – supposedly an eternal, very deeply-rooted, unchangeable and seemingly 'natural' feature of Black African societies. Terms like 'tribal massacres' continue to be very frequently used in the West – as it seems, only while speaking of Black Africa – reinforcing and perpetuating the racist image of Black Africans, supposedly reveling in 'tribal' slaughter since immemorial times.[60] The famous last paragraph of Chinua Achebe's novel *Things Fall Apart* (1956) marvelously reveals the absurdity and grotesqueness of such a vision of Africa: when the British Commissioner hears about Okonkwo's tragedy, he views it only as an interesting episode which he might include in a book on "The Pacification of the Primitive Tribes of the Lower Niger".[61]

In *The West and the Rest of Us*, Chinweizu shows in a compelling manner how the West is exploiting the greed of the African petit-bourgeois elites to intimidate leaders committed to the liberation of Africa. In consequence, even the Senghorian *négritude* paradoxically turned into "a handmaid of French imperialism".[62] Senegal's first Prime Minister Mamadou Dia, more radical than Senghor, supported popular participatory democracy, but was removed from power and imprisoned in 1962, and Senegal's political elites took an elitist approach to the

60 For a few recent examples of headlines and media content referring to 'tribal massacres' in Africa that stem from various Western country sources, cf. Hague Court Sentences Congolese Warlord to 12 Years for Role in Tribal Massacre. In: *The New York Times*, 23.05.2014. http://www.nytimes.com/2014/05/24/world/africa/hague-court-sentences-congolese-warlord-to-12-years.html; "massacres tribaux" in South Sudan. In: *La Croix*, 22.11.2014. http://www.la-croix.com/Actualite/Sport/JO-Un-athlete-appelle-aux-dons-pour-etre-le-1er-a-representer-le-Soudan-du-Sud-2014-11-22-1241296; the 2007–2008 post-election violence in Kenya was described as "tribal bloodshed". In: *The Telegraph*, 23.03.2013. http://www.telegraph.co.uk/news/worldnews/africaandindianocean/kenya/9952534/Kenya-Supreme-Court-orders-recount-at-22-polling-centres.html (all accessed 15.08.2015).

61 Chinua Achebe: *Things Fall Apart*. London: Heinemann 1971, p. 183.

62 Chinweizu: *The West and the Rest of Us*, p. 364.

issue of national development.[63] Mamadou Dia and Ben Mady Cissé, the director of *Animation Rurale*, the ambitious program of rural development, intended peasants – the majority of Senegalese population – to play an active and decisive way in this genuinely socialist program. France was fully aware of its dangers, and ready to exploit Senegal's economic dependence on the former colonial power. In fact, peanuts are this country's main export crop, and when France threatened to buy less of them and at lower prices, it meant a grave danger to the salaries of the Senegalese bureaucracy, hungry for Western cars and other imported consumer goods, and used to free government housing and other privileges – a typical petit bourgeois behavior. It was clear that France had no intention of tolerating "any pattern of development that would undermine the colonial economic relationship."[64] In consequence, Senghor felt forced to choose the neocolonial path of "maldevelopment"[65] financed from foreign aid and loans, and steered by technocrats. It is worth noting the striking similarity between the language used by Chinweizu and the English title of a very influential work on economic neocolonialism, *Maldevelopment: Anatomy of a Global Failure*, a book written by Egyptian political economist Samir Amin.[66]

Even though the second edition of *The West and the Rest of Us* was published in 1987, today, almost 30 years later, his analysis of the economic relationship between the former colonial powers and the former colonies in Africa remains to a large extent disturbingly valid. Africa is not as dependent on imported consumer goods as in the 1980s – to take a very recent example, in November 2014 the Nigerian company Innoson Vehicle Manufacturing Company Limited, hailed as the first indigenous car manufacturer in Nigeria, officially unveiled 500 newly-made cars,[67] but it seems that many former

63 Chinweizu: *The West and the Rest of Us*, pp. 364–379.

64 Ibid., p. 375.

65 This term is used by Chinweizu in his article "Cargo Cult Maldevelopment" (in *Decolonising the African Mind*, pp. 13–30) to argue that neo-colonial "development" has nothing to do with real development and only perpetuates the economic dependence of the Third World on the West.

66 Samir Amin: *Maldevelopment: Anatomy of a Global Failure*. Capetown: Pambazuka 2011. The French original is *La faillite du développement en Afrique et dans le Tiers Monde*. Paris: L'Harmattan 1989.

67 Chidi Nnadi: Innoson Rolls out 500 Made in Nigeria Cars Today. In: *The Sun: Voice of the Nation*, 29.11.2014. http://sunnewsonline.com/new/?p=93132 (accessed 19.02.2015).

colonies remain on the path of Chinweizian "maldevelopment" to a much larger extent than his native country.

In an article published in a recent issue of *Le Monde Diplomatique* and written by the Senegalese economist Sanou Mbaye,[68] one can read about an undeniably grotesque example of 'development' which serves the interests of the former colonial power. The *Agence Française de développement* lent Senegal 58 billion of CFA francs (88.5 million of euro) as part of its Emerging Senegal Plan (*Plan Sénégal émergent*). The loan was to be spent on constructing a highway section leading from Diamniadio (the place of the November summit of the International Organisation of La Francophonie) to the planned new Blaise-Diagne airport.[69] The construction contract was awarded without a tender to one of the largest French companies, Eiffage; and this company is going to profit for 30 years from the highway toll. Mbaye sums up the situation in these words: the Emerging Senegal Plan "lulls the Senegalese with dreams without any link with reality".[70]

Of course, this grotesque story would not in any way surprise Chinweizu. It fits very well with his general theory on the relationship between the West and Africa which he portrayed paradigmatically by reference to the 1966 coup d'état in Ghana. According to Chinweizu, Nkrumah was overthrown as a consequence of a "pro-western revolt by neocolonial agents and petit-bourgeois liberals."[71] As it was discussed earlier, Kofi Busia and Colonel Afrifa are portrayed in *The West and the Rest of Us* as completely alienated, "Europeanised" Africans,[72] and thus became eager and loyal servants of Western interests. The Nigerian thinker views Busia, Afrifa and all the other "African Ariels" as the modern, neocolonial equivalents of the "Black slavers" – those African rulers and elites who derived profits from the slave trade, showing in this way how blinded they were by selfishness and greed. He laconically sums up his idea in *Decolonising the African Mind*, where

68 Sanou Mbaye: L'Afrique francophone piégée par sa monnaie unique. In: *Le Monde Diplomatique*, November 2014, pp. 12–13.

69 Cf. Sabine Cessou: A Dakar, restaurants chics et bidonvilles poussent comme des champignons. In: *Le Monde Diplomatique*, November 2014, p. 12.

70 Mbaye: L'Afrique, p. 13, my translation.

71 Chinweizu: *The West and the Rest of Us*, p. 356.

72 Chinweizu: *Decolonizing the African Mind*, p. 3, presents Busia as a perfect example of an "Europeanised African".

he devotes a lot of attention to the much less known Islamic slave trade out of Africa: "These are today's equivalents of the old slaving elites who destroyed Africa while hunting slaves for sale to Arabs and Europeans."[73]

IV.

In conclusion, it is definitely worth paying some attention to Chinweizu's views on racism which are both original and refreshing. In a world where some researchers publish books where they claim that Blacks are supposedly intellectually inferior to whites,[74] it may well seem that it is vitally important to refute their claims. The Nigerian author believes, however, that such efforts will be fruitless as long as Black Africa is not powerful enough to force the rest of the world (and especially the West) to respect Blacks. It is Chinweizu's firm belief that whites always despise those whom they view as weak, and no amount of intellectual argumentation can make them admit that Black people are their equals. As he humourously explains, when racists claim that Africa has no art, it is not worth shouting: "Hey, white man! You lie! Here is an abundance of African artworks. Tip your hat to African creativity, African life force."[75]

Such efforts are doomed to failure because racists will immediately find other ways to 'prove' the inferiority of Black people. Chinweizu sarcastically wonders what will happen if the IQ tests used by racist researchers are proven to be worthless: "Will the monstrous accusation not rise once more, like an evil phoenix, from the ashes of the old charges, in a new form? Orgasmic quotients, perhaps?"[76] In his view, all attempts at refuting racist claims are, in reality, a waste of

73 Chinweizu: *Decolonizing the African Mind*, p. 3. In this connection see particularly his polemic with the eminent Guinean historian Djibril Tamsir Niane (Chinweizu: *Decolonising the African Mind*, pp. 109–135). Chinweizu (somewhat bafflingly) portrays Arabs as whites, so both Arabs and Europeans are in his eyes "white invaders". He states, for instance, that both Europeanised and Arabised African Ariels "believe in the intrinsic superiority of the white invaders of Africa" (*Decolonising the African Mind*, p. 3).

74 Many racist researchers are financially supported by the Pioneer Fund, established in 1937, cf. William H. Tucker: *The Funding of Scientific Racism: Wickliffe Draper and the Pioneer Fund.* Chicago: University of Illinois Press 2007.

75 Chinweizu: *The West and the Rest of Us*, p. 394.

76 Ibid.

time, an activity which distracts Africans from a far more important issue: the necessity to turn Africa into a powerful and respected continent. As he emphasizes, the Japanese came to be viewed as "honorary whites" in apartheid South Africa because of the impressive economic power of Japan.[77] One is tempted to add that the Japanese still seem to be perceived in this way by white Westerners, and it may be indeed largely due to the fact that Japan is one of the wealthiest countries on the planet.

To make his analysis of the real source of anti-Black racism as vivid and powerful as possible, Chinweizu even makes a very provocative suggestion to the "professional refuters" of claims made by racists: "Why not get out, abandon the whole enterprise and drop a nuclear bomb on Pretoria, South Africa?"[78] Though these words may shock some readers and are, of course, not to be taken seriously, they perfectly sum up his views on what is absolutely necessary to overcome the neo-colonial exploitation and oppression of Africa, mass poverty on the African continent, and global anti-Black racism: Africa must become powerful. And it will never become powerful if Africans do not liberate their mind from the damaging influence of colonial conditioning; if they do not put an end to what Bob Marley so aptly named "mental slavery" in his *Redemption Song*.[79] And to put an end to this kind of state of slavery, they have to learn to think critically and to realize that white culture is not in any way superior to African culture; that the former is even shockingly inhuman in many respects: "America's pets and dogs [...] eat much better than most of humanity",[80] as Chinweizu bitterly remarks.

Some scholars have been led to view Chinweizu as an "anti-white" intellectual and poet.[81] In my opinion, however, this is a severe misreading of Chinweizu, a basic misunderstanding of the disappointments and frustrations with blocked decolonization – on all levels: from politics to economics to mentality – which inform his work and might well be the roots for Chinweizu's fierce outbursts. Eventually,

77 Ibid., pp. 403–404.

78 Ibid., p. 394.

79 Bob Marley and the Wailers: Redemption Song. On: *Uprising*. Island Records 1980.

80 Chinweizu: *The West and the Rest of Us*, p. xx.

81 R. Victoria Arana: Chinweizu. In: *The Facts on File Companion to World Poetry*, p. 102.

he intends to wake up Africans and get them ready for liberation. To me it seems even more unfair to label the Nigerian thinker "anti-white" than to label him "sexist" or "misogynist" – for after all *The West and the Rest of Us* is dedicated not only to the victims of Western invasion and oppression and to "all Third World liberation fighters and martyrs", but also "to the people of the West, to the extent that they refuse to tolerate western control over the rest of us".[82] Chinweizu speaks to all of us.

82 Chinweizu: *The West and the Rest of Us*, p. v.

Which Way Africa?

Re-Reading George Padmore's *Pan-Africanism or Communism*

Arno Sonderegger

In 1956, George Padmore, one of the most inspiring African intellectuals of the time, published *Pan-Africanism or Communism? The Coming Struggle for Africa.* He dedicated this book "to the Youth of Africa – the Torchbearers of Pan Africanism".[1] Dying suddenly in 1959, while working in the newly independent Ghana as Kwame Nkrumah's advisor on African affairs,[2] this was to be his last book. Padmore was a prolific writer, publishing 10 books between 1931 and 1956 and thousands of journalistic articles.[3] He was a Trinidadian

1 George Padmore: *Pan-Africanism or Communism? The Coming Struggle for Africa.* London: Dobson 1956, p. iv. The second edition omitted both subheading and question mark. By the early 1970s, then, that conflict was neither considered on the verge nor in question; cf. *Pan-Africanism or Communism.* Garden City, NY: Anchor Books, Doubleday 1972, p. v. Henceforth I refer to the second edition.

2 On Padmore's Ghana connection, see C. L. R. [Cyril Lionel Robert] James: *Nkrumah and the Ghana Revolution.* London: Allison & Busby 1982 [1977]; Leslie James: *George Padmore and Decolonization from Below: Pan-Africanism, the Cold War, and the End of Empire.* Basingstoke: Palgrave Macmillan 2015, pp. 164–190.

3 In course of the 1930s he published three books: George Padmore: *The Life and Struggles of Negro Toilers.* London: RILU 1931. https://www.marxists.org/archive/padmore/1931/negro-toilers/index.htm (accessed 30.01.2015); id.: *How Britain Rules Africa.* New York: Negro Universities Press 1969 [1936]; id.: *Africa and World Peace.* London: Cass 1972 [1937]. Leslie Elaine James: *"What we put in black and white": George Padmore and the Practice of Anti-Imperial Politics.* PhD-Thesis (LSE), London 2012, pp. 263–313, lists almost all of his contributions to journals appearing in British colonies. Besides, he wrote regularly for several American newspapers and for British papers too.

born in 1903 who, as a young man, studied in the US. There he joined the Communist Party and made a quick career that brought him to continental Europe in late 1929. He broke from the Party in 1933 (and was officially expulsed from it in 1934), but he carried on with his work as both an excellent "intellectual activist" and a gifted "political organiser".[4] In his journalism and writing, he

> was much more forensic and report-based, rather than theoretical. Padmore laboured to imprint the evidence that could serve as the basis for a sustained attack upon the hypocrisy of benevolent empire. He worked to make things concrete, understandable, and therefore attackable. Yet Padmore was also deeply engaged in political thought of his own, even if he derided the status of intellectualism.[5]

He settled permanently in London in 1935, and henceforth became the key figure of pan-African reorganization, building networks and associations to counter imperialism and colonialism as well as racism – not only on theoretical grounds but in very practical terms. There he mentored a bulk of young Africans who would soon come to prominence in the national movements then emerging in the colonies. His influence on Kwame Nkrumah and Jomo Kenyatta, for instance, was considerable.[6] With the end of World War II, Padmore intensified his anti-imperialist and pan-African efforts even more, organizing the first Pan-African Congress since 1927, that is, the Fifth Pan-African Congress held in Manchester in October 1945. Subsequently, he published several anti-colonial books in swift succession.[7]

4 The terms are used by Leslie James: *Decolonization from Below*, p. 10. On Padmore's early (Communist) organizational work, see Holger Weiss: *Framing a Radical African Atlantic: African American Agency, West African Intellectuals and the International Trade Union Committee of Negro Workers*. Leiden: Brill 2014.

5 James: *Decolonization from Below*, p.11.

6 On the relationship between Padmore and Nkrumah, see Arno Sonderegger: How the Empire Wrote Back: Notes on the Struggle of George Padmore and Kwame Nkrumah. In: Bea Lundt / Christoph Marx (eds): *Kwame Nkrumah (1909–1972) Today*. Stuttgart: Steiner 2015, forthcoming. Cf. Fitzroy Baptiste / Rupert Lewis (eds): *George Padmore: Pan-African Revolutionary*. Kingston / Miami: Randle 2009. On his pan-African work since the 1930s, see Susan D. Pennybacker: *From Scottsboro to Munich: Race and Political Culture in 1930s Britain*. Princeton / Oxford: Princeton UP 2009; Jonathan Derrick: *Africa's 'Agitators': Militant Anti-Colonialism in Africa and the West, 1918–1939*. London: Hurst 2008; James: *What we put in*; James R. Hooker: *Black Revolutionary: George Padmore's Path from Communism to Pan-Africanism*. New York: Praeger 1967.

7 Nancy Cunard / George Padmore: The White Man's Duty: An Analysis of the Colonial Question in Light of the Atlantic Charter [1943]. In: Maureen Moynagh

What follows is my re-reading of Padmore's final book *Pan-Africanism or Communism?*

The book is structured in five sections of uneven length. "Part One" considers the 19th century "back to Africa Movements", the history of "Liberia" and the birth of ideas of a "Black Nationhood". "Part Two" discusses the scramble for Africa and its impact, and then proceeds with a very critical polemic against Marcus Garvey, depicted negatively in terms of "Black Zionism or Garveyism". "Part Three" deals with what Padmore considered Pan-Africanism proper, recounting the Booker Washington vs. W. E. B. DuBois debate, the founding of the National Association for the Advancement of Colored People (NAACP, 1909), the Pan-African congresses, and highlighting the Manchester Congress of 1945 and Kwame Nkrumah's subsequent anticolonial Pan-African activities on the Gold Coast. The workings of the "Colonial Systems and Native Policies" since 1945 are at issue in "Part Four". The last section is by far the longest. "Part Five" looks first at Kenya and Nigeria in the late 1940s and early 1950s. They serve as case studies for multi-racial policies, constitutional development and tribalism. It is clear from the attention paid to the events of the preceding ten years that, in Padmore's view, the year 1945 marked a decisive point in time – important that is in what he sensed the coming struggle for Africa, inevitably resulting from the profound changes triggered by the end of the Second World War.

World War II signalled a decisive break in at least two respects. First, a new international order had been implemented, dominated by the US and structured by the logic of the Cold War. As Noam Chomsky put it recently, "At the end of the Second World War, the United States was absolutely at the peak of its power. It had half of the world's wealth and every one of its competitors [that is, the old empires of Britain and France, Germany and Japan, plus the USSR] was seriously

(ed.): *Essays on Race and Empire.* Ormskirk: Broadview 2002, pp. 127–177; George Padmore (ed.): *Voice of Coloured Labour.* Manchester: Panaf 1945; George Padmore, in collaboration with Dorothy Pizer: *How Russia Transformed Her Colonial Empire: A Challenge to the Imperialist Powers.* London: Dobson 1946; George Padmore (ed.): *Colonial and...Coloured Unity: A Programme of Action: History of the Pan-African Congress.* London: Hammersmith 1963 [1947]; id.: *Africa: Britain's Third Empire.* New York: Negro Universities Press 1969 [1949]; id.: *The Gold Coast Revolution: The Struggle of an African People from Slavery to Freedom.* London: Dobson 1953; id.: *Pan-Africanism or Communism? The Coming Struggle for Africa.* London: Dobson 1956.

damaged or destroyed. It had a position of unimaginable security and developed plans to essentially rule the world".[8] Part of the outcome was the extremist propaganda for 'anti-communism' and the global policies of 'containment', so characteristic of the Cold War logic implemented since 1947. This was the first breaking point. Secondly, the old empires were in a process of vanishing, colonial people were increasingly successful in their efforts to get rid of the colonial yoke. Decolonization in Asia had already begun, and Africans too were on the way "out of Empire" and in search of "redefining Africa's place in the world".[9] It was, however, altogether unclear what would be the ultimate outcome of such efforts. As Frederick Cooper reminds us, there was "the acute uncertainty of the post-war moment, in Europe as well as in Africa. […] the uncertainty of those times, when people realized the world was about to change but did not know in what direction it would move."[10]

George Padmore seems atypical in this respect, for he was indeed quite certain about what should be done. Padmore certainly knew what ideals he was going to realize, and he was well acquainted with the organizational and ideological means necessary for realization. He had much confidence in his abilities of social historical analysis, and therefore no objections to give directions and set out guidelines. According to Padmore's analysis, the post-war era changed everything. The global power system, as it used to be, was severely crashed. The cards in the play were about to be mixed anew. Now, Africans had to make a decisive choice – a radical ideological commitment, in order to achieve a life worth living. For Padmore that meant a life characterized by economic and political freedom, social equality and solidarity. In order to rejuvenate, realize the hopes for freedom and lead a good and self-determined life, Africa and Africans had to decide what path to take. The question, *Which Way Africa?*, became therefore

8 Noam Chomsky: *Power Systems: Conversations on Global Democratic Uprisings and the New Challenges to U.S. Empire: Interviews with David Barsamian.* New York: Metropolitan Books 2013, p. 56.

9 Frederick Cooper: *Out of Empire: Redefining Africa's Place in the World.* Göttingen: Vienna UP 2013, pp. 6–7. David Birmingham: *The Decolonization of Africa.* London: UCL Press 1995, gives a short but vivid account of the political decolonization processes in different regions of Africa, as does Frederick Cooper: *Africa since 1940: The Past of the Present.* Cambridge: Cambridge UP 2002.

10 Ibid., pp. 5–6.

paramount in Padmore's discussion of the relation between Pan-Africanism and its alternatives, especially so in his chapter "Communism and Black Nationalism" that takes up most of the final "Part Five" of the book.

The Options Not to Be Taken: Capitalism and Tribalism

Theoretically, there were four options available to commit to in the 1950s: 'Capitalism', 'Communism', 'Nation-state autonomy', and 'Pan-Africanism'. Practically, Padmore did not bother with the alternatives of nationalist and capitalist development for long. Concerning successful long-time perspectives of development, both were out of question. Given the colonial situation and its main mechanism of divide-and-rule exploiting ethnic and regional differences, any thought of a nation-state that would free its people seemed utterly unrealistic to Padmore. "Tribalism", as it came to be called back then, was to Padmore hardly different from what he frequently called "bourgeois nationalism", for both these '-isms' worked in the interests of the already powerful, against the interests of the many. So, Padmore recognized from the beginning the crucial dilemma of any notion of African nation-state, of what Basil Davidson would call, almost four decades later, "the curse of the nation-state" upon Africa[11] – rejecting it outright. He recognized, however, the importance of national movements in the colonies; their success in ending colonial rule in territories one by one, was considered an important strategic step on the way to freedom. But the political success of African national movements was, in Padmore's analysis, only a step in a greater game towards a grander goal, not an end in itself. I will return to this point below.

Capitalist development could not be regarded an option for social and political improvement either, due to one very basic reason. In a capitalist world system there are and must be, by systemic rule, both "haves" and "have-nots", there must exist centres and peripheries at the same time, oppressors and oppressed. "War" is at the root of capitalism, "capitalist anarchy", as Padmore called it in his book

11 Basil Davidson: *The Black Man's Burden: Africa and the Curse of the Nation-State.* London: Currey 1992.

Africa and World Peace in 1937.[12] Warning against the threat of renewed imperialism, as evident by Italy's occupation of Abyssinia, Japan's war against China, and Nazi-Germany's expansionist policies, Padmore had this to say,

> the fundamental problem of to-day, like yesterday, is still the Colonial Question. That is to say, a renewed struggle for a redivision of the world has once more become the main political objective of certain great Powers who are at present dissatisfied with the *status quo*.
> This problem, the quintessence of capitalism in its imperialist stage, influences more than any factor the issue of war or peace. […]
> World Imperialism can be divided into two main camps: 'The Haves', those who possess colonies, and the 'Have-Nots', those who seek to possess. The distinction, however, is not a new manifestation. It is merely a continuation of the pre-war relation of forces, and reflects the unequal development of capitalism.[13]

That is to say that, within capitalist world order, there are no peaceful means of changing a given position within the system's logic, at least none that could be applied by choice and free will of the system's underdogs, the colonized, exploited and oppressed. It may be sensed how Padmore's historically informed analysis of capitalism on a world scale, developed in the inter-war years, anticipates many ideas which today are more readily identified with writers like Fernand Braudel and Immanuel Wallerstein.[14] Recounting and largely following Lenin's argument that "Imperialism" is "the Highest Stage of Capitalism",[15] Padmore declared in the mid-1950s with full confidence that "Imperialism is a discredited system, completely rejected by Africans."[16] Imperialism, like fascism, was just another mask of capitalism. Therefore, it had to be rejected right away.

His stance on nationalism is more nuanced, as he saw some national awakening as a pre-requisite to the new internationalism he had in mind, but he recognized its immediate dangers. He warned against their inherent reactionary, egotistical and opportunistic character:

12 Padmore: *Africa and World Peace*, p. 6.

13 Ibid., pp. 3–4.

14 Fernand Braudel: *Die Dynamik des Kapitalismus*. Stuttgart: Klett-Cotta [3]1997 [1985]; Immanuel Wallerstein: *Historical Capitalism* [1983] *with Capitalist Civilization*. London / New York: Verso 2011.

15 Padmore: *Pan-Africanism*, pp. 269–283; see Vladimir Ilyich Lenin: Der Imperialismus als höchstes Stadium des Kapitalismus: Gemeinverständlicher Abriss. In: Id.: *Ausgewählte Werke*. Moscow: Progress 1987 [1916–1917], pp. 164–257.

16 Padmore: *Pan-Africanism*, p. xviii.

> It is the fashion among coloured students to be 'left'. But they are never so 'left' as to let themselves be left behind when politicians in office offer them jobs! In fact, most of them shed their Marxist garments on returning home and revert to what they have always been at heart – bourgeois nationalists. Some even degenerate into out-and-out tribalists [...]. With these professional Africans, it is largely a case of being 'revolutionary' at twenty, moderate at thirty, conservative at forty, and reactionary at fifty.[17]

Nationalism then was a double-edged sword. If seen as an end in itself, nationalism would of necessity lead either to the strengthening of capitalism and imperialism or to tribalist chauvinism. In either case, it would lead to the rule of a few against the interests of the many. Therefore, Padmore could not allow for seeing nationalism as an end in it, but only as a means to prepare the ground for a future internationalism. This was in line with the strategy for "world revolution" proposed by Lenin during World War One:

> Having come to the conclusion that bourgeois nationalism constitutes a revolutionary reserve that could be turned to their advantage, the Bolsheviks went all out to arouse revolt among the coloured races of the Orient. When, therefore, the Third (Communist) International, popularly known as the Comintern, was established [in 1919], it became incumbent upon all newly-formed Communist parties in the Western world which sought affiliation to it, to accept the Leninist programme on the National and Colonial Question.[18]

While the Soviet-led Communists changed directions repeatedly and finally dissolved the Comintern altogether in 1943, Padmore himself adhered to this programme of national self-awakening and self-determination first, realization of socialist ideals second, all his life. It is quite clear then that according to Padmore, there must be a fundamental break from the bourgeois capitalist system. And this brings us to the two options he discussed in his last book as the sole alternatives to be taken seriously. Which way then Africa? – Pan-Africanism, or Communism?

17 Ibid., p. 307.

18 Ibid., p. 281. Cf. Vladimir Ilyich Lenin: *Critical Remarks on the National Question* [1913]. *The Right of Nations to Self-Determination* [1914]. Moscow: Progress 1974 [1951].

Communism, Social Democracy and Pan-Africanism

His answer was unconditionally 'yes' to Pan-Africanism, and a qualified 'no' to Communism. In *Pan-Africanism or Communism*, he argued elaborately against Communism as a suitable way for Africa. As he was a professing Marxist, this may seem a strange attitude. But, in fact, it was not strange at all, given his undogmatic understanding of Marxism and his distinctive historical-mindedness, for "Pan-Africanism recognizes much that is true in the Marxist interpretation of history, since it provides a rational explanation for a good deal that would otherwise be unintelligible."[19] What then was his stance on Communism, and what were his reasons for refusing it? – In 1956, he described himself "a socialist and democrat".[20] This self-image refers to a certain set of ideas and attitudes which are revered: self-government and self-determination, solidarity and co-operation, individual liberty and collective freedom, equality of chances, and rights to a decent living. This self-description might surprise at the first glance, for it is well known that he had been a high cadre among the Communists until his break with the Party in 1933/34.[21] Since then he never repudiated his firm trust in Marxist social historical analysis. Having worked within Communist organizations, and persistent in his Marxism, Padmore's critique of Communism is by no means coming from an unsympathetic angle, and therefore it is even more severe and, anyway, much more trustworthy than those of stern anti-communists. Although to the point, his critique stems from his own first-hand experience and personal disillusionment with, what I would call, the imperialism of the USSR.

With regard to the Soviet party line and its satellites, he wrote of "doctrinaire Communism"[22] preaching "some myopic pseudo-Marxist doctrinaire policy"[23], and asserted that "Dogmatism is the disease of parvenu-Communists."[24] This was one of the reasons for his rejection of Communism. He "refuses to accept the pretentious claims

19 Padmore: *Pan-Africanism*, p. xvi.

20 Ibid., p. 348.

21 Hooker: *Black Revolutionary*, pp. 27–29, 32–33; James: *What we put in*; James: *Decolonization from Below*; Derrick: *Africa's Agitators*; Pennybacker: *From Scottsboro to Munich*.

22 Padmore: *Pan-Africanism*, p. 317.

23 Ibid., p. xvi.

24 Ibid., pp. 322–323.

of doctrinaire Communism, that it alone has the solution to all the complex racial, tribal, and socio-economic problems facing Africa."[25] A second reason was what he called at one point very concisely "the Communist intolerance of those who do not subscribe to its ever-changing party line even to the point of liquidating them […]. Democracy and brotherhood cannot be built upon intolerance and violence."[26] In reviewing the history of anti-colonial struggles all over Africa, he showed time and again how untrustworthy allies Communists proved to be in matters of self-determination.[27] This was due to the fact that Communists were pawns of Soviet foreign policy which was ever changing according to Russia's national interests.

Such an attitude was never to his taste. Moreover, he reported the history of unsuccessful attempts of Communist infiltration into African anti-colonial circles in order to counter the anti-communist propaganda by the capitalists-colonialists. He emphasized that there is no communist threat in Africa, amongst Africans: "At the moment none of the African independence movements is influenced by Communism."[28]

> Again I repeat, Communism is no immediate threat to Africa. […] What the majority of Africans know about Communism is what their imperialist rulers have told them on the red bogey. Even the handful of West African intellectuals claiming to be Communists are of a kind that orthodox Marxists would find it difficult to recognize as true disciples of Marx, Lenin and Stalin. The term 'Communist' is just a term of abuse, used loosely by Europeans and reactionary Black politicians to smear militant nationalists whose views they dislike. There is hardly a colonial leader worth his salt who at some time or another has not been branded a 'dangerous Communist agitator'. […] As long as the African leaders remain true to the people, they have nothing to fear but fear. Destiny is in their own hands.[29]

To talk of a Communist threat to Africa was, therefore, humbug. It was not grounded in African realities at the time:

> For if there is one thing which events in Africa, no less than in Asia, have demonstrated in the post-war years, it is that colonial peoples are resentful of the attitude of Europeans, of both Communist and anti-Communist persuasion,

25 Ibid., p. xvi.
26 Ibid.
27 Ibid., pp. 310–340.
28 Ibid., p. xiii.
29 Ibid., p. 355.

> that they alone possess the knowledge and experience necessary to guide the advancement of dependent peoples.[30]

However, under conditions of the Cold War, there was Communist as well as Western propaganda to deal with in Africa. His book, published amidst the Western world and appealing to an international audience, was very conscious of this fact. Navigating his own Pan-African agenda, Padmore told his Western readers that "Africans only lend ear to Communist propaganda when they feel betrayed and frustrated".[31]

> If the Western Powers are really afraid of Communism and want to defeat it, the remedy lies in their own hands. First, it is necessary to keep one step ahead of the Communists by removing the grievances of the so-called backward peoples, which the Communists everywhere seek to exploit for their own ends. Secondly, there must be a revolutionary change in the outlook of the colonizing Powers, who must be prepared to fix a date for the complete transfer of power […] and to give every technical and administrative assistance to the emerging colonial nations during the period of transition from internal self-government to complete self-determination.[32]

In short, then, his way of achieving African independence pursued two rationales. First, ending or, at least, diminishing imperialism as represented not only by the old empires but also by US capitalism; secondly, containing Communism *à la* Soviet model because it is not adequate to local needs. Ways of development cannot be exported from one place to another, but have to be realized by the people themselves. This was an insight very dear to Padmore: "Development plans cannot be drawn up *in vacuo*, but must reflect the concrete situation and needs in each territory – and Africa is a vast continent"; therefore one "shall not attempt to sketch any economic and social blue prints".[33]

Padmore made a substantial argument for concreteness and flexibility, quoting Mao Tse-tung approvingly: "[D]ogmas are more useless than cow dung. Dung can be used as fertilizer."[34] Sowing seeds, planting roots, weeding and watering; in a word, cultivating the soil carefully,

30 Padmore: *Pan-Africanism*, p. xv.

31 Ibid., p. 317.

32 Ibid.

33 Ibid., p. 353.

34 Ibid., p. 323.

struggling permanently with given conditions and thereby, changing them to the better – that's the way to secure rich harvest. This is what his ideas and practices are all about: the world is in the making, and it is made by us – by our deeds and thoughts. To him, the sole seminal option for Africa's improvement is Pan-Africanism. It is the one to be embraced wholeheartedly:

> In our struggle for national freedom, human dignity and social redemption, Pan-Africanism offers an ideological alternative to Communism on the one side and Tribalism on the other. It rejects both white racialism and black chauvinism. It stands for racial co-existence on the basis of absolute equality and respect for human personality.
> Pan-Africanism looks above the narrow confines of class, race, tribe and religion. In other words, it wants equal opportunity for all. Talent to be rewarded on the basis of merit. Its vision stretches beyond the limited frontiers of the nation-state. Its perspective embraces the federation of regional self-governing countries and their ultimate amalgamation into a *United States of Africa.*[35]

Conclusion

As everyone knows, the options taken by most African countries since the times of independence were those ruled out by Padmore on principle. The ways of the narrow 'nation-state' model and 'development' along capitalist lines, i. e. according to the given international *neo-colonial* rules, were the routes actually taken by most leading figures of independence and after. There are, of course, comprehensible reasons for this lack in breaking down the chains of dependency, but I do not want to go into them now. Instead I would like to propose an answer as to why Padmore was able to see so clearly in the mid-20th century that those paths ultimately chosen were no seminal options at all. – It was first and foremost his critical understanding of capitalism, imperialism and colonialism on the one hand, of nationalism and racism on the other hand. That allowed him develop a proper reasonable perspective. He could rightly interpret on-going developments with great perspective because of the quality of his social historical analysis. It was based on broad knowledge and wide networks of informants and friends, and rooted in his firm belief in men's duty to make the world a better place for everyone. His unrelenting practical work of bringing solidarity to life, both by networking and

35 Ibid., pp. 355–356.

publishing, prove Padmore a paradigm of an 'engaged intellectual'. He was critical to the bones *and* deeply human. Padmore has a lot of historical insight to offer. If we are to read him again, we will discover that he speaks to us with a voice still strong. The question which Padmore advanced in his last book in 1956 is one of perpetual importance, *Which Way Africa?* And his analysis sounds still fresh, original and well-founded.

Bibliography

Abafita, Jemal / Fikadu Mitiku / Kim Kyung Ryang: Korea's Saemaul Undong (New Village Movement): A Model for Rural Development in Ethiopia? In: *Journal of the Korean Society of International Agriculture* 25,3 (2013), pp. 217–230.

Abbink, Jon: Ethnicity and Conflict Generation in Ethiopia: Some Problems and Prospects of Ethno-Regional Federalism. In: *Journal of Contemporary African Studies* 24,3 (2006), pp. 389–413.

Abram, Morris: *The Day is Short: An Autobiography.* New York: Harcourt, Bruce, Jovanovich 1982.

Achebe, Chinua: *Things Fall Apart.* London: Heinemann 1971.

Adem, Seifudein: Is Japan's Cultural Experience Relevant for Africa's Development? In: Id. (ed.): *Japan, a Model and a Partner: Views and Issues in African Development.* Leiden / Boston: Brill 2006, pp. 187–222.

Adorno, Theodor W.: *Negative Dialectics* [1966]. New York: Continuum 1983.

Adusei-Poku, Nana: The Multiplicity of Multiplicities – Post-Black Art and Its Intricacies. In: *Darkmatter Journal* 9,2 (2012): Post-Racial Imaginaries. http://www.darkmatter101.org/site/2012/11/29/the-multiplicity-of-multiplicities-%E2%80%93-post-black-art-and-its-intricacies/ (accessed 18.08.2015).

Agarwal, Manmohan: South-South Economic Cooperation for a Better Future. In: Sachin Chaturvedi / Thomas Fues / Elizabeth Sidiropoulos (eds): *Development Cooperation and Emerging Powers: New Partners or Old Patterns?* London: Zed Books 2012, pp. 37–63.

Alemayehu Geda: The Political Economy of Growth in Ethiopia. In: Jean-Paul Azam / Robert H. Bates / Stephen A. O'Conell / Augustin K. Fosu / Jan Willem Gunning / Benno J. Ndulu / Dominique Nijinkeu (eds): *The Political Economy of Economic Growth in Africa, 1960–2000*, vol. 2: Country Case Studies. Cambridge: Cambridge UP 2008, pp. 116–142.

Altbach, Philipp (ed.): *Publishing and Development in the Third World.* London: Zell 1992.

Amin, Samir: *Unequal Development: An Essay on the Social Formations of Peripheral Capitalism.* New York: Monthly Review Press 1976 [1973].

—: *Maldevelopment: Anatomy of a Global Failure.* Cape Town / Dakar / Nairobi / Oxford: Pambazuka 2011.

Anderson, Perry: *Considerations on Western Marxism.* London: Verso 1979.

Appadurai, Arjun: Globale kulturelle Flüsse. In: Fernand Kreff / Eva-Maria Knoll / Andre Gingrich (eds): *Lexikon der Globalisierung.* Bielefeld: Transcript 2011, pp. 111–113.

Appiah, Kwame Anthony: *In My Father's House: Africa in the Philosophy of Culture.* Oxford: Oxford UP 1992.

—: *Lines of Descent: W. E. B. Du Bois and the Emergence of Identity.* Cambridge, MA / London: Harvard UP 2014.

Arana, R. Victoria: Chinweizu. In: *The Facts on File Companion to World Poetry, 1900 to Present.* New York: Facts on File 2008, pp. 102–103.

—: Professor Derrida Eshu. In: *The Facts on File Companion to World Poetry, 1900 to Present.* New York: Facts on File 2008, pp. 364–365.

Arnold, Millard (ed.): *Apartheid: The International Legal Implications.* A Report of the November 1978 Conference on the International Legal Effects of South Africa's System of Apartheid. Washington, D.C.: Southern Africa Project 1979.

— (ed.): *Steve Biko: Black Consciousness in South Africa.* New York: Random House 1979.

Asante, Molefi Kete: Location Theory and African Aesthetics. In: Kariamu Welsh-Asante (ed.): *The African Aesthetic: Keeper of the Traditions.* Westport, CT / London: Greenwood 1993, pp. 53–62.

Atieno-Odhiambo, Elisha Stephen: The Production of History in Kenya: the Mau Mau Debate. In: *Canadian Journal of African Studies* 25,2 (1991), pp. 300–307.

Atieno-Odhiambo, Elisha Stephen / John Lonsdale (eds): *Mau Mau & Nationhood: Arms, Authority & Narration.* Athens: Ohio State UP 2003.

Badie, Bertrand: *L'Etat importé: Essai sur l'occidentalisation de l'ordre politique.* Paris: Fayard 1992.

Baptiste, Fitzroy / Rupert Lewis (eds): *George Padmore: Pan-African Revolutionary.* Kingston / Miami: Randle 2009.

Bassong, Mbog Mbombog: *La Méthode de la Philosophie Africaine.* Paris: L'Harmattan 2007.

—: *Esthétique de l'Art Africain.* Paris: L'Harmattan 2007.

Bavaj, Riccardo: Intellectual History, Version: 1.0. In: *Docupedia-Zeitgeschichte*, 13.09.2010, pp. 1–19. http://docupedia.de/zg/Intellectual_History (accessed 13.02.2015).

Bayart, Jean-François: *L'État au Cameroun.* Paris: Presses de la Fondation nationale des sciences politiques 1979.

—: *Les études postcoloniales: un carnaval académique.* Paris: Karthala 2010.

Beier, Ulli: *Yoruba Myths.* Cambridge: Cambridge UP 1980.

Beresford, David: David Soggot Obituary: Civil Rights Lawyer Connected with Several of South Africa's Most Famous Cases. In: *The Guardian*, 27.06.2010. http://www.theguardian.com/world/2010/jun/27/david-soggot-obituary (accessed 30.10.2013).

Berlinerblau, Jaques: *Heresy in the University: The Black Athena Controversy and the Responsibilities of American Intellectuals.* New Brunswick: Rutgers UP 1999.

Berman, Bruce: Ethnography as Politics, Politics as Ethnography: Kenyatta, Malinowski, and the Making of Facing Mount Kenya. In: *Canadian Journal of African Studies* 30,3 (1996), pp. 313–344.

Berman, Bruce / John M. Lonsdale: *Unhappy Valley: Conflict in Kenya & Africa.* Athens: Ohio UP 1992.

—: The Labors of Muigwuithania: Jomo Kenyatta as Author, 1928–45. In: *Research in African Literatures* 29,1 (1998), pp. 16–42.

—: Custom, Modernity, and the Search for Kihooto: Kenyatta, Malinowski, and the Making of Facing Mount Kenya. In: Robert J. Gordon / H. Tilley (eds): *Anthropology, European Imperialism and the Ordering of Africa.* Manchester: Manchester UP 2007, pp. 173–198.

Bernal, Martin: *Black Athena: The Afroasiatic Roots of Classical Civilization.* New Brunswick: Rutgers UP 1987.

Bertoncini-Zúbková, Elena / Mikhail D. Gromov / Said A.M. Khamis / Kyallo W. Wamitila: *Outline of Swahili Literature. Prose Fiction and Drama.* Leiden / Boston: Brill 2009.

Bewaji, John Ayotunde Isola: *Beauty and Culture: Perspectives in Black Aesthetics: An Introduction to African and African Diaspora Philosophy of Art.* Ibadan: Spectrum 2003.

— : *Black Aesthetics: Beauty and Culture: An Introduction to African and African Diaspora Philosophy of Arts.* Trenton, NJ: Africa Research and Publications 2013.

Bgoya, Walter: Introduction – Scholarly Publishing: An Overview. In: Alois Mlambo (ed.): *African Scholarly Publishing: Essays.* Oxford: African Books Collective 2006, pp. 1–11.

Biko, Steve: *I Write What I Like: Steve Biko, a Selection of his Writings*, ed. by Aelred Stubbs. London: Heinemann 1987.

Birmingham, David: *The Decolonization of Africa.* London: UCL Press 1995.

Bizos, George: *No One to Blame: In Pursuit of Justice in South Africa.* Cape Town: Phillip 1998.

Blanchard, Pascale / Sandrine Lemaire (eds): *Culture Coloniale: La France conquise par son empire, 1871–1931.* Paris: Éditions Autrement 2003.

— (eds): *Culture Coloniale: Les colonies au cœur de la République, 1931–1961.* Paris: Éditions Autrement 2004.

Boahen, A. Adu: *African Perspectives on Colonialism.* Baltimore: Johns Hopkins UP 1987.

Brahm, Felix: 40 Jahre Vereinigung für Afrikawissenschaften in Deutschland (VAD), 1969–2009. VAD-Online-Paper 2009. http://www.vad-ev.de/fileadmin/user_upload/pdf/FelixBrahm-40JahreVAD.pdf (accessed 14.02.2015).

— : *Wissenschaft und Dekolonisation. Paradigmenwechsel und institutioneller Wandel in der akademischen Beschäftigung mit Afrika in Deutschland und Frankreich, 1930–1970.* Stuttgart: Steiner 2010.

Branigin, Bill: Chetty Quits South Africa: Prominent Civil Rights Activist Fears Ban on Law Practice, Seeks British Asylum. In: *The Washington Post*, 11.08.1979, p. A12.

Braudel, Fernand: *Die Dynamik des Kapitalismus.* Stuttgart: Klett-Cotta [3]1997 [1985].

Bräutigam, Deborah / Tang Xiaoyang: African Shenzhen: China's Special Economic Zones in Africa. In: *Journal of Modern African Studies* 49,1 (2011), pp. 27–54.

Broun, Kenneth S.: *Black Lawyers, White Courts.* Athens: Ohio UP 1999.

Brownmiller, Susan: *Against Our Will: Men, Women and Rape.* New York: Fawcett 1993.

Buijtenhuijs, Robert: *Mau Mau Twenty Years After: the Myth and the Survivors.* The Hague: Mouton 1973.

Burke, Peter: *What is Cultural History?* Cambridge / Malden: Polity 2008.

Casely Hayford, Joseph Ephraim: *Ethiopia Unbound: Studies in Race Emancipation.* London: Cass 1969 [1911].

Castells, Manuel: *The Information Age: Economy, Society and Culture*, vol. 1: The Rise of the Network Society. 2nd ed. Oxford: Wiley Blackwell 2010.

Césaire, Aimé: *Discourse on Colonialism.* New York: Monthly Review Press 2000 [1955].

Cessou, Sabine: A Dakar, restaurants chics et bidonvilles poussent comme des champignons. In: *Le Monde Diplomatique*, November 2014, pp. 12–13.

Chabal, Patrick: *Africa: The Politics of Suffering and Smiling*. London / New York: Zed Books 2009.

Chachage, Chachage Seithy L.: *Makuadi wa Soko Huria* ['The Pimps of the Free Market']. Dar es Salaam: E & D 2002.

Charle, Christophe: *La crise des sociétés impériales. Allemagne, France, Grande-Bretagne (1900–1945): Essai d'histoire sociale comparée*. Paris: Éditions du nouveau monde 2001.

Cheka, Cosmas: The State of the Process of Decentralisation in Cameroon. In: *Africa Development* XXXII,2 (2007), pp. 181–196.

Chinweizu: *The West and the Rest of Us: White Predators, Black Slavers and the African Elite*. Lagos: Pero 1987 [1975].

—: *Decolonising the African Mind*. Lagos: Pero 1987.

—: *Anatomy of Female Power: A Masculinist Dissection of Matriarchy*. Lagos: Pero 1990.

—: Lugardism, UN Imperialism and the prospect of African power. A public lecture delivered at the Agip Recital Hall, Muson Centre, Onikan, Lagos, 18.02.2006. http://www.thepatrioticvanguard.com/lugardism-un-imperialism-and-the-prospect-of-african-power (accessed 16.02.2015).

Chomsky, Noam: *Power Systems: Conversations on Global Democratic Uprisings and the New Challenges to U.S. Empire: Interviews with David Barsamian*. New York: Metropolitan Books / Henry Holt 2013.

Clapham, Christopher: Controlling Space in Ethiopia. In: Wendy James / Donald L. Donham / Eisei Kurimoto / Alessandro Triulzi (eds): *Remapping Ethiopia: Socialism & After*. Oxford: Currey 2002, pp. 9–30.

—: Post-War Ethiopia: The Trajectories of Crisis. In: *Review of African Political Economy* 36,120 (2009), pp. 181–192.

Clarke, J. Calvitt: *Alliance of the Colored Peoples: Ethiopia and Japan before World War II*. Rochester, NY: Currey 2011.

Clough, Marshall S.: *Fighting Two Sides: Kenyan Chiefs and Politicians, 1918–1940*. Niwott: UP of Colorado 1990.

Cocks, Paul: The Rhetoric of Science and the Critique of Imperialism in British Social Anthropology, c. 1870–1940. In: *History and Anthropology* 9,1 (1995), pp. 93–119.

Cooper, Frederick: *Africa since 1940: The Past of the Present*. Cambridge: Cambridge UP 2002.

—: *Colonialism in Question: Theory, Knowledge, History*. Berkeley / Los Angeles / London: University of California Press 2005.

—: Writing the History of Development. In: *The Journal of Modern European History* 8 (2010), pp. 5–23.

—: *Out of Empire: Redefining Africa's Place in the World*. Göttingen: Vienna UP 2013.

—: *Africa in the World: Capitalism, Empire, Nation-State*. Cambridge, MA: Harvard UP 2014.

—: Development, Modernization, and the Social Sciences in the Era of Decolonization: the Examples of British and French Africa. In: *Revue d'Histoire des Sciences Humaines* 10,1 (2014), pp. 9–38.

—: *Citizenship between Empire and Nation: Remaking France and French Africa, 1945–1960*. Princeton: Princeton UP 2014.

Cox, Kevin R. / Rohit Negi: The State and the Question of Development in Sub-Saharan Africa. In: *Review of African Political Economy* 37,123 (2010), pp. 71–85.

Culler, Jonathan: Structure of Ideology and Ideology of Structure. In: *New Literary History* 4,3 (1973), pp. 471–482.

Cunard, Nancy / George Padmore: The White Man's Duty: An Analysis of the Colonial Question in Light of the Atlantic Charter [1943]. In: Maureen Moynagh (ed.): *Essays on Race and Empire*. Ormskirk: Broadview 2002, pp. 127–177.

Davidson, Basil: *The Black Man's Burden: Africa and the Curse of the Nation-State*. Ibadan: Spectrum / London: Currey 2000 [1992].

Day, Richard J. F.: *Gramsci Is Dead: Anarchist Currents in the Newest Social Movements*. London: Pluto 2005.

Denning, Michael: Wageless Life. In: *New Left Review* 66 (2010), pp. 79–97.

Dereje Feyissa: The Ethnic Self and the National Other: Anywaa Identity Politics in Reference to the Ethiopian State System. In: Bahru Zewde (ed.): *Society, State, and Identity in African History*. Addis Ababa: Forum for Social Studies 2008, pp. 123–153.

Derrick, Jonathan: *Africa's 'Agitators': Militant Anti-Colonialism in Africa and the West, 1918–1939*. London: Hurst 2008.

Diegner, Lutz: *Die Ausweitung der Gesellschaftskritik in den swahilisprachigen Romanen von Euphrase Kezilahabi und Said Ahmed Mohamed* ['The Swahili Novel Beyond Criticizing Society: A Comparative Dialogical Reading of Euphrase Kezilahabi and Said Ahmed Mohamed'] Köln: Selbstverlag 2007.

—: The Kenyan Challenge (?): Dis/Continuities in Swahili Novel Writing 50 Years after Independence. In: Hannelore Vögele / Uta Reuster-Jahn / Raimund Kastenholz / Lutz Diegner (eds): *From the Tana River to Lake Chad: Research in African Oratures and Literatures. In memoriam Thomas Geider*. Köln: Köppe 2014, pp. 341–356.

Dimier, Véronique: Enjeux institutionnels autour d'une science politique des colonies en France et en Grande-Bretagne, 1930–1950. In: *Genèses* 37,1 (1999), pp. 70–92.

Diop, Cheikh Anta: *Nations nègres et culture: de l'Antiquité nègre égyptienne aux problèmes culturels de l'Afrique noire d'aujourd'hui*. Paris: Présence Africaine 1954.

Dissanayake, Ellen: *Home Aestheticus: Where Art Comes from and Why*. Washington: University of Washington Press 1995.

Doh, Emmanuel Fru: *Africa's Political Wastelands: The Bastardization of Cameroon*. Bamenda / Mankon: Langaa 2008.

Dorsch, Hauke: *Globale Griots: Performanz in der afrikanischen Diaspora*. Berlin / Münster / Wien / Zürich: Lit 2006.

Droz, Yvan: *Migrations Kikuyus: des pratiques sociales à l'imaginaire*. Paris: Editions MSH 1999.

—: L'Ethos du Mûramati Kikuyu: Schème migratoire, différenciation sociale et individualisation au Kenya. In: *Anthropos* 95,1 (2000), pp. 87–98.

Drummond Mbalia, Doreatha: *Toni Morrison's Developing Class Consciousness*. Cranbury: Rosemont 2004.

Eckert, Andreas: Wem gehört das Alte Ägypten? Die Geschichtsschreibung zu Afrika und das Werk Cheikh Anta Diops. In: Wolfgang Reinhard (ed.): *Die fundamentalistische Revolution: Partikularistische Bewegungen der Gegenwart und ihr Umgang mit der Geschichte*. Freiburg i. Brsg.: Rombach 1995, pp. 189–214.

—: Universitäten und die Politik des Exils. Afrikanische Studenten und antikoloniale Politik in Europa. 1900–1960. In: Rüdiger vom Bruch / Rainer C. Schwinges (eds): *Universitäten und Kolonialismus*. Stuttgart: Steiner 2004, pp. 129–145.

Eckert, Andreas / Ingeborg Grau / Arno Sonderegger (eds): *Afrika 1500–1900: Geschichte und Gesellschaft*. Vienna: Promedia 2010.

Efer, Thomas / Ninja Steinbach-Hüther: Quantitative Analyses in Global and Area Studies Using Graph-based Filtering of Heterogeneous Catalogue Data. In: Lars Grunske /Erhard Plöderer / Eric Schneider / Dominik Ull (eds): *Proceedings of INFORMATIK 2014*. Bonn: Gesellschaft für Informatik 2014, pp. 1027–1037.

Eko'o Akouafane, Jean Claude: *La décentralisation administratives au Cameroun*. Paris: L'Harmattan 2009.

Ela, Jean-Marc / Marie-Sidonie Zoa: *Fécondité et migrations africaines: les nouveaux enjeux*. Paris: L'Harmattan 2006.

Ellis, Stephen: *Season of Rains: Africa in the World*. London: Hurst 2011.

Engel, Ulf / Gorm Rye Olsen: Introduction: The African Exception: Conceptual Notes on Governance in Africa in the New Millennium. In: Iid. (eds): *The African Exception*. Aldershot: Ashgate 2005, pp. 1–13.

Eribon, Didier: *Michel Foucault (1926–1984)*. Paris: Flammarion 1989.

Eshete, Andreas: Modernity: Its Title to Uniqueness and its Advent in Ethiopia. In: *Northeast African Studies* 13,1 (2012), pp. 1–17.

Espagne, Michel: *Les transferts culturels Franco-Allemands*. Paris: PUF 1999.

—: Comparison and Transfer: A Question of Method. In: Matthias Middell / Lluis Roura i Aulinas (eds): *Transnational Challenges to National History Writing*. Basingstoke: Palgrave Macmillan 2013, pp. 36–53.

Falola, Toyin: African Historical Writing. In: Alex Schneider / Daniel Woolf (eds): *The Oxford History of Historical Writing*, vol. 5: Historical Writing since 1945. Oxford: Oxford UP 2011, pp. 399–421.

Fanon, Frantz: *Black Skin, White Masks*. New York: Grove 1967 [1952].

—: *The Wretched of the Earth*. New York: Grove 2004 [1961].

Fauvelle, François-Xavier: *L'Afrique de Cheikh Anta Diop: Histoire et idéologie*. Paris: Karthala 1996.

Fauvelle, François-Xavier / Jean-Pierre Chrétien / Claude-Hélène Perrot (eds): *Afrocentrismes: L'histoire des Africains entre Égypte et Amérique*. Paris: Karthala 2000.

Ferguson, James: Globalizing Africa? Observations from an Inconvenient Continent. In: Id.: *Global Shadows: Africa in the Neoliberal World Order*. Durham: Duke UP 2006, pp. 25–49.

Fonchingong, Tangie Nsoh: *Cameroon: The Stakes and Challenges of Governance and Development*. Bamenda / Mankon: Langaa 2009.

Fonjong, Lotsmart N.: *The Challenges of Nongovernmental Organisations in Anglophone Cameroon*. New York: Nova Science 2007.

Foucault, Michel: *L'ordre du discours*. Paris: Gallimard 1972.

—: *The Archaeology of Knowledge*. London / New York: Routledge 2002 [1969].

Frederiksen, Bodil F.: The Present Battle is the Brain Battle. Writing and Publishing a Kikuyu Newspaper in the Pre-Mau Mau Period in Kenya. In: Karin Barber (ed.): *Africa's Hidden Histories: Everyday Literacy and Making the Self*. Bloomington: Indiana UP 2006, pp. 278–313.

—: Jomo Kenyatta, Marie Bonaparte and Bronislaw Malinowski on Clitoridectomy and Female Sexuality. In: *History Workshop Journal* 65,1 (2008), pp. 23–48.

Fröbel, Folker / Jürgen Heinrichs / Otto Kreye: *The New International Division of Labour*. Cambridge: Cambridge UP 1980.

Garnier, Xavier: *Le roman Swahili. La notion de 'littérature mineure' à l'épreuve*. Paris: Karthala 2006.

Garretson, Peter: *A Victorian Gentleman and Ethiopian Nationalist: The Life and Times of Hakim Wärqenäh, Dr. Charles Martin*. Rochester, NY: Currey 2012.

Getachew Felleke: Education and Modernization: An Examination of the Experiences of Japan and Ethiopia. In: Seifudein Adem (ed.): *Japan, a Model and a Partner: Views and Issues in African Development*. Leiden / Boston: Brill 2006, pp. 67–104.

Gibbs, James / Jack Mapanje / Flora Rees (eds): *The African Writers' Handbook*. Oxford: African Books Collective 1999.

Gilroy, Paul: *The Black Atlantic: Modernity and Double Consciousness*. Cambridge, MA: Harvard UP 1993.

Gocking, Roger S.: *The History of Ghana*. Westport: Greenwood 2005.

Goody, Jack: *The Expansive Moment: The Rise of Social Anthropology in Britain and Africa 1918–1970*. Cambridge / New York / Melbourne: Cambridge UP 1995.

Graham, Mark / Scott Hale / Monica Stephens: Die Orte akademischen Wissens. In: Corinne M. Flick (ed.): *Eine Geographie des Wissens der Welt*. Oxford: Oxford Internet Institute, University of Oxford 2011, pp. 14–16. www.oii.ox.ac.uk/publications/convoco_geographies_de.pdf (accessed 20.02.2015).

Grassin, Antoine (ed.): La mobilité des étudiants d'Afrique sub-saharienne et du Maghreb. In: *Les notes du Campus France, Hors-série* 7, June 2013. http://www.campusfrance.org/sites/default/files/note_07_hs_Afrique.pdf (accessed 13.02.2015).

Gromov, Mikhail D.: Visions of the Future in the 'New' Swahili Novel: Hope in Desperation? In: *Tydskrif vir Letterkunde* 51,2 (2014), pp. 40–51.

Gros, Jean-Germain (ed.): *Cameroon: Politics and Society in Critical Perspective*. Lanham: UP of America 2003.

Harding, Leonhard / Brigitte Reinwald (eds): *Afrika – Mutter und Modell der europäischen Zivilisation? Die Rehabilitierung des schwarzen Kontinents durch Cheikh Anta Diop*. Berlin: Reimer 1990.

Hegel, Georg Wilhelm Friedrich: Introduction to the Philosophy of History, trans. from the German by John Sibree. In: *Great Books of the Western World*, ed. by Robert M. Hutchins. London: Encyclopedia Britannica 1952, pp. 151–201.

Hiwet, Addis: *Ethiopia: From Autocracy to Revolution*. London: Review of African Political Economy 1975.

Honke, Gudrun: Verlagswesen und Buchhandel. In: Jacob Mabe (ed.): *Das Afrika Lexikon: Ein Kontinent in 1000 Stichwörtern*. Stuttgart: Hammer 2004, pp. 674–676.

Hooker, James R.: *Black Revolutionary: George Padmore's Path from Communism to Pan-Africanism*. New York: Praeger 1967.

Hountondji, Paulin J.: *African Philosophy, Myth and Reality*. Bloomington / Indianapolis: Indiana UP 2002.

Hugon, Philippe: Cooperation: New Players in Africa. In: *International Development Policy* 1 (2010), pp. 95–113.

Hunt, Nancy Rose: The Affective, the Intellectual, and Gender History. In: *Journal of African History* 55,3 (2014), pp. 331–345.

Iggers, Georg C.: *Geschichtswissenschaft im 20. Jahrhundert: Ein kritischer Überblick im internationalen Zusammenhang*. Göttingen: Vandenhoeck & Ruprecht 2007.

Illy, Hans F.: *Politik und Wirtschaft in Kamerun: Bedingungen, Ziele und Strategien der staatlichen Entwicklungspolitik*. Munich: Weltforum 1976.

Jackson, Robert: *Quasi-States: International Relations, Sovereignty and the Third World*. Cambridge: Cambridge UP 1990.

Jahn, Janheinz: *A History of Neo-African Literature*. London: Faber 1968.

James, C. L. R. [Cyril Lionel Robert]: *Nkrumah and the Ghana Revolution*. London: Allison & Busby 1982 [1977].

James, Leslie Elaine: *"What we put in black and white": George Padmore and the Practice of Anti-Imperial Politics*. PhD Thesis, Department of International History of the London School of Economics (LSE) 2012.

—: *George Padmore and Decolonization from Below: Pan-Africanism, the Cold War, and the End of Empire*. Basingstoke / New York: Palgrave Macmillan 2015.

Jameson, Frederic: *Postmodernism or the Cultural Logic of Late Capitalism*. London: Verso 1991.

Janis, Michael: *Africa after Modernism: Transitions in Literature, Media, and Philosophy*. New York: Routledge 2008.

Johnson, Chalmers: *Miti and the Japanese Miracle: The Growth of Industrial Policy, 1925–1975*. Stanford: Stanford UP 1982.

Judt, Tony: *Reappraisals: Reflections on the Forgotten Twentieth Century*. New York: Penguin 2008.

Judt, Tony, with Timothy Snyder: *Thinking the Twentieth Century*. New York: Penguin 2012.

Jules-Rosette, Bennetta: *Black Paris: The African Writers' Landscape*. Urbana / Chicago: University of Illinois Press 2000.

Käbbädä, Mikael: *Ityopyanna mərabawi sələṭṭane / Ethiopia and Western Civilization / L'Éthiopie et la civilisation occidentale* [trilingual publication]. Addis Ababa: Bərhanənna Sälam 1949.

Kaggia, Bildad Mwaganu / W. de Leeuw / M. Kaggia: *The Struggle for Freedom and Justice*. Nairobi: Transafrica 2012.

Kamé, Bouopda Pierre: *Cameroun du protectorat vers la Démocratie 1884–1992*. Paris: L'Harmattan 2008.

Kareithi, Peter: *Kaburi Bila Msalaba* ['Grave without a Cross']. Nairobi: East African Publishing House 1969.

Katrak, Ketu H.: *Politics of the Female Body: Postcolonial Women Writers of the Third World.* New Brunswick / London: Rutgers UP 2006.

Kenyatta, Jomo: *My People of Gikuyu and the Life of Chief Wangombe.* London: Luttersworth 1942.

—: *The Land of Conflict.* London: Panaf 1945.

—: *Facing Mount Kenya.* New York: Vintage 1965 [1938].

—: *Jomo Kenyatta: Suffering Without Bitterness: The Founding of the Kenya Nation.* Nairobi: East African Publishing House 1968.

Kershaw, Greet: *Mau Mau From Below.* Oxford: Currey 1997.

Kezilahabi, Euphrase: *Dunia Uwanja wa Fujo* ['The World an Arena of Chaos']. Dar es Salaam / Nairobi / Kampala: East African Literature Bureau 1975.

—: *African Philosophy and the Problem of Literary Interpretation.* Unpublished PhD Thesis, University of Wisconsin, Madison 1985.

—: *Nagona* ['Nagona']. Dar es Salaam: Dar es Salaam UP 1990 [1987].

—: *Mzingile* ['Labyrinth']. Dar es Salaam: Dar es Salaam UP 1991.

Khamis, Said A. M.: *Uhuru wa Watumwa* de James Mbotela (Kiswahili, 1934): un premier roman politiquement trop correct. In: Xavier Garnier / Alain Ricard (eds): *L'effet roman. Arrivée du roman dans les langues d'Afrique.* Paris: L'Harmattan 2006, pp. 127–138.

Koselleck, Reinhart: *Vergangene Zukunft: Zur Semantik geschichtlicher Zeiten.* Frankfurt am Main: Suhrkamp 1989.

Krenčeyová, Miša: *Africa and the Rest: Imaginations Beyond a Continent in African Scholarship on Human Rights and Development.* PhD Thesis, University of Vienna 2013.

—: Who is allowed to Speak about Africa? A Reflection on Knowledge, Positionality, and Authority in Africanist Scholarship. In: *Africa Insight* 44,1 (2014): Development Through Knowledge, pp. 7–21.

Krieger, Milton: *Cameroon's Social Democratic Front: Its History & Prospects as an Oppostion Politcal Party (1990–2011).* Bamenda / Mankon: Langaa 2008.

La Fontaine, Dana de: *Neue Dynamiken in der Süd-Süd-Kooperation: Indien, Brasilien und Südafrika als Emerging Donors.* Wiesbaden: Springer VS 2013.

Laclau, Ernesto: The Death and Resurrection of the Theory of Ideology. In: *MLN* 112,3 (1997), pp. 297–321.

Lefkowitz, Mary R. / MacLean, Rogers Guy (eds): *Black Athena Revisited.* Chapel Hill / London: University of North Carolina Press 1996.

Leftwich, Adrian: Democracy and Development: Is there Institutional Incompatibility? In: *Democratization* 12,5 (2005), pp. 686–703.

Lenin, Vladimir Ilyich: *Critical Remarks on the National Question* [1913]. *The Right of Nations to Self-Determination* [1914]. Moscow: Progress 1974 [1951].

—: Der Imperialismus als höchstes Stadium des Kapitalismus: Gemeinverständlicher Abriss. In: Id.: *Ausgewählte Werke.* Moscow: Progress 1987 [1916–1917], pp. 164–257.

Lepenies, Wolf (ed.): *Entangled Histories and Negotiated Universals.* Frankfurt am Main: Campus 2003.

Lepsius, Rainer M.: Kritik als Beruf. Zur Soziologie der Intellektuellen. In: Id.: *Interessen, Ideen und Institutionen.* Opladen: Westdeutscher Verlag 1990, pp. 270–285.

Levine, Donald: Ethiopia and Japan in Comparative Civilizational Perspective. In: Katsuyoshi Fukui / Eisei Kurimoto / Masayoshi Shigeta (eds): *Ethiopia in Broader Perspective: Papers of the 13th International Conference of Ethiopian Studies.* Kyoto: Shokado 1997, pp. 652–675.

—: Ethiopia, Japan, and Jamaica: A Century of Globally Linked Modernizations. In: *International Journal of Ethiopian Studies* 3,1 (2007), pp. 41–51.

LeVine, Victor T.: *The Cameroons from Mandate to Independence.* Westport: Greenwood 1964.

Leys, Colin: *Underdevelopment in Kenya.* London: Heinemann 1975.

Lindfors, Bernth: The Early Writings of Wole Soyinka. In: James Gibbs (ed.): *Critical Perspectives on Wole Soyinka.* Washington, D. C.: Three Continents Press 1980, pp. 19–44.

—: Beating the White Man at His Own Game: Nigerian Reactions to the 1986 Nobel Prize in Literature. In: James Gibbs / Bernth Lindfors (eds): *Research on Wole Soyinka.* Trenton, NJ: Africa World Press 1993, pp. 341–354.

Lobban, Michael: *White Man's Justice: South African Political Trials in the Black Consciousness Era.* London: Clarendon 1996.

Lonsdale, John M.: The Prayers of Waiyaki: Political Uses of the Kikuyu Past. In: David M. Anderson / Douglas Hamilton Johnson (eds): *Revealing Prophets: Prophecy in Eastern African History.* London: Currey 1995, pp. 240–291.

—: "Listen While I Read": The Orality of Christian Literacy in the Young Kenyatta's Making of the Kikuyu. In: Hamilton Johnson de la Gorgendière / Kenneth King / Sarah Vaughan (eds): *Ethnicity in Africa: Roots, Meanings and Implications.* Edinburgh: Centre of African Studies, University of Edinburgh 1996, pp. 7–53.

—: KAU's Cultures: Imaginations of Community and Constructions of Leadership in Kenya after the Second World War. In: *Journal of African Cultural Studies* 13,1 (2000), pp. 107–124.

—: Jomo Kenyatta, God & the Modern World. In: Jan-Georg Deutsch / Peter Probst / Heike Schmidt (eds): *African Modernities: Entangled Meanings in Current Debate.* London: Currey 2002, pp. 31–66.

—: Contest of Time: Kikuyu Historiography, Old and New. In: Axel Harneit-Sievers (ed.): *A Place in the World: New Local Historiographies from Africa and South Asia.* Leiden: Brill 2002, pp. 201–254.

—: Les Procès de Jomo Kenyatta. Destruction et construction d'un Nationaliste Africain. In: *Politix* 17,66 (2004), pp. 163–197.

—: Ornamental Constitutionalism in Africa: Kenyatta and the Two Queens. In: *The Journal of Imperial and Commonwealth History* 34,1 (2006), pp. 87–103.

—: Henry Muoria, Public Moralist. In: Wangari Muoria-Sal / Bodil F. Frederiksen / John Lonsdale / Derek R. Peterson (eds): *Writing for Kenya: The Life and Works of Henry Muoria.* Leiden: Brill 2009, pp. 3–58.

Madumulla, Joshua S.: *Riwaya ya Kiswahili. Nadharia, Historia na Misingi ya Uchambuzi* ['The Swahili Novel: Theory, History and Foundations of Analysis']. Dar es Salaam: Mture / Nairobi: Phoenix 2009.

Malcolm X: Message to the Grass Roots. In: Marcus D. Pohlmann (ed.): *African American Political Thought: Confrontation vs. Compromise, from 1945 to the Present.* London / New York: Taylor & Francis 2003, pp. 115–129.

Mamdani, Mahmood: *Citizen and Subject: Contemporary Africa and the Legacy of Late Colonialism.* London: Currey / Princeton UP 1996.

Marable, Manning / Peniel Joseph: Steve Biko and the International Context of Black Consciousness. In: Andile Mngxitama / Amanda Alexander / Nigel C. Gibson (eds): *Biko Lives! Contesting the Legacies of Steve Biko.* New York: Palgrave Macmillan 2008, pp. vii–x.

Maupeu, Hervé: Kikuyu Capitalistes. Réflexions sur un Cliché Kenyan. In: *Outre-Terre* 2,11 (2005), pp. 493–506.

Mbaku, John Mukum / Joseph Takougang: *The Leadership Challenge in Africa: Cameroon under Paul Biya.* Trenton: Africa World Press 2004.

Mbatiah, Mwenda: *Wimbo Mpya* ['New Song']. Nairobi: Jomo Kenyatta Foundation 2004.

Mbaye, Sanou: L'Afrique francophone piégée par sa monnaie unique. In: *Le Monde Diplomatique*, November 2014, pp. 12–13.

Mbembe, Achille: *On the Postcolony.* Berkeley / Los Angeles / London: University of California Press 2001.

—: African Modes of Self-Writing. In: *Public Culture* 14,1 (2002), pp. 239–273.

—: *Critique de la raison nègré.* Paris: Éditions la Découverte 2013.

Mbotela, James: *Uhuru wa Watumwa.* London: Sheldon 1934 (trans. from the English as: *The Freeing of the Slaves in East Africa*, London: Evans 1956).

Mbuagbo, Timothy / Robert Mbe Akoko: Roll Back: Democratization and Social Fragmentation in Cameroon. In: *Nordic Journal of African Studies* 13,1 (2004), pp. 1–12.

Médard, Jean-Francois: L'État sous-développé au Cameroun. In: *Année africaine*, June 1977, pp. 33–84.

Melber, Henning: What is African in Africa(n) Studies? Confronting the (Mystifying) Power of Ideology and Identity. In: Terry A. Barringer (ed.): *Africa Bibliography 2013.* Cambridge: Cambridge UP 2014, pp. vii–xvii.

Meles Zenawi: States and Markets: Neoliberal Limitations and the Case for a Developmental State. In: Akbar Norman / Kwesi Botchwey / Howard Stein / Joseph E. Stiglitz (eds): *Good Growth and Governance in Africa: Rethinking Development Strategies.* Oxford: Oxford UP 2011, pp. 140–174.

Memmi, Albert: *Portrait du colonisé précédé du Portrait du colonisateur.* Paris: Buchet-Chastel 1957.

Merid W. Aregay: Japanese and Ethiopian Reactions to Jesuit Missionary Activities in the Sixteenth and Seventeenth Centuries. In: Katsuyoshi Fukui / Eisei Kurimoto / Masayoshi Shigeta (eds): *Ethiopia in Broader Perspective: Papers of the 13th International Conference of Ethiopian Studies.* Kyoto: Shokado 1997, pp. 676–698.

Meseret Chekol Reta: *The Quest for Press Freedom: One Hundred Years of History of the Media in Ethiopia.* Lamham, MD / Plymouth, UK: UP of America 2013.

Messay Kebede: Japan and Ethiopia: An Appraisal of Similarities and Divergent Courses. In: Katsuyoshi Fukui / Eisei Kurimoto / Masayoshi Shigeta (eds): *Ethiopia in Broader Perspective: Papers of the 13th International Conference of Ethiopian Studies.* Kyoto: Shokado 1997, pp. 639–651.

Middell, Matthias: *Self-reflexive Area Studies*. Leipzig: Leipziger Universitätsverlag 2000.

—: Kulturtransfer und historische Komparatistik: Thesen zu ihrem Verhältnis. In: *Comparativ* 10,1 (2000), pp. 7–41.

Mkandawire, Thandika: Thinking about Developmental States in Africa. In: *Cambridge Journal of Economics* 25,3 (2001), pp. 289–313.

Mkangi, Katama: *Walenisi* ['They Are Us']. Nairobi / Kampala / Dar es Salaam: East African Educational Publishers 1995.

Mkufya, William: *Ziraili na Zirani* ['Asrael and Zirani']. Dar es Salaam: Hekima 1999. (Translated by the author as: 'Pilgrims from Hell', yet unpublished.)

Mngxitama, Andile / Amanda Alexander / Nigel C. Gibson: Biko Lives. In: Iid. (eds): *Biko Lives! Contesting the Legacies of Steve Biko.* New York: Palgrave Macmillan 2008, pp. 1–20.

— (eds): *Biko Lives! Contesting the Legacies of Steve Biko.* New York: Palgrave Macmillan 2008.

Mohamed, Said Ahmed: *Babu Alipofufuka* ['When Grandfather Came to Life Again']. Nairobi: Jomo Kenyatta Foundation 2001.

—: *Dunia Yao* ['Their World']. Nairobi: Oxford UP 2006.

—: *Nyuso za Mwanamke* ['Faces of Woman']. Nairobi / Kampala / Dar es Salaam: Longhorn / Sasa Sema 2010.

Molvaer, Reidulf K.: *Black Lions: The Creative Lives of Modern Ethiopia's Literary Giants and Pioneers.* Lawrenceville, NJ: Red Sea 1997.

Mudimbe, V. Y.: *The Invention of Africa: Gnosis, Philosophy, and the Order of Knowledge.* Bloomington: Indiana UP 1988.

Mulokozi, Mugyabuso M.: Utangulizi ['Introduction']. In: Shaaban Bin Robert: *Siku ya Watenzi Wote* ['The Day of All Doers']. Dar es Salaam: Taasisi ya Uchunguzi wa Kiswahili, Chuo Kikuu cha Dar es Salaam 2008 [[1]1968], pp. iv–vii.

— (ed.): *Tenzi Tatu za Kale* ['Three Ancient Epic Poems']. Dar es Salaam: Taasisi ya Uchunguzi wa Kiswahili 1999.

— / Tigiti S. Y. Sengo: *History of Kiswahili Poetry, A. D. 1000–2000: A Report.* Dar es Salaam: Taasisi ya Uchunguzi wa Kiswahili, Chuo Kikuu cha Dar es Salaam 1995.

Murphy, Caryle: Jesse Jackson's Tour Angers South African Government. In: *The Washington Post*, 29.07.1979, p. A27.

Murray-Brown, Jeremy: *Kenyatta.* London: Allen & Unwin 1972.

Mveng, Engelbert: *Histoire du Cameroun.* Paris: Présence Africaine 1963.

—: Problématique d'une esthétique negro-africaine, 2ième partie: Culture et civilisations. In: *Ethiopiques, Revue négro-africaine de litterature et de philosophie* 3, (Juillet 1975). http://ethiopiques.refer.sn/spip.php?article490 (accessed 25.01.2015) [Reproduction of a lecture held at the *Colloque sur littérature et esthétique négro-africaines* at Abidjan University, Côte d'Ivoire, December 1974].

—: *L'art et l'artisanat africains.* Yaoundé: Clé 1980.

Ndegwa, Duncan: *Walking in Kenyatta Struggles: My Story.* Nairobi: Kenya Leadership Institute 2011.

Ngenge, Tata Simon: The Institutional Roots of the 'Anglophone Problem' in Cameroon. In: Jean-Germain Gros (ed.): *Cameroon: Politics and Society in Critical Perspective*. Lanham: UP of America 2003, pp. 61–86.

Ngobeni, Solani: Scholarly Publishing in South Africa. In: Id. (ed.): *Scholarly Publishing in Africa: Opportunities & Impediments*. Pretoria: African Institute of South Africa 2010, pp. 69–83.

Ngoh, Victor Julius: *Constitutional Developments in Southern Cameroons 1946–1961*. Yaoundé: Pioneer 1990.

Njoh, Ambe J.: *Plannig Rules in Post-Colonial States: The Political Economy of Urban and Regional Planning in Cameroon*. New York: Nova Science 2001.

Nkrumah, Kwame: *Neo-Colonialism: The Last Stage of Imperialism*. London: Panaf 1971 [1965].

—: *Revolutionary Path*. London: Panaf 1973.

Nyerere, Julius: *Binadamu na Maendeleo*. Dar es Salaam: Oxford UP 1974. (Simultaneously published Swahili version of *Man and Development*. Dar es Salaam: Oxford UP 1974.)

Obenga, Théophile: *La philosophie africaine de la période pharaonique: 2780–330 avant notre ère*. Paris: L'Harmattan 1980.

Onwueme, Osonye Tess: *Tell it to Women: An Epic Drama for Women*. Detroit: Wayne State UP 1994.

Oshinsky, David M.: *Polio: An American Story: The Crusade that Mobilized the Nation against the 20th Century's Most Feared Disease*. Oxford: Oxford UP 2005.

Ozumba, Godfrey O.: Outlines of African Aesthetics. In: *Sophia: An African Journal of Philosophy and Public Affairs* 9,2 (April 2007), pp. 153–158. http://unical-ng.academia.edu/GodfreyOzumba (accessed 19.10.2012).

—: *Philosophy and Method of Integrative Humanism*. Calabar, Nigeria: Jochrisam 2010.

Ozumba, Godfrey O. / S. Y. Alabi: *Landmarks in Aesthetic Studies: A Book of Reading*. Makurdi, Nigeria: Microteacher 2007.

Padmore, George: *The Gold Coast Revolution: The Struggle of an African People from Slavery to Freedom*. London: Dobson 1953.

—: *Pan-Africanism or Communism? The Coming Struggle for Africa*. London: Dobson 1956.

—: *How Britain Rules Africa*. New York: Negro Universities Press 1969 [1936].

—: *Africa: Britain's Third Empire*. New York: Negro Universities Press 1969 [1949].

—: *Pan-Africanism or Communism*. Garden City, NY: Anchor / Doubleday 1972 [1956].

—: *Africa and World Peace*. London: Cass 1972 [1937].

—, in collaboration with Dorothy Pizer: *How Russia Transformed Her Colonial Empire: A Challenge to the Imperialist Powers*. London: Dobson 1946.

— (ed.): *Voice of Coloured Labour*. Manchester: Panaf 1945.

— (ed.): *Colonial and... Coloured Unity: A Programme of Action: History of the Pan-African Congress*. London: Hammersmith 1963 [1947].

Pankhurst, Richard: Misoneism and Innovation in Ethiopian History. In: *Ethiopia Observer* 7,4 (1964), pp. 287–320.

—: The Foundations of Education, Printing, Newspapers, Book Production, Library and Literacy in Ethiopia. In: *Ethiopia Observer* 6,3 (1962), pp. 241–290.

—: *The Ethiopians: A History*. Oxford: Blackwell 2001.

Paul, James C. N. / Christopher Clapham: *Ethiopian Constitutional Development*. Addis Ababa: Haile Selassie I UP 1967.

Paulus, Christoph G.: Die Handhabung von Wissen im Recht. In: Corinne M. Flick (ed.): *Wem gehört das Wissen der Welt*. Frankfurt am Main: Frankfurter Verlagsanstalt 2011, pp. 151–163.

Peatrik, Anne-Marie: Un système composite: l'organisation d'age et de génération des Kikuyu précoloniaux. In: *Journal des Africanistes* 64,1 (1994), pp. 3–36.

Pennybacker, Susan D.: *From Scottsboro to Munich: Race and Political Culture in 1930s Britain*. Princeton / Oxford: Princeton UP 2009.

Peterson, Derek R.: *Creative Writing: Translation, Bookkeeping, and the Work of Imagination in Colonial Kenya*. Portsmouth: Heinemann 2004.

Pityana, N. Barney: Medical Ethics and South Africa's Security Laws: A Sequel to the Death of Steve Biko. In: N. Barney Pityana / Mamphela Ramphele / Malusi Mpumlwana / Lindy Wilson (eds): *Bounds of Possibility: The Legacy of Steve Biko and Black Consciousness*. Atlantic Highlands, NJ: Zed Books 1992, pp. 78–98.

—: Revolution within the Law? In: N. Barney Pityana / Mamphela Ramphele / Malusi Mpumlwana / Lindy Wilson (eds): *Bounds of Possibility: The Legacy of Steve Biko and Black Consciousness*. Atlantic Highlands, NJ: Zed Books 1992, pp. 201–212.

Pityana, N. Barney / Mamphela Ramphele / Malusi Mpumlwana / Lindy Wilson (eds): *Bounds of Possibility: The Legacy of Steve Biko and Black Consciousness*. Atlantic Highlands, NJ: Zed Books 1992.

Pocock, J. G. A.: What is Intellectual History? In: *History Today* 35,10 (1985). http://www.historytoday.com/stefan-collini/what-intellectual-history (accessed 11.02.2015).

Polakow-Suransky, Sasha: *The Unspoken Alliance: Israel's Secret Relationship with Apartheid South Africa*. New York: Pantheon 2010.

Pollack, Dean Louis H.: *The Inquest into the Death of Stephen Bantu Biko*. A Report to the Lawyers' Committee for Civil rights Under Law, Prepared for the Southern Africa Project. February 24, 1978. University of Cape Town Archives, Biko Doctors Case Collection (BC 822), Folder B2 (Legal).

Prouzet, Michel: *Le Cameroun*. Paris: Librairie générale de droit et de jurisprudence 1974.

Ramphele, Mamphela: *Across Boundaries: The Journey of a South African Woman Leader* New York: The Feminist Press at CUNY 1999.

Ranger, Terence O.: From Humanism to the Science of Man: Colonialism in Africa and the Understanding of Alien Societies. In: *Transactions of the Royal Historical Society (Fifth Series)* 26 (1976), pp. 115–141.

Reichart-Burikukiye, Christiane: Erinnerungsräume und Wissenschaftstransfer. Die Erfindung Afrikas. In: Winfried Speitkamp (ed.): *Erinnerungsräume und Wissenstransfer: Beiträge zur afrikanischen Geschichte*. Göttingen: V&R unipress 2008, pp. 11–34.

Reid, Richard: Review of Peter Garretson's 'A Victorian Gentleman & Ethiopian Nationalist: the Life and Times of Hakim Warqenah, Dr Charles Martin'. In: *Reviews in History* 1388 (2013). http://www.history.ac.uk/reviews/review/1388 (accessed 23.01.2014).

Reiss, Timothy J.: *Against Autonomy: Global Dialectics of Cultural Exchange.* Stanford: Stanford UP 2002.

Robert, Shaaban: *Kusadikika. Nchi Iliyo Angani.* ['A Place to Believe in. A Country in the Sky']. London: Nelson 1951 (trans. from the English by David C. Sperling in 1973, but presumably unpublished).

—: *Adili na Nduguze* ['Adili and His Brothers']. London: Macmillan 1952 [written pre-1946?].

—: *Kufikirika* ['A Place to Imagine']. Nairobi: Oxford UP 1967 [written 1946].

—: *Utubora Mkulima* ['Utubora the Farmer']. Nairobi: Nelson 1968.

—: *Siku ya Watenzi Wote* ['The Day of all Doers']. Nairobi: Nelson 1968.

Robinson, Cedric J.: *Black Marxism: The Making of the Black Radical Tradition.* Chapel Hill: University of North Carolina Press 2000.

Rodney, Walter: *How Europe Underdeveloped Africa.* Abuja / Lagos / Pretoria: Panaf 2009 [1973].

Rodrik, Dani: Political Economy and Development Policy. In: *European Economic Review* 36 (1992), pp. 329–336.

Rollins, Jack Drake: *A History of Swahili Prose*, part I: From Earliest Times to the End of the Nineteenth Century. Leiden: Brill 1983.

Ross, Jay: Key S. African Black Dies in Custody: U.S. Officials Criticize Death in Custody of Moderate Black Leader in S. Africa. In: *The Washington Post*, 14.09.1977, p. A1.

Ruhumbika, Gabriel: *Miradi Bubu ya Wazalendo* ['The Silent Projects of the Patriots']. Dar es Salaam: Tanzania Publishing House 1995 [1992].

—: *Silent Empowerment of the Compatriots*, trans. from Kiswahili by the author. Dar es Salaam: E & D Vision 2009.

Said, Edward W.: *Orientalism: Western Conceptions of the Orient.* London: Penguin 1995 [1978].

Sandbrook, Richard: *The Politics of Africa's Economic Stagnation.* Cambridge: Cambridge UP 1985.

Schneider, Norbert: Ästhetische Geltungsansprüche. In: Friedrich Jaeger / Burkhard Liebsch / Jürgen Straub / Jörn Rüsen (eds): *Handbuch der Kulturwissenschaften*, vol. 1. Grundlagen und Schlüsselbegriffe. Stuttgart: Metzler 2004, pp. 266–276.

—: *Geschichte der Ästhetik: Von der Aufklärung bis zur Postmoderne.* Ditzingen: Reclam 2005.

Schütz, Alfred: Husserls Importance for the Social Science. In: Id.: *Collected Papers*, vol. I: The Problem of Social Reality, ed. by Maurice Natanson. The Hague: Nijhoff 1962, pp. 140–149.

Senghor, Léopold Sédar: L'Esthétique négro-africaine. In: *Diogène, Revue trimestrielle* 16 (October 1956), p. 50.

Senkoro, Fikeni E. M. K: *Fasihi. Toleo Jipya.* Dar es Salaam: KAUTTU 2011 ['Literature. New Edition'; it only deals with prose, and concentrates on novels].

Shitemi, Naomi: *Ushairi wa Kiswahili kabla ya Karne ya Ishirini* ['Swahili Poetry before the 20th Century']. Eldoret: Moi UP 2010.

Shivji, Issa G.: *Silences in NGO Discourse: The Role and Future of NGOs in Africa.* Nairobi: Fahamu 2007.

—: *Insha za Mapambano ya Wanyonge.* Kimehaririwa na Bashiru Ally ['Essays on the Battle for the Poor', ed. by Bashiru Ally; written 2003–2011]. Dar es Salaam: Taasisi ya Taaluma za Kiswahili, Chuo Kikuu cha Dar es Salaam 2012.

Shohat, Ella / Robert Stam: *Unthinking Eurocentrism: Multiculturalism and the Media.* London / New York: Routledge 1994.

Sidiropoulos, Elizabeth / Thomas Fues / Sachin Chaturvedi: Introduction. In: Iid. (eds): *Development Cooperation and Emerging Powers: New Partners or Old Patterns?* London: Zed Books 2012, pp. 1–10.

Siegrist, Hannes: Perspektiven der vergleichenden Geschichtswissenschaft: Gesellschaft, Kultur und Raum. In: Hartmut Kaelble / Jürgen Schriewer (eds): *Vergleich und Transfer: Komparatistik in den Sozial- Geschichts- und Kulturwissenschaften.* Frankfurt am Main: Campus 2003, pp. 305–340.

Simo, David: Was ist Afrika? Postkoloniale Konstruktionen von Afrikabildern. In: Aïssatou Bouba / Detlev Quintern (eds): *Das Bild von Afrika. Von kolonialer Einbildung zu transkultureller Verständigung.* Berlin: Weißensee 2010, pp. 75–88.

Sindjoun, Luc: *L'État ailleurs: Entre noyau dur et case vide.* Paris: Agence intergouvernementale de la francophonie / Economica 2002.

Skinner, Quentin: What is Intellectual History? In: *History Today* 35,10 (1985). http://www.historytoday.com/stefan-collini/what-intellectual-history (accessed 11.02.2015).

Slater, Montagu: *The Trial of Jomo Kenyatta.* London: Secker & Warburg 1955.

Smethurst, James Edward: *The Black Arts Movement: Literary Nationalism in the 1960s and 1970s.* Chapel Hill / London: University of North Carolina Press 2005.

Smith, Tom W.: Changing Racial Labels: from 'Colored' to 'Negro' to 'Black' to 'African American'. In: *Public Opinion Quarterly* 56,4 (1992), pp. 496–514.

Sonderegger, Arno: *Die Dämonisierung Afrikas: Zum Despotiebegriff und zur Geschichte der Afrikanischen Despotie.* Saarbrücken: VDM 2008.

—: Nachbetrachtung zur Kolonialgeschichte und Historiographie Afrikas. In: Birgit Englert / Ingeborg Grau / Arno Sonderegger (eds): *Afrika im 20. Jahrhundert: Geschichte und Gesellschaft.* Vienna: Promedia 2011, pp. 228–254.

—: African Thoughts on (Neo-)Colonial Worlds: Steps towards an Intellectual History of Africa 06.11.2014–07.11.2014 Wien. In: *H-Soz-Kult*, 16.12.2014. http://www.hsozkult.de/conferencereport/id/tagungsberichte-5732 (accessed 13.02.2015).

—: How the Empire Wrote Back: Notes on the Struggle of George Padmore and Kwame Nkrumah. In: Bea Lundt / Christoph Marx (eds): *Kwame Nkrumah (1909–1972) Today.* Stuttgart: Steiner 2015, forthcoming.

— / Grau, Ingeborg / Englert, Birgit (eds): *Afrika im 20. Jahrhundert: Geschichte und Gesellschaft.* Vienna: Promedia 2011.

Soyinka, Wole: *Myth, Literature and the African World.* Cambridge: Cambridge UP 1978.

Speitkamp, Winfried: Erinnerungsorte und Erinnerungskulturen in Afrika. In: Sonja Klein / Vivian Liska / Karl Solibakke / Bernd Witte (eds): *Gedächtnisstrategien und Medien im interkulturellen Dialog.* Würzburg: Königshausen & Neumann 2011, pp. 273–282.

Spivak, Gayatri Chakravorty: More on Power/Knowledge. In: Ead.: *Outside in the Teaching Machine.* New York: Routledge 1993, pp. 25–51.

—: *Other Asias.* Oxford: Blackwell 2008.

Stäheli, Urs: Spezialeffekte als Ästhetik des Globalen. In: Gregor Schwering / Carsten Zelle (eds): *Ästhetische Positionen nach Adorno.* Paderborn: Fink 2002, pp. 191–213.

Steinbach-Hüther, Ninja / Matthias Middell: Zur Präsenz akademischer Literatur aus Afrika in Deutschland – eine Bestandsaufnahme. In: Steffi Marung / Matthias Middell (eds): *Transnational Actors – Crossing Borders: Transnational History Studies.* Leipzig: Leipziger Universitätsverlag 2015, pp. 243–261.

Tamarkin, Moderchai: The Roots of Political Stability in Kenya. In: *African Affairs* 77,308 (1978), pp. 297–320.

Tetzlaff, Rainer / Cord Jakobeit: *Das nachkoloniale Afrika. Politik, Wirtschaft, Gesellschaft.* Wiesbaden: VS 2005.

Thiong'o, Ngugi wa: *Something Torn and New: An African Renaissance.* New York: Basic Civitas 2009.

—: The Myth of Tribe in African Politics. In: *Transition* 101 (2009), pp. 16–23.

Thomas, Scott: *The Diplomacy of Liberation: The Foreign Relations of the ANC since 1960.* New York: IB Tauris 1996.

Throup, David W.: The Construction and Destruction of the Kenyatta State. In: Michael G. Schatzberg (ed.): *The Political Economy of Kenya.* Portsmouth: Praeger 1987, pp. 33–74.

Tibebu, Teshale: Modernity, Eurocentrism, and Radical Politics in Ethiopia 1961–1991. In: *African Identities* 6,4 (2008), pp. 345–371.

Tijssen, Robert J. W.: Africa's Contribution to the Worldwide Research Literature: New Analytical Perspectives, Trends and Performance Indicators. In: *Scientometrics* 71,2 (2007), pp. 303–327.

Tucker, William H.: *The Funding of Scientific Racism: Wickliffe Draper and the Pioneer Fund.* Chicago: University of Illinois Press 2007.

Tudor, Henry: *Political Myth.* Portsmouth: Praeger 1972.

Turner, Frederick: *Beauty: The Value of Values.* Charlottesville: University of Virginia Press 1991.

Ulimwengu, Jenerali: *Rai ya Jenerali.* Dar es Salaam: E & D n. d. [2005]. ['Jenerali's Viewpoint'; newspaper articles and essays, most of them written 1993–1995].

Université d'Abidjan, Institut de littérature et d'esthétique négro-africaines [ILENA]: *Colloque sur littérature et esthétique négro-africaines, Abidjan, Côte d'Ivoire 1974.* Abidjan: Les Nouvelles Editions Africaines 1979.

Van Binsbergen, Wim M. J.: Black Athena and Africa's Contribution to Global Cultural History. In: *Quest, Philosophical Discussions: An International African Journal of Philosophy* 9,2/10,1 (1996), pp. 100–137.

Villalón, Leonardo A: The African State at the End of the Twentieth Century: Parameters of the Critical Juncture. In: Id. / Phillip A. Huxtable (eds): *The African State at a Critical Juncture: Between Disintegration and Reconfiguration.* Boulder / London: Lynne Rienner 1998, pp. 3–25.

Vubo, Emmanuel Yenshu: *Civil Society and the Search for Development Alternatives in Cameroon.* Dakar: CODESRIA 2008.

Walker, Alice: *In Search of Our Mothers' Gardens: Womanist Prose.* Boston: Mariner 2003.

Wallerstein, Immanuel: *Historical Capitalism* [1983] *with Capitalist Civilization.* London / New York: Verso 2011.

Wamitila, Kyallo W.: Reading the Kenyan Swahili Prose Works: A Terra Incognita in Swahili Literature. In: *Afrikanistische Arbeitspapiere (AAP)* 51 – *Swahili Forum* IV (1997), pp. 117–125.

—: *Msimu wa Vipepeo* ['Season of Butterflies']. Nairobi: Vide~Muwa 2006.

Welsch, Wolfgang: *Blickwechsel: Neue Wege der Ästhetik.* Stuttgart: Reclam 2012.

Whitaker, Joseph: Lawyers' Group Here Works for Civil Rights in South Africa. In: *The Washington Post,* 19.12.1977, p. A6.

Williams, Gareth: *Paralysed with Fear: The Story of Polio.* Basingstoke: Palgrave 2013.

Woods, Donald: *Biko: The True Story of the Young South African Martyr and His Struggle to Raise Black Consciousness.* New York: Henry Holt 1978.

Woodson, Carter G.: *The Miseducation of the Negro.* Washington: Associated Publishers 1933.

Wrong, Michaela: *It's Our Turn to Eat: The Story of a Kenyan Whistle Blower.* London: Fourth Estate 2009.

Young, Robert J. C.: *Postcolonialism: An Historical Introduction.* Malden / Oxford / Victoria: Blackwell 2001.

Zeleza, Paul Tiyambe: The African Academic Diaspora in the United States and Africa: The Challenges of Productive Engagement. In: *Comparative Studies of South Asia, Africa and the Middle East* 24,1 (2004), pp. 261–275.

—: *In Search of African Diasporas: Testimonies and Encounters.* Durham: Carolina Academic Press 2012.

Zell, Hans: Professional Reading (Review of *African Scholarly Publishing*). In: *The African Book Publishing Record* 33,2 (2007), pp. 106–110.

Zewde, Bahru: *A History of Modern Ethiopia, 1855–1974.* London: Currey 1991.

—: *Pioneers of Change in Ethiopia: the Reformist Intellectuals of the Early Twentieth Century.* Oxford: Currey / Addis Ababa: Addis Ababa UP / Athens: Ohio UP 2002.

—: *Society, State and History: Selected Essays.* Addis Ababa: Addis Ababa UP 2008.

—: The Concept of Japanization in the Intellectual History of Modern Ethiopia. In: Id.: *Society, State and History: Selected Essays.* Addis Ababa: Addis Ababa UP 2008, pp. 198–214.